SO YOU WANT TO SING CHAMBER MUSIC

So You Want to Sing

Guides for Performers and Professionals

A Project of the National Association of Teachers of Singing

So You Want to Sing: Guides for Performers and Professionals is a series of works devoted to providing a complete survey of what it means to sing within a particular genre. Each contribution functions as a touchstone work not only for professional singers but also for students and teachers of singing. Titles in the series offer a common set of topics so readers can navigate easily the various genres addressed in each volume. This series is produced under the direction of the National Association of Teachers of Singing, the leading professional organization devoted to the science and art of singing.

So You Want to Sing Music Theater: A Guide for Professionals, by Karen S. Hall, 2013
So You Want to Sing Rock 'n' Roll: A Guide for Professionals, by Matthew Edwards, 2014
So You Want to Sing Jazz: A Guide for Professionals, by Jan Shapiro, 2015
So You Want to Sing Country: A Guide for Performers, by Kelly K. Garner, 2016
So You Want to Sing Gospel: A Guide for Performers, by Trineice Robinson-Martin, 2016
So You Want to Sing Sacred Music: A Guide for Performers, edited by Matthew Hoch, 2017
So You Want to Sing Folk Music: A Guide for Performers, by Valerie Mindel, 2017
So You Want to Sing Barbershop: A Guide for Performers, by Diane M. Clarke & Billy J. Biffle, 2017
So You Want to Sing A Cappella: A Guide for Performers, by Deke Sharon, 2017
So You Want to Sing Light Opera: A Guide for Performers, by Linda Lister, 2018
So You Want to Sing CCM (Contemporary Commercial Music): A Guide for Performers, edited by Matthew Hoch, 2018
So You Want to Sing for a Lifetime: A Guide for Performers, by Brenda Smith, 2018
So You Want to Sing the Blues: A Guide for Performers, by Eli Yamin, 2018
So You Want to Sing Chamber Music: A Guide for Performers by Susan Hochmiller, 2019

SO YOU WANT TO SING CHAMBER MUSIC

A Guide for Performers

Susan Hochmiller

Allen Henderson
Executive Editor, NATS

Matthew Hoch
Series Editor

A Project of the National Association of Teachers of Singing

ROWMAN & LITTLEFIELD
Lanham • Boulder • New York • London

Published by Rowman & Littlefield
An imprint of The Rowman & Littlefield Publishing Group, Inc.
4501 Forbes Boulevard, Suite 200, Lanham, Maryland 20706
www.rowman.com

6 Tinworth Street, London SE11 5AL

British Library Cataloguing in Publication Information Available

Library of Congress Cataloging-in-Publication Data

Names: Hochmiller, Susan, 1981– author.
Title: So you want to sing chamber music : a guide for performers / Susan Hochmiller.
Description: Lanham : Rowman & Littlefield, [2018] | Series: So you want to sing | Includes bibliographical references and index.
Identifiers: LCCN 2018035877 (print) | LCCN 2018038155 (ebook) | ISBN 9781538105177 (electronic) | ISBN 9781538105160 (pbk. : alk. paper)
Subjects: LCSH: Singing—Instruction and study.
Classification: LCC MT820 (ebook) | LCC MT820 .H724 2018 (print) | DDC 783.1/143—dc23
LC record available at https://lccn.loc.gov/2018035877

∞™ The paper used in this publication meets the minimum requirements of American National Standard for Information Sciences—Permanence of Paper for Printed Library Materials, ANSI/NISO Z39.48-1992.

Printed in the United States of America

CONTENTS

SERIES EDITOR'S FOREWORD

So You Want to Sing Chamber Music: A Guide for Performers is the fourteenth book in the NATS/Rowman & Littlefield So You Want to Sing series and the eleventh book to fall under my editorship. Susan Hochmiller, assistant professor of voice and coordinator of vocal studies at the Sunderman Conservatory of Music at Gettysburg College, is the author of this volume. Deeply committed to chamber music, she brings a wealth of knowledge, formal study, and experiences to the pages you are about to read. Her breadth of background in the field of chamber music makes her the ideal author for this title.

Although many chamber pieces in the Western classical canon require a technique that is similar to art song, rehearsing and performing chamber music is a different animal. Even the addition of only one *obbligato* instrument to a voice and piano duo changes the landscape immensely, affecting intonation, ensemble, and balance. The rehearsal dynamic is also altered—how do three people interact with one another as opposed to two, and who "takes charge" of the rehearsal then (if anyone)? And what happens when there are four, five, six, or more musicians? This book will address all of these issues and more.

In addition, *So You Want to Sing Chamber Music* will provide a comprehensive overview of the chamber music repertoire, introducing new works to readers who are less likely to have studied chamber music for voice in their formal schooling. Stylistic shifts that occur as one navigates various eras and vocal techniques necessary to sing both early and contemporary in a healthy and stylistically correct way will also be discussed. Finally, singing alongside others in duets, trios, and quartets will also be addressed—an important topic for singers who in their studies focus overwhelmingly on being soloists as opposed to generous collaborators alongside fellow singers.

Like other books in the series, there are several "common chapters" that are included across multiple titles. These chapters include a chapter on voice science by Scott McCoy and one on vocal health by Wendy LeBorgne. These chapters help to bind the series together, ensuring consistency of fact when it comes to the most essential matters of voice production. A foreword by NATS Lifetime Achievement Award winner Joan Boytim—who happens to be Hochmiller's first voice teacher—adds a touching note to this volume.

The collected volumes of the So You Want to Sing series offer a valuable opportunity for performers and teachers of singing to explore new styles and important pedagogies. I am confident that voice specialists, both amateur and professional, will benefit from Susan Hochmiller's important resource on singing chamber music. It has been a privilege to work with her on this project. This book is an invaluable resource for performers who are interested in adding chamber music to their repertoire.

Matthew Hoch

FOREWORD

This book deserves to be on every voice teacher's bookshelf. Collaborative music making has been the most treasured aspect of my musical life for the past sixty years. Susan Hochmiller has thoroughly researched this form of singing with her dedication to provide a scholarly discussion of the development of the art of collaborative vocal music.

As a former semiprofessional horn performer, I enjoyed my years of performing with one to four horns and other instrumental players more than my forty-five years of playing in symphony orchestras.

My nine years of teaching music in junior and senior high schools led me to explore duet and trio singing with quality octavos. The personal joys and singing independence developing within my students were gratifying. In addition, I noticed the demand for great sensitivity also improved the quality of excellent solo singing.

When I devoted my full-time teaching to the private community voice studio, I started to form compatible pairs and trios in my studio. In the 1970s, 1980s, and 1990s, I accepted the challenge of providing special music for almost all of the 8:30 a.m. services in my church for thirty-one years.

With this opportunity, I was able to use my students in solo, duets, and trios plus research the vast amount of available quality music in the choral field. As an aside, I published "Why Neglect the Sacred Solo Duet?" in the *NATS Bulletin* (February 1972) and "Duet Literature for the Christmas Season" in the same journal (October 1976).

There was a time when I had eight performing duet pairs in my studio. In today's age, with the advent of every school performing musicals, many churches providing fewer opportunities for special music, and students being overprogrammed, this rarely happens. Several of my former sister duos still perform together after more than forty years.

Susan's book should prove to be very useful for college students searching for duet literature to fit in with literature performed in joint recitals. This volume should entice many singers to explore the opportunities that are available for the serious performer willing to branch out into this most interesting music for both the performer and the listening audience.

I was flattered when Susan asked me to write the foreword for her book. She entered my voice studio while beginning eighth grade. She was gifted with a high soprano voice, a good piano background, and the desire to excel. She was a "dream" student and accepted all I had to offer. As a beginner, her intellect and ability were way ahead of her emotional maturity, but gradually within the next two years, these aspects began to blend and there was no way of stopping her overall development as a singer, scholar, teacher, and—now—the coordinator of the voice area at Gettysburg College in Gettysburg, Pennsylvania.

Joan Frey Boytim

ACKNOWLEDGMENTS

I am grateful to the following people who generously played a significant role in inspiring and supporting this book with their time, expertise, guidance, comments, questions, and encouragement: Matthew Hoch for all of his work and insightful input as my editor extraordinaire; Allen Henderson, executive director of the National Association of Teachers of Singing; Natalie Mandziuk, associate acquisitions editor at Rowman & Littlefield; all of my music teachers, who motivated me to pursue a career in music and strive for excellence every day; my former and current students for studying, singing, and performing chamber music, especially Heather McConnell for your repertoire assistance; the music faculty of the Sunderman Conservatory of Music at Gettysburg College, whose input has been invaluable; Nyela Basney for the opportunity of directing Orvieto Musica's Art of Song, which has led to treasures of discoveries in coaching and performing vocal chamber music repertoire; Jeffrey Fahnestock for encouraging me to sit in the stacks and explore music at Sibley Library—your influence on my career cannot be overstated; Russell Miller and Carol Webber for an illuminating course on vocal chamber music; Ari Isaacman-Beck and Adam Cordle for our helpful conversations about strings; Vimbayi Kaziboni for a conductor's philosophical thoughts on chamber music; Chuck Chandler for your brilliance and endless encouragement; the Eastman mafia, which has united me with mentors and friends of exceptional talent and generosity.

To Joan Boytim, my first and most influential voice teacher, who introduced me to the vocal duets that inspired my research interest in this area. I am so proud to be a student of your teaching legacy.

To my family, who has supported and encouraged my love of music since day one. You've never missed a concert, and I couldn't have done this without you.

To Steve Marx, my first proofreader and a tireless source of support, clarity, and humor.

INTRODUCTION

In her article, "Promoting 'Minds-On' Chamber Music Rehearsals," Margaret H. Berg writes, "Chamber music provides myriad opportunities to develop students' ability to think like professional musicians while engaged in the authentic task of working closely with and learning from peers."[1] Most people recognize the term "chamber music," but what distinguishes *vocal chamber music* and why is it an important inclusion in a singer's repertoire and performance experience? Christina Bashford defines "chamber music" in her Oxford Music Online entry:

> In current usage the term "chamber music" generally denotes music written for small instrumental ensemble, with one player to a part, and intended for performance either in private, in a domestic environment with or without listeners, or in public in a small concert hall before an audience of limited size. In essence, the term implies intimate, carefully constructed music, written and played for its own sake; and one of the most important elements in chamber music is the social and musical pleasure for musicians of playing together.[2]

This description does little to improve our understanding of what parameters define *vocal chamber music* unless we delve much deeper into the genre. When one does a library search for chamber music, hundreds of entries for recordings, articles, and books will be discovered, but most are solely instrumental. Only a handful of scholarly resources exist on the topic of vocal chamber music. Few explore how or why vocal chamber music fit into composers' oeuvres, nor the significance of this repertoire as a genre. How does one characterize *vocal chamber music*? Does it include Handel's *Neun Deutsche Arien* for soprano, violin, and continuo? Yes. Does it include Brahms's *Neue Liebeslieder* for four solo voices and four-hand piano? Yes. Does it include Schoenberg's *Pierrot Lunaire* for voice, flute and piccolo, clarinet and bass clarinet, violin, viola, cello, and piano? Yes. Vocal chamber music has been celebrated for hundreds of years, with compositions dating from the medieval period through the twenty-first century. In the thirteenth century, early chamber music was composed in the form of Latin motets, Italian and English madrigals, and French airs de coeur and developed into the popular baroque solo vocal cantata.[3] Classical and romantic composers, increasingly influenced by the development and performance of art song, wrote vocal chamber pieces that reflected the evolving musical and cultural landscape of the middle class. Vocal chamber music in the twentieth century became a vehicle for experimental sounds as composers explored new ways to combine the timbres of modern instruments and, in some instances, electronic music with the voice. Vocalists learned to use nontraditional techniques like Sprechtstimme and percussive sounds, in addition to exploring microtonality. The function of this genre over time has served performers' collaborative interests and composers' exploration of innovative timbral combinations. Because of this, one may find vocal chamber repertoire to complement almost any style and combination of voices, with or without instruments. Many are surprised to discover that composers who are best known for other genres—Brahms, Mendelssohn, Fauré, Lalo, Duparc, Poulenc, Beach, Massenet, for example—also wrote chamber music. This list of repertoire is extensive and has great potential for singers who are looking to enhance their performing and/or teaching repertoire.

Outstanding and invaluable resources on vocal chamber repertoire include *Vocal Chamber Music: A Performer's Guide* by Barbara Winchester and Kay Dunlap, *Chamber Music for Solo Voice and Instruments, 1960–1989: An Annotated Guide* by Kenneth Klaus, *The Art of the Song Recital* by Shirlee Emmons and Stanley Sonntag, *American Vocal Chamber Music, 1945–1980: An Annotated Bibliography* compiled by Patricia Lust, *Vocal Chamber Duets: An Annotated Bibliography* by Corre Berry, *The Comprehensive Catalogue of Duet Literature for Female Voices* by Marilyn S. M. Newman, and *Art Songs with Obligato Instruments* compiled by Richard LeSueur. *So You Want to Sing Chamber Music* serves a different purpose: to help vocalists gain knowledge of repertoire and confidence in their ability to perform chamber music. It provides instruction on practical considerations like preparing scores for rehearsal, how to identify repertoire that suits the technical and artistic needs of a chamber ensemble, how to communicate with instrumentalists in a chamber setting, and how to use chamber music as a pedagogical tool in the vocal studio.

Why is vocal chamber music an important addition to the current canon of familiar art song and operatic repertoire? First, it offers singers the opportunity to collaborate soloistically with other singers and/or instrumentalists while expanding their knowledge of other voice types and instruments. Students of voice spend much of their education training their voices with solo literature in the art song, musical theater, and operatic oeuvres with the intention of pursuing a solo career. This generates a musical focus on individual lines rather than an understanding and appreciation of a score and the synthesis of its parts. Such a specific concentration limits students from practicing critical skills like collaborative awareness, resourcefulness, collective decisions, leadership, time management, and teamwork, which can be learned through studying and performing vocal chamber music.

Second, it provides an intimate musical environment for students to expand their musicianship in ways that include performing music with greater scope as they anticipate other lines and leading through nonverbal communication. In vocal chamber music, which traditionally has no conductor, vocalists and instrumentalists must learn to lead each other through recognizable cues that happen through physical movement, aural indication, or inhalatory gesture as they view every part in the score simultaneously. This physical and emotional awareness develops sensitivity and expands a singer's ability to lead and follow with equal confidence, creating a mutually shared performance of "give and take."

Third, it not only expands repertoire possibilities that offer technical, artistic, and collaborative challenges to the performers but also presents exciting new repertoire to audiences. Although familiar, many art songs and arias have equally strong counterparts in vocal chamber music that offer beautiful melodies within the context of more complex textures. Additional voices and/or instruments increase aural and visual stimulation as the collaborative relationship engages audiences and performers in delightful new ways.

Fourth, it provides a new network of colleagues and helps to diversify a career avenue for those who are looking to expand their professional opportunities. It is no secret that pursuing a solo vocal career in either art song or opera can be economically challenging due to the limited number of opera companies, orchestras, and professional musical organizations. Conversely, vocal chamber music presents itself as a wonderful addition to a professional career. With strong collaborative skills, singers can flexibly work with numerous chamber ensembles based on the specific job, venue, or geographic location. Whether singing professionally with an ensemble or freelancing, gaining knowledge of the different aspects of performing in a vocal chamber music group will augment an individual's vocal skill set, collaborative skills, and professional opportunities.

How does one research and choose vocal chamber music? This book will help singers discover repertoire resources according to their interests and abilities. Many excellent resources exist that have organized vocal chamber music according to instrumentation and voicing, but how does a singer know where to begin? Similar to choosing art song, vocal chamber music repertoire can be identified according to technical and artistic ability, poetic interest, or simply as a pragmatic decision based on the vocalists and instruments interested in performing together. A selection could be as simple as a Carissimi vocal duet with harpsichord, as vocally collaborative as a song cycle for vocal quartet and piano, or as complex as a twentieth-century work with multiple instrumentalists and extended vocal technique. While considering repertoire options, singers will discover different vocal and artistic demands created by performing with large and small ensembles, which can strongly influence decisions. This text will help singers develop vocabulary that enables them to effectively communicate about phrasing, vibrato, timbre, articulation, and style with a string player, a wind player, or other singers and will give them confidence to choose repertoire with any combination of musicians.

Another valuable aspect of vocal chamber music is its pedagogical purpose within the voice studio. Teachers of voice can utilize vocal chamber music by singing duets with their students and learn how this form of instruction can improve diction, phrasing, breath management, vowel modification, and so forth. Instead of employing verbal instruction as the primary medium of communication, the teacher can use visual and aural cues to model musical or technical concepts. Research suggests that a vocal curriculum that effectively integrates modeled vocal chamber music augments traditional solo art song and verbal instruction by equipping students with critical tools such as enhanced collaborative awareness; the ability to read music with greater speed, scope, and comprehension; and the facility to make subtle technical and musical changes in the moment. Performing vocal chamber music may also lessen performance anxiety when students feel like personal responsibility and attention from the audience are spread among more artists. Modeling duets affords teachers and learners a new perspective that acknowledges the experiences, strengths, and areas for growth of students within a supportive environment. It also presents a new teaching tool for those who wish to include vocal chamber music in their curriculum or repertoire portfolio.

This volume serves as a resource on the preparation, rehearsal, performance, and teaching of vocal chamber music for singers, teachers, pianists, instrumentalists, and conductors. Communication and collaboration across studios, departments, and instrumental disciplines are the pathway to stronger musicianship, more performances, deeper interpersonal awareness, and greater professional opportunities. Shirlee Emmons and Stanley Sonntag wrote, "Doubtless there will come a time in your singing career when the pleasures of collaboration with another singer will entice you. Our advice is: succumb immediately!"[4] Including instrumentalists in this sentiment, let's begin our exploration of vocal chamber music.

NOTES

1. Margaret H. Berg. "Promoting 'Minds-On' Chamber Music Rehearsals," *Music Educators Journal* (2008): 48, www.jstor.org/stable/30219664, accessed February 26, 2016.

2. Christina Bashford, "Chamber Music," Oxford Music Online, www.oxfordmusiconline.com/subscriber/article/grove/music/05379, accessed September 14, 2016.

3. Shirlee Emmons and Stanley Sonntag, *The Art of the Song Recital* (Prospect Heights, IL: Waveland Press, 1979), 251.

4. Ibid., 256.

ONLINE SUPPLEMENT NOTE

So You Want to Sing Chamber Music features an online supplement courtesy of the National Association of Teachers of Singing. Visit the link below to discover additional exercises and examples, as well as links to recordings of the songs referenced in this book.

http://www.nats.org/So_You_Want_To_Sing_Book_Series.html

A musical note symbol ♪ in this book will mark every instance of corresponding online supplement material.

1

A BRIEF HISTORY OF CHAMBER MUSIC

An exciting aspect of vocal chamber music is its evolution in function, scope, form, text, voicing, and instrumentation over the course of history. Its development over nine centuries began with traveling amateur musicians who accompanied their courting songs with lute and matured into an art form that can be performed by professional singers in a concert hall with electronic sounds and an ensemble of instrumentalists. While numerous resources exist on the development and analysis of instrumental chamber music as a major genre in the lives of many composers, far fewer exist that focus on vocal chamber music. This chapter will explore the major forms of vocal chamber music, representative repertoire from different time periods, cultural context, and the future of contemporary vocal chamber music.

EARLY CHAMBER MUSIC

The earliest notated vocal music was monophonic, commonly in the sacred form of liturgical chant. Outside of the church, trouvères, troubadours, and German Minnesingers of the eleventh through thirteenth centuries were the earliest traveling musicians who composed and performed secular monophonic melodies. They were often accompanied (or accompanied themselves) on instruments like viol, which provided variety through melodic doubling, repetition, or counterpoint. Matthew Steel writes:

> The troubadours, considered the earliest vernacular song composers, resided in the south of what is largely now France, spoke the regional vernacular now known as "Occitan," and chiefly wrote their texts in the Old Provençal dialect. The trouvères lived in the north of France, writing poetry in Old French. Although the repertories of the troubadours and trouvères appear to have much in common, i.e., themes of love and betrayal, similar poetic genres and even melodies, the songs reflect the considerable differences in politics, religion, and social history between the two contiguous regions.[1]

As interest in secular music and *musica ficta* continued to evolve in the fourteenth century; monophonic song and newly developing polyphonic *formes fixes*, which included the ballade, rondeau, and virelai, were performed mainly in courts before shifting to middle-class patronage. Many types of instrumentation were used:

> At medieval courts a distinction existed between "loud" music (*alto musica, haute musique*), played by such instruments as trumpets, pipes and drums, used for ceremonial and festive events, and "soft music" (*bassa musique, basse musique*), performed by such instruments as harps, fiddles, chamber organs and flutes, sometimes with voices, used at banquets and on more intimate social occasions.[2]

The motet was a significant development for early polyphony. The tenor was derived from chant, and upper voices created a contrapuntal or melismatic complement. Two prominent composers during the medieval period who codified and contributed to the development of the motet and other accompanied secular song forms include Philippe de Vitry (1291–1361), author of the influential Ars Nova treatise, and Guillaume de Machaut (1300–1377), whose revolutionary motets mixed sacred and secular texts. In these works, solo voices were often accompanied by an instrument, which provided melodic support, but Gilbert Reaney clarifies, "The actual instrumental parts are evidently textless tenors and *contratenors*. They are never marked with the names of definite instruments in the manuscripts, but this is not surprising, since the fourteenth century did not rigidly confine its music to one type of instrument."[3] Recordings referenced throughout this chapter can be found by clicking on the "resources" link on the www.nats.org website.

1. "O canenda vulgo per compita" by Philippe de Vitry (Motet) ♪
2. "Ay, amours! tant me dure" by Philippe de Vitry (Chanson) ♪
3. "De ma dolour" by Guillaume de Machaut (Motet) ♪
4. "Se quanque amours" by Guillaume de Machaut (Ballade) ♪

THE RENAISSANCE

With the transition to the Renaissance, a rebirth of cultural, religious, philosophical, and artistic ideas contributed to a new landscape for music. The invention of the printing press enabled manuscripts to become more widely available, which supported music making in the home for those who were able to afford early instruments. During the sixteenth century, Italian strophic songs for voice and instruments called *frottole* flourished, but the leading form during the late Renaissance was the through-composed madrigal for four, five, or six voices. As composers like Orlando di Lasso (1532–1594), Luca Marenzio (1553–1599), and Carlo Gesualdo (1561–1613) wrote more sophisticated and technically challenging madrigals, professional vocal chamber ensembles were formed in many Italian courts:

> A large proportion of the repertory heard in courtly and domestic contexts in the late 15th and 16th centuries was polyphonic vocal music, in particular madrigals. Where such music was performed by voices alone in small or medium-size rooms, it was normal to have one singer per part; however, flexible performing practices meant that instruments, such as lutes and viols, often replaced or doubled some of the voices, probably in accordance with the forces and skills that were available, producing what are commonly called "mixed" or "broken" consorts.[4]

In England, British secular part songs inspired by Italian madrigals were popular, but composers John Dowland (1563–1626) and Thomas Campion (1567–1620) gained notoriety for their lute songs, which are often performed today with lute, classical guitar, or piano arrangement, due to the sophistication of text setting and word painting. In 2006, British singer Sting recorded an album of John Dowland songs entitled *Songs from the Labyrinth* with lutenist Edin Karamazov, reintroducing contemporary audiences to music written four hundred years ago.

1. "Vaghi e lieti fanciulli a 6 voci" by Luca Marenzio ♪
2. "Moro, e mentre sospiro" by Carlo Gesualdo ♪
3. "Tell Me, True Love" by John Dowland ♪

BAROQUE PERIOD

The Florentine Camerata and Claudio Monteverdi's impact on the importance of text declamation and harmonic freedom paved the way for the newly defined *seconda prattica* to strongly influence the changing style of vocal chamber music at the cusp of the baroque period. Affect, chromaticism, a newly dominant vocal line, and basso continuo were all prominent developments at this time. Basso continuo, an accompaniment in the form of a figured bass line, was performed by instrumentalists who improvised harmonies based on given numeric and accidental symbols. "The instruments used included keyboard (organ, harpsichord), plucked string (chitarrone/theorbo, lute, guitar, harp) and bowed string (lirone, bass viol, violoncello)."[5] Monteverdi's eight books of madrigals stand out as a significant historical achievement in chamber music. The concitato-style madrigals in the eighth book "are not traditional five-part madrigals. Rather, they are one to six-part vocal concertos with basso continuo. The theme of love predominates in the collection wherein Monteverdi reshapes the madrigal for a number of different voice pairings—most notably tenor duets with instruments."[6] These vocal concertos, with progressive text painting, harmonies, and forms, illustrate the innovative ways in which text and music could be synthesized.

The multimovement solo cantata with continuo slowly replaced the madrigal and drew attention from many Italian composers like Barbara Strozzi (1619–1677). Her works strongly characterize the seconda prattica with word painting supported by melodic fioratura and harmonic dissonance. In Susan J. Mardinly's excellent article about Barbara Strozzi, she writes:

> [Strozzi] replaces the genre of madrigals with arias, cantatas, and duets, requiring a higher degree of vocal *fioritura* and dramatic characterization than opus one. Although the seeds of Barbara Strozzi's mature style exist in her earlier works, her ability to derive dramatic structure through an independent bass motive emerged graphically in opus two. A large proportion of opus two are strophic arias, generated by the poetic structure. Motives are used for each line of text, often in a duet gesture shared by the gamba. Attention to emotional impact is the basis for metrical construction.[7]

Other Italian composers of cantatas include Luigi Rossi (1597–1653), Giacomo Carissimi (1605–1674), Antonio Cesti (1623–1669), Giovanni Legrenzi (1626–1690), Alessandro Stradella (1639–1682), Antonio Caldara (1670–1736), Benedetto Marcello (1686–1739), Giovanni Bononcini (1670–1747), Nicola Antonio Porpora (1686–1768), and Antonio Vivaldi (1678–1741). Detailed information about Vivaldi's cantatas can be found in Michael Talbot's book *The Chamber Cantatas of Antonio Vivaldi*. Alessandro Scarlatti (1660–1725) achieved new heights in his six hundred cantata compositions:

> These works crown the history of a genre which over more than a century of vigorous growth held a rank second only to opera; indeed contemporaries generally placed it above opera in refinement and regarded it as the supreme challenge to a composer's artistry. Scarlatti was among the last to contribute significantly to its literature.[8]

Numerous French and German composers contributed to the development and popularization of the cantata. In France, the *cantata française* was popular.

> These secular cantatas were composed both for small informal gatherings and for larger events in fashionable society. They were performed by both amateurs and professionals. Like their Italian counterparts, French cantatas were written for one or more solo singers and continuo, with or without obbligato instruments. . . . They became wildly popular in Paris in the period between Lully and Rameau. Most composers of the time, including André Campra, Nicolas Bernier, Louis-Nicolas Clérambault, Montéclair, and Rameau, were drawn to the form.[9]

Chief among the German cantata composers was Johann Sebastian Bach, who wrote secular cantatas like the *"Coffee" Cantata* (BWV 211), *"Peasant" Cantata* (BWV 212), and *"Hunting" Cantata* (BWV 208), among others. These multimovement cantatas integrate dance forms of the period; vary in form between solo arias, recitatives, and multivoice movements; and utilize instrumental ensembles in addition to continuo. Lesser known than J. S. Bach for their output, Dietrich Buxtehude (1637–1707), Georg Philipp Telemann (1681–1767), and Christoph Graupner (1683–1760) also wrote numerous secular cantatas that were performed for various audiences.

> In German and Dutch towns, *collegia musica*, small groups of musicians who gathered regularly to play music, were common. A *collegium musicium* under Sweelinck's direction was established in Amsterdam in the early 17th century for a small group of well-to-do amateur musicians; in Leipzig *collegia* were popular with students eager to read through ensemble music under the guidance of a professional musician.[10]

In addition to cantatas, serenatas and vocal chamber arias and duets with continuo were composed during this period by Giacomo Carissimi (1605–1674), Giovanni Clari (1677–1754), Francesco Durante (1684–1755), George Frideric Handel (1685–1759), and Agostino Steffani (1654–1728). Henry Purcell (1659–1695) published an extensive list of duets in his *Orpheus Britannicus* that "are somewhat uneven in interest, exhibiting instances of the commonplace as well as the magnificent."[11]

1. "Zefiro torna" SV 251 by Claudio Monteverdi ♪
2. "Duo belli occhi fur larmi, onde traffitta" SV 155 by Claudio Monteverdi ♪
3. "Begl'occhi superbi" by Barbara Strozzi ♪
4. "Ardo, è ver, per te d'amore" H62 by Alessandro Scarlatti ♪
5. "Die Katze lässt das Mausen nicht" from *"Coffee" Cantata* BWV 211 by Johann Sebastian Bach ♪
6. "Meine Seele hört im Sehen" from *Neun Deutsche Arien* HWV 207 by George Frideric Handel ♪
7. "Lost Is My Quiet for Ever" by Henry Purcell ♪

CLASSICAL PERIOD

In the mid-eighteenth century, a newly established *galant* style led composers away from basso continuo accompaniment with florid vocal lines to a simpler style with melodic emphasis, newly established harmonic structure, definition of form, and subordinate accompaniment supported by the fortepiano. Haydn's and Mozart's string quartets were the crowning achievement of instrumental chamber music during this period, but vocal chamber music was still an important and evolving genre. The commercialization of published music enabled middle-class families and amateur musicians to perform this music in their homes or in public spaces, particularly as aristocratic patronage began its decline.

Composers of this genre include Franz Joseph Haydn (1732–1809), Johann Christian Bach (1735–1782), Giovanni Paisiello (1740–1816), Wolfgang Amadeus Mozart (1756–1791), Vincenzo Righini (1756–1812), and Luigi Cherubini (1760–1842). Haydn's *Zwei Italienische Duette* for soprano and tenor were composed in 1796 and are a delightful set of duets. He also composed cantatas and songs for two, three, and four voices with keyboard. Johann Christian Bach's *Sei Canzonetta a due*, Opus 4, and *Sei Canzonettas*, Opus 6, are appealing and surprisingly underperformed works. Vincenzo Righini, a vocal pedagogue born in the same year as Mozart, composed chamber duets that exemplify the classical style because of the simple piano accompaniment and formulaic harmonic progressions. Introduced to me by Joan Boytim, *Dodici Duetti da Camera*, Opus 8, served as the inspiration for my doctoral lecture recital and initial research on the pedagogical benefits of using duets in an applied lesson setting.

Four transitional figures between the classical and romantic periods include Ludwig van Beethoven (1770–1827), Louis Spohr (1784–1859), Carl Loewe (1796–1869), and Franz Schubert (1797–1828). Beethoven, in particular, wrote a number of vocal chamber works including *25 Scottish Songs*, *25 Irish Songs*, and *26 Welsh Songs* for one or two voices with violin and cello. Louis Spohr composed duets and quartets and a haunting chamber version of *Erlkönig*, from *6 Gesänge*, Op. 154, for baritone, violin, and piano. In this fourth song, the Erlkönig is represented by an obbligato violin, weaving menacingly throughout the vocal and piano textures before concluding with a solo postlude. In addition to his influential *lieder*, Franz Schubert wrote beautiful duets entitled *Licht und Liebe* and *Mignon und der Harfner* for soprano and tenor and numerous works for vocal quartet. Schubert's commonly performed *Der Hirt auf dem Felsen* for soprano and clarinet and *Auf dem Strom* for soprano, horn, and piano illustrate the burgeoning dramatic equality between all voices.

1. "Pur nel sonno" from *Sei Canzonetta a due*, Op. 4, No. 3 by Johann Christian Bach ♪
2. "Oh! Thou Art the Lad of My Heart" from 25 *Scottish Songs*, Op. 108, No. 11 by Ludwig van Beethoven ♪
3. "Erlkönig" from 6 *Deutsche Lieder*, Op. 154, No. 4 by Louis Spohr ♪
4. *Licht und Liebe* D352 by Franz Schubert ♪
5. *Der Hirt auf dem Felsen* D965 by Franz Schubert ♪

ROMANTIC PERIOD

While the output of vocal chamber music seemed to wane during the classical period due to the focus on instrumental genres such as the string quartet and trio sonata, the early romantic period saw a renewed interest in vocal works with the emergence of German *lieder* and French *mélodie*. The development of the modern piano led to more expressive possibilities while composers were inspired to synthesize poetry and harmony in innovative ways. This included composing a large canon of duets, trios, quartets, and songs with instruments to satisfy both amateur musicians engaging in domestic *Hausmusik* or performing with men's choral societies and professional musicians performing in larger public venues. In the nineteenth century, the study of chamber music served as an important platform for education, recreation, sense of community, social propriety, and intellectual engagement.

During the early romantic period, many composers such as Hector Berlioz (1803–1869), Peter Cornelius (1824–1874), César Franck (1822–1890), Gioachino Rossini (1792–1868), Gaetano Donizetti (1797–1848), Charles Gounod (1818–1893), Édouard Lalo (1823–1892), Giacomo Meyerbeer (1791–1864), Robert Schumann (1810–1856), Felix

Mendelssohn (1809–1847), and Fanny Mendelssohn (1805–1847) wrote chamber music in the form of duets, trios, and quartets for different combinations of voices. Franz Abt (1819–1885), a composer whose extensive song output is often underappreciated, composed nearly one hundred duets that are especially useful for young singers because of limited ranges, simple harmonies, and homorhythmic text settings. Of particular interest are two sets composed specifically for bass voice. Friedrich Curschmann (1805–1841), another lesser-known German composer, also composed accessible and melodic duets and trios. Fanny and Felix Mendelssohn's contribution to duets is extensive, and these melodic songs often feature homophonic textures and rhythms, making them approachable for younger singers.

Robert Schumann, well-known for his *lieder* and solo song cycles like *Frauenliebe und Leben* and *Dichterliebe*, also made significant contributions to vocal chamber music. There is speculation that his *Spanisches Liederspiel*, Opus 74, for vocal quartet and piano, deserves recognition as the first song cycle for four voices.[12] He wrote specific sets of duets and trios, but additional duet, trio, and quartet groupings can be found within larger cycles like *Spanische Liebeslieder*, Opus 138, for four voices and four-hand piano; *Minnespiel*, Opus 101; and *Spanisches Liederspiel*, Opus 74. These pieces expand on the expressive compositional style present in Robert Schumann's solo songs and are outstanding recital repertoire that redefine chamber music as multiple voices of equal melodic significance performing in a soloistic style within a harmonically intertwined narrative.

Later in the nineteenth century, as nationalistic tendencies increased and the relationship between harmony and text gained increasing importance in art song, composers like Johannes Brahms approached vocal duets, trios, and quartets in a collaboratively more meaningful way and they became the zenith of Romantic vocal chamber music. A valuable resource for Brahms's chamber music is Lucien Stark's *Brahms's Vocal Duets and Quartets with Piano: A Guide with Full Texts and Translations*. This book provides information about the history of each chamber work, thorough analysis, vocal range, and approximate duration. Stark writes,

> But generally speaking, Brahms seemed to view the vocal quartet as a sonorously expanded song combined with the linear independence of the

> string quartet. Certainly a major factor in the enduring pleasure provided by the *Liebeslieder* waltzes, for example, is their chamber-music quality—the ever-changing relationships of counterpoint and timbre among the four voices and four-hand piano.[13]

In addition to his famous *Liebeslieder-Walzer*, Opus 52; *Neue Liebeslieder*, Opus 65; and *Zigeunerlieder* quartets, Opus 103, Brahms wrote a number of opuses for two voices (in various combinations) and other lesser-known quartets. Stark laments, "Consequently all of this repertoire except the three large sets is virtually unknown at present because it is performed so rarely, and even those cycles are familiar primarily through the choral performance that Brahms occasionally tolerated but never intended or encouraged."[14] In addition to these works, Brahms also complemented his vocal chamber music with the affecting *Zwei Gesänge*, Opus 91, for voice, viola, and piano.

Other composers who made notable contributions to chamber music in the late romantic period, either in quality or quantity, include Ernest Chausson (1855–1899), Jules Massenet (1842–1912), Max Reger (1873–1916), Henri Duparc (1848–1933), Anton Rubinstein (1829–1894) and his student Pyotr Tchaikovsky (1840–1893), and Gabriel Fauré (1845–1924). Camille Saint-Saëns (1835–1921) wrote duets, but his *Violons dans le soir* for soprano, violin, and piano and *Une flûte invisible* chamber pieces are especially worth exploring because they demonstrate the virtuosic ways in which the voice and instrument share equally dramatic roles in a passionate musical narrative. Antonín Dvořák's (1841–1904) three sets of Moravian duets offer students an opportunity to explore his repertoire (in German or Czech) outside of, or in addition to, his standard solo art song repertory.

1. "La Regata Veneziana" from *Soirée musicales* by Gioachino Rossini ♪
2. "Herbstlied" from *6 Zweistimmige Lieder*, Op. 63, No. 4 by Felix Mendelssohn ♪
3. "Dunkler Lichtglanz" from *Spaniches Liebeslieder*, Op. 138 by Robert Schumann ♪
4. "Verzicht, o Herz auf Rettung" from *Neue Liebeslieder Waltzer*, Op. 65 by Johannes Brahms ♪

5. "Tarantelle" from 2 Duets, Opus 10, No. 2 by Gabriel Fauré ♪
6. "La Fuite" by Henri Duparc ♪
7. "Violons dans le soir" by Camille Saint-Saëns ♪

TWENTIETH AND TWENTY-FIRST CENTURIES

In the twentieth century, chamber music evolved into a medium for modernist conceptions of sounds and artistic vision as a response to the musical excesses of the late nineteenth century, emancipated tonal language, nationalism, technological advancement, world wars, and globalization. This led to exciting new combinations of voices and instruments, using both traditional and extended techniques. James McCalla differentiates compositional periods before World War I, after 1945, and after the 1950s in his book *Twentieth-Century Chamber Music*. He writes:

> For various historical or musical reasons, composers begin to hear new timbres and new timbral combinations, which are as important to the new music of the twentieth century as the so-called breakdown of functional tonality or the inclusion of the voice or of literary or dramatic programs in the previously "pure," absolute genres of chamber music. Works that were new in many ways, such as Schoenberg's *Pierrot lunaire*, sounded that much newer, and were that much more important historically, because of their new sounds.[15]

Chamber music performed by amateur musicians in the home diminished as new repertoire demanded the expertise of professional musicians. Schoenberg's hallmark chamber work, *Pierrot lunaire* (written for voice, flute and piccolo, clarinet and bass clarinet, violin and viola, cello, and piano), is regarded as one of the most pivotal and influential chamber works in the twentieth century because it introduced the singing voice in the avant-garde form of *Sprechstimme* (speech-sing). McCalla states:

> Much more radically than *Verklärte Nacht* or the second quartet, *Pierrot* is the cusp between the nineteenth and twentieth centuries, between Romanticism and modernism. The work was an immediate event in 1912, first in Berlin and then throughout Europe. It gave rise to Ravel's *Three*

> *Poems of Stéphane Mallarmé* (1913) and Stravinsky's *Three Japanese Lyrics* (also 1913), transmuting Schoenberg's "expressionism" into a contemporary French idiom. It resonates still through Boulez's *Le marteau sans maître* of 1957 and thereafter.[16]

A wide range of chamber pieces were written during this period, varying in scope, dramatic intention, style, and instrumentation. Influential twentieth-century chamber works and those that are particularly accessible for recitals or chamber music concerts are highlighted in this resource. For those readers who want to explore musically and interpretively difficult works, please explore repertoire by Karlheinz Stockhausen (1928–2007), Luciano Berio (1925–2003), György Ligeti (1923–2006), George Crumb (b. 1929), and John Cage (1912–1992), whose unconventional works were revolutionary. It is best to consult a reference like Barbara Winchester and Kay Dunlap's book *Vocal Chamber Music: A Performer's Guide*, a comprehensive resource organized by composer and scoring. For those looking to identify chamber music from the second half of the twentieth century, Kenneth S. Klaus's book, *Chamber Music for Solo Voice and Instruments 1960–1989*, is an indispensable resource for repertoire that is lesser-known and offers unique artistic and technical challenges.

The following section moves chronologically through other twentieth and twenty-first century composers who help represent the changing musical landscape of vocal chamber music. It is meant to serve as a point of departure for those who are new to the genre or looking for listening or repertoire suggestions. In addition to melodic duets, Amy Beach composed works for voice with violin or cello and piano, notably *Two Songs*, Opus 100, and the highly romantic *Chanson d'amour*, Opus. 21, No. 1. Ralph Vaughan William wrote numerous songs for voice and instruments including *Along the Field* for high voice and violin; *Four Hymns* for tenor, piano, and viola; *On Wenlock Edge* for tenor, piano, and string quartet; and *Ten Blake Songs* for tenor, soprano, and oboe among others. Igor Stravinsky's *Three Japanese Lyrics* for soprano, two clarinets, two flutes, piano, and string quartet is an important early twentieth-century work that expanded the scope of vocal chamber music in brevity, virtuosity, tonal language, timbral combinations, and text setting. He also composed *Berceuses du chat* for voice and three clarinets and *In memoriam Dylan Thomas* for tenor, four trombones, and string quartet, among other works. Anton Webern wrote a small selection of works with various instrumentation if one is looking for a pointillistic musical challenge. Although her vocal chamber output was small, British composer Rebecca Clarke's *Three Old English Songs* and *Three Irish Country Songs* for voice and violin are an accessible and charming addition to a recital program.

If a soprano can locate eight cellists, Brazilian composer Heitor Villa-Lobos's *Bachianas Brasileira no. 5* creates a memorable chamber music experience. Darius Milhaud wrote chamber works for duets, solo vocal quartet, and numerous chamber pieces with various instruments. Mario Castelnuovo-Tedesco composed the stunning *Romancero Gitano* for vocal quartet and guitar, which would make an intriguing addition to a recital. Two standout works for solo voice and string quartet include Virgil Thomson's *Stabat Mater* for soprano, Ottorino Respighi's *Il Tramonto* for soprano, and Samuel Barber's *Dover Beach* for baritone. Francis Poulenc, in his recognizable tonal language, wrote works with instruments, a stark duet for soprano and baritone (in which the two voices never sing together) entitled *Colloque*, and a chamber cantata for six voices entitled *Un soir de neige*.

For singers wanting to collaborate with a particular instrument, the following resources will be of help: Richard LeSueur's *Art Songs with Obligato Instruments* and articles from the *Journal of Singing*, which include Shelly Batt Archambo's "Music for Voice and Harp" and "Singing on the Horn: A Selective Survey of Chamber Music for Voice, Horn, and Keyboard" by Laurie S. Shelton.

Regarding the future of vocal chamber music, the genre is well-supported and well-represented by a number of living composers who have written chamber music, including Ned Rorem (b. 1923), Andre Prévin (b. 1929), William Bolcom (b. 1938), John Corigliano (b. 1938), John Harbison (b. 1938), Joseph Schwantner (b. 1943), Libby Larsen (b. 1950), Eric Ewazen (b. 1954), Lori Laitman (b. 1955), Ricky Ian Gordon (b. 1956), Jake Heggie (b. 1961), and Jennifer Higdon (b. 1962), among many, many others. Numerous ensembles have been founded that dedicate themselves to the performance of vocal chamber music, both early and contemporary, such as Anonymous 4, TENET, Grammy-nominated Seraphic Fire, and the Grammy-winning Roomful of Teeth.

Jeffrey Gavett, director of the professional vocal chamber ensemble Ekmeles, describes why he performs and commissions new vocal chamber pieces:

> While I love the rich classical tradition of vocal music, I have always felt a certain cultural distance from it. Commissioning and performing new works is a way of making music that is innately of my time and place. My focus on chamber music is partly the result of the DIY nature of the contemporary music scene I joined when I came to New York. Rather than auditioning and waiting for someone to cast me in something I found interesting, I could work with my friends to commission new works and put on our own concerts.

College curricula are increasingly adding chamber music as a requirement, recognizing that twenty-first-century musicians must be not only versatile but able to communicate and collaborate with each other in a meaningful way. Although many chamber music festivals are thriving, few focus on vocal chamber music. Orvieto Musica, a summer music festival in Orvieto, Italy, has dedicated itself to the study of chamber music through an intensive strings program and vocal chamber music program. Founder Nyela Basney remarks:

> I launched "Art of Song" in 2008 as the culmination of an ongoing conversation with Dale Morehouse, a friend who is on the faculty at UMKC, about the need to provide more opportunities for pre-professional singers to further develop interpretive and collaborative musical skills. So often young vocal artists focus their summer study solely on opera repertoire, perhaps long before their voices or their musical instincts are fully ready for the challenge. Studying vocal chamber music enables them to discuss and then to make independent choices (under the tutelage of teachers and coaches) about tempo, rubato, phrasing, text, and style in rehearsals with like-minded colleagues. They learn to express their ideas clearly in rehearsal, to listen carefully, to collaborate, to defend their musical ideas and compromise, and, in the end, to present a performance unique to their combined musical sensibilities. They are challenged to lead when singing with younger colleagues and rise to the occasion when paired with more experienced singers. And they grow in musical sophistication as they participate in rehearsals with string and wind players and collaborative pianists. They grow in confidence and in their joy in music making.

As the current director of Orvieto Musica's Art of Song, I delight in choosing chamber repertoire for a select group of singers and watching them learn exciting new repertoire they can share with each other as they collaborate in rehearsals and in performance, knowing that their collaborative and interpretive skills have been expanded. While the scope, characteristics, and skill level of vocal chamber music composers and performers may have evolved over centuries, the value of an intimate musical conversation has retained its distinction, purpose, inspiration, and allure over centuries.

1. "Mondestrunken" from *Pierrot Lunaire*, Op. 21, No. 1 by Arnold Schönberg ♪
2. "Tsaraiuki" from *Three Japanese Lyrics*, No. 3 by Igor Stravinsky ♪
3. *On Wenlock Edge* by Ralph Vaughan Williams ♪
4. *Three Old English Songs* by Rebecca Clarke ♪
5. "Cantilena" from *Bachianas Brasileiras no. 5* by Heitor Villa-Lobos ♪
6. *Dover Beach*, Op. 3 by Samuel Barber ♪
7. "Bourreaux de solitude" from *Le Marteau sans Maître* by Pierre Boulez ♪
8. "The Butterfly" from *I Never Saw Another Butterfly* by Lori Laitman ♪

NOTES

1. Matthew Steel, "Troubadours and Trouvères," Oxford Bibliographies in Medieval Studies, www.oxfordbibliographies.com/view/document/obo-9780195396584/obo-9780195396584-0148.xml, accessed June 25, 2017.

2. Christina Bashford, "Chamber Music," Oxford Music Online, www.oxfordmusiconline.com/subscriber/article/grove/music/05379, accessed July 1, 2017.

3. Gilbert Reaney, "The Middle Ages," in *A History of* Song, ed. Denis Stevens (New York: WW Norton & Company, 1960), 48–49.

4. Bashford, "Chamber Music."

5. Peter Williams and David Ledbetter, "Continuo," Oxford Music Online, www.oxfordmusiconline.com/subscriber/article/grove/music/06353, accessed July 2, 2017.

6. Sabine Ehrmann, Liner notes for *Madrigali Concertati* (Teldec, 1993).

7. Susan J. Mardinly, "Barbara Strozzi: From Madrigal to Cantata," *Journal of Singing* 58, no. 5 (2002): 382.

8. Malcolm Boyd, Roberto Pagario, and Edwin Hanley. "Scarlatti," Oxford Music Online, www.oxfordmusiconline.com/subscriber/article/grove/music/24708pg1, accessed July 2, 2017.

9. Martha Elliott, *Singing in Style: A Guide to Vocal Performance Practices* (New Haven, CT: Yale University Press, 2006), 86.

10. Steven Zohn, "Telemann, Georg Philipp," Oxford Music Online, www.oxfordmusiconline.com/subscriber/article/grove/music/27635pg6, accessed July 2, 2017.

11. Corre Berry, *Vocal Chamber Duets: An Annotated Bibliography* (Huntsville, TX: Sam Houston State University Press, 1981), 36.

12. Jeffrey Brinton Unger, "Robert Schumann's *Spanisches Liederspiel*" (DMA dissertation, University of Southern California, 1991), 1.

13. Lucien Stark, *Brahms's Vocal Duets and Quartets with Piano: A Guide with Full Texts and Translations* (Bloomington: Indiana University Press, 1998), 2.

14. Ibid., 3.

15. James McCalla, *Twentieth-Century Chamber Music* (New York: Schirmer Books, 1996), 103.

16. Ibid., 67.

2

WHY SING CHAMBER MUSIC?

Singers have long been enamored with art song and opera. Nothing quite compares to the experience of hearing a voice that captures the listener's attention with its singular beauty. When we hear the names of great artists like Luciano Pavarotti, Maria Callas, Dietrich Fischer-Dieskau, Elly Ameling, and Renee Fleming, we associate them with specific repertoire, roles, or performances. This can inspire us to sing the repertoire they have championed, and this is especially true for singers who long to pursue an operatic or solo vocal career. It is no surprise then that vocal curricula and private studios train singers using operatic and art song repertoire because it satisfies technical, artistic, dramatic, and linguistic goals, either as a teaching tool or in performance. So why sing chamber music?

THE TWENTY-FIRST-CENTURY SINGER

Perhaps a good place to begin is with the burgeoning interest in the question, "What does it mean to be a musician in the twenty-first century?" One only needs to type the phrase "twenty-first-century musician" into a search engine or examine the mission statements of conservatories and music programs to realize its ubiquity and impact on collegiate curricula and the current job market. Music and the ways in which we perform, learn, program, share, and listen to it are evolving, and musicians must be ready to adapt in creative and meaningful ways. Chamber music is perhaps an ideal medium for this charge.

DePauw University School of Music launched the 21st-Century Musician Initiative (21CM) and is embracing our changing musical landscape with innovative ideas for performance, education, and community engagement:

> The 21st-Century Musician Initiative is a complete reimagining of the skills, tools and experiences necessary to create musicians of the future instead of the past—flexible, entrepreneurial musicians who find diverse musical venues and outlets in addition to traditional performance spaces, develop new audiences, and utilize their music innovatively to impact and strengthen communities.[1]

The Conservatory of Music at Lawrence University has a web page dedicated to 21st Century Musicianship and uses a diagram to illustrate the qualities that support a modern vision of core musicianship: creative impulse, multimusicality, performance reimagined, social engagement, and an entrepreneurial mindset.[2]

In her 1997 address at the National Association of Schools of Music (NASM) national convention, composer Libby Larsen contributed this thought to "The Role of the Musician in the 21st Century: Rethinking the Core":

> All of them will need to have active listening skills. Many of them, but not all of them, will need technical performance skills. All of them will need skills in critical thinking, about music, about its purpose in our lives, about how well it is or is not performed, and about its place in our cultural environment. They will need to know about our cultural environment and the place of the musician in that environment. And finally, those who move on to teach music will need pedagogical training in both the acoustic core and the produced sound core.[3]

In fall 2014, the College Music Society (CMS) published a report entitled "Transforming Music Study from Its Foundations: A Manifesto for Progressive Change in the Undergraduate Preparation of Music

Majors." Within its suggested considerations for ensembles, the authors write:

> At the same time, it is essential to identify a broad continuum of ensemble formats and correlate these with real-world experience. For example, small groups in which members improvise and compose are arguably some of the most prevalent ensemble types both in the United States and across the globe. Small ensembles of improvising musicians, in any and all styles, could complement the standard classical chamber music model, or provide the basis for an entirely new model that achieves new kinds of diverse synthesis.[4]

Chamber music, a genre which has existed since music's origin, provides the means through which the twenty-first-century musician can achieve many of the professional skills that employers and audiences are seeking. Working alongside other singers or instrumentalists builds pathways for networking and expands a knowledge base of technique, artistry, improvisation, and repertoire. This can create entrepreneurial doorways for innovative performances within the community. It is a collaborative, versatile, enriching, and rewarding path that more vocalists could experience. Some instrumentalists study within chamber ensembles as a curricular requirement, and numerous festivals and programs exist to train instrumental chamber groups. What is the value of performing in small groups, and why does vocal chamber music provide a unique learning environment?

MUSICAL LEADERSHIP AND COLLABORATION

Communication is at the heart of what we as musicians strive to achieve. The question is twofold: With whom are we communicating, and how do we strengthen these skills? If we compare music to theater arts, performing as a soloist is analogous to presenting a monologue to an audience. This dramatically important skill provides insight into the character's psychological profile, personal feelings, and emotional motivation but is only one aspect of the actor's portfolio. The actor must also be able to improvise and convincingly communicate with other actors onstage, reacting in real time to expressions, gestures, timing, and emotions. The ability to respond and engage in dialogue enhances an actor's flexibility, sensitivity, and intention. These virtues are at the heart of chamber music, which allows musicians to lead, respond, learn, and communicate with each other in a personal way that facilitates unparalleled musical, artistic, and *collaborative* growth.

Singers who work with supportive collaborative pianists already understand the value of performing and communicating with another musician. This collaborative relationship is the starting point of departure for sharing musical and artistic ideas, learning how to balance leadership with being an active listener, and responding to musical cues. Within the context of chamber music, however, these skills can be augmented as singers explore repertoire with other instruments and singers.

In her *Journal of Singing* column, collaborative pianist Margo Garrett writes about the importance and relevancy of chamber music:

> Chamber music makes demands on singers that aid them in everything else they do, but cannot be learned in opera or song solely. The humbling experience of not being able to accurately find pitch or rhythm when heard by a string quartet or a wind quintet, rather than a piano, is step one toward amassing the highest musicianship, rarest skills, and personal satisfaction chamber music can and will give to those who seriously and frequently mount this large, beautiful, rich, and varied repertoire.[5]

Expanding collaborative relationships can be an enlightening and enriching experience for singers. Working with instrumentalists will enhance singers' musicianship skills and challenge their understanding of their own technique as they make choices regarding phrasing, vibrato, intonation, and balance in response to an instrument. These decisions can be impacted differently depending on the instrument and its player, the demands of the music, the intricacy of the melodic lines, and the ability to synthesize artistic vision. While wind instrumentalists and singers share breath as the engine of sound, the degree of differences between phrasing, intonation, and articulation can be surprising. Meanwhile, string and percussion instruments require no air to create sound, which necessitates a different conversation and understanding of sound production regarding timing, phrasing, intonation, and articulation. This requires the ability to not only verbally communicate technical goals and ideas but have an understanding of how they are being demonstrated visually and aurally during a rehearsal or performance.

COMPREHENSIVE MUSICIANSHIP

Because of the vast amount of chamber repertoire, singers have the option of performing with almost any combination of instruments and voice types. Some chamber pieces include piano, which provides harmonic support and collaborative stability, and other pieces are composed for voice and a solo instrument. This form of chamber music demands a different type of creative risk because, without the reinforcement of the piano, rhythms, pitches, and phrasing are mutually determined by the singer and the instrumentalist. It requires the desire for shared leadership and a working knowledge of the instrument's technical capabilities so that two equal lines of equal solo importance can converse and respond to each other in a co-constructed musical environment. It also enhances singers' music-reading skills, intonation, and accountability for learning correct rhythms and pitches. Margo Garrett recalls Jan DeGaetani's interest in chamber music as a tool for improving intonation.

> Jan DeGaetani sang a *lot* of chamber music. She was a noted recitalist and fearless and fabulous in new music. Her ear, not just her tuning, was *sine qua non*, and she said she developed her ear from working with so many different instrumentalists and from a lifetime of tuning herself.[6]

Gaining familiarity with the technical abilities of an instrumentalist within the context of a chamber piece can also increase singers' appreciation for the compositional construction of orchestral and operatic scores. Although most singers train their voices with the intention of being able to perform with an orchestra, many never get the opportunity. For others who do, it can be overwhelming the first time new timbres are introduced. As they rehearse and perform in chamber ensembles, singers will increase familiarity with the different tone qualities, ranges, and volume of individual or small groups of instruments. Furthermore, they will learn how to read a score more comprehensively, paying attention not only to the vocal line but to the ways in which the voice and instruments interact and influence each other. This may be from a technical standpoint, in which singers work to match timbre, phrasing, vibrato, or intensity, or expressively as artistic viewpoints and musical ideas are shared and debated. Subsequently, singers will begin to develop a more complete understanding of score reading and discover how to read, value, and anticipate other lines while singing their own.

Concentration, independence, and the ability to respond and adjust to sounds are paramount to the success of a chamber ensemble. These skills are also transferable to performances of solo repertoire, large ensemble works, and opera roles. This can assist in augmenting a singer's versatility, adaptability, and musicianship. While chamber music provides an outstanding opportunity to enhance collaborative skills, it must stem from the most important attribute that is required of all professional twenty-first-century musicians: intellectual curiosity. The most successful collaborators are stimulated by the desire for knowledge about instruments, have an interest in analyzing the sum parts of a score for a more inclusive performance, and possess enthusiasm for boldly expressing oneself within the context of a cooperative musical dialogue.

BUILDING A PROFESSIONAL NETWORK

Not only is performing chamber music a personally satisfying and challenging experience, it builds an important network of professional relationships that generate numerous entrepreneurial opportunities. As musicians in the twenty-first century, we cannot expect to perform exclusively within one genre, in one location, or with one other musician. Instead, we must be prepared to learn what we do not know, create our own opportunities, become flexible, and represent ourselves as versatile musicians. This comes from experiences performing in many different ensembles and with many different musicians. Sharing new musical experiences and gathering new musical perspectives enhance us as musicians, artists, and communicators. Chamber music has assisted in the expansion and popularity of many burgeoning arts entrepreneurship workshops, certificate programs, and degree programs.

As musicians, we are often practicing and training for collective experiences, like orchestra or choir, where a musical goal is to assimilate gesture, sound, vision, and timing. While these learning and performance experiences are important for musicians, they can be difficult to replicate as a freelancer or recent collegiate graduate looking to maintain a performance schedule. Each time a singer embraces the opportunity to perform chamber music with a new colleague, instrumentation, or style of repertoire, they have expanded their resumé, repertoire list, and list of professional contacts. This equates to an expanded network of potential employers and increased performance opportunities.

Performing with a chamber ensemble, or multiple chamber ensembles, also provides singers with the opportunity to be at the helm of their musical career. A small ensemble can provide enough autonomy and support that musicians can set and negotiate fees for gigs, choose appropriate repertoire, maintain a desirable performance schedule, and generate marketing materials for professional exposure. Additionally, the intimate nature and size of a chamber ensemble enables singers to pursue new audiences, venues, outreach opportunities, and community engagement possibilities. One of the best aspects about chamber ensembles is that they simultaneously provide accountability and inspiration. Collaborative growth and the ability to take risks, both artistically and entrepreneurially, depend upon trusting partners to lead with a shared vision. It is this trust and support that enable creative risk, empowered leadership, and synthesis of musical ideas that creates a unique musical environment for performers and audiences. The unique benefits gained from performing with chamber ensembles should incentivize every singer to pursue them.

CAREER VERSATILITY

The technical and artistic demands of performing with other singers in a solo ensemble are wide-ranging. Singers should consider their own vocal production and expression and synthesize it in a soloistic way alongside other performers. This is different than blending or matching sounds, as a singer might in a choral setting. While some attributes must complement other singers' voices, such as diction, dynamics, phrasing, and vibrato, blending of timbres is not paramount. The distinctness of each voice is a distinguishing element of chamber music, and it requires confidence and musical independence to be successful at it. Listen to the Deutsche Grammophon recording of Brahms's *Liebeslieder-Walzer*, Op. 52, performed by Edith Mathis, Brigitte Fassbaender, Peter Schreier, Dietrich Fischer-Dieskau, Karl Engel, and Wolfgang Sawallisch ♪ to experience the thrilling sound of four solo voices and four-hand piano coming together with one artistic vision.

Chamber ensemble singing is a springboard for the cultivation of collaborative and entrepreneurial skills that can be applied to many solo careers in music, and it can serve as a career in and of itself. Pianist Raymond Beegle founded the award-winning New York Vocal Arts Ensemble in 1971, and this quartet, which comprised various singers over the course of its history, performed and recorded vocal chamber music to great acclaim. In a *New York Times* article from 1981, Beegle is quoted as saying:

> The demands on a solo quartet of singers are incredible. They have to know more styles, more languages, more ways of coloring their voices and more kinds of vibrato than any other kind of vocalist. Balance and listening to others is so important.[7]

One of the New York Vocal Arts Ensemble's recordings, *Vocal Chamber Music of the Russian Imperial Court*, expresses the value of chamber music:

> There are many distinguished musical organizations today presenting the great string quartets of Beethoven, Brahms, Schubert, and Schumann on a regular basis to warmly receptive audiences. But what of the equally magnificent works composed by these and other great masters for vocal rather than instrumental quartets—a rich and vast literature that has long been neglected because it falls somewhere between the solo song repertoire and that for large choral groups? Like the string quartet, the vocal quartet calls for artists of outstanding talent and musicianship who are willing and able to blend their individualities into an ensemble that is the best of each of them yet different from any one of them; to achieve a cohesive and moving interpretation of the music to which all of them contribute equally and which no conductor or director dominates.[8]

A contemporary group with a similar pursuit is the Grammy Award–winning vocal ensemble Roomful of Teeth, whose website states,

"Through study with masters from vocal traditions the world over, the eight-voice ensemble continually expands its vocabulary of singing techniques and, through an ongoing commissioning process, forges a new repertoire without borders." This vocal ensemble is redefining vocal chamber music for contemporary audiences by reimagining its scope and function. Founder Brad Wells says:

> My aim with Roomful of Teeth was twofold: to create an arena in which trained classical singers could expand their functional capacities based on focused study with practitioners and teachers of other singing techniques and traditions and second, for that arena to provide composers a more expansive instrument with which to work. The "chamber" aspect of the project comes in various ways. Each singer's capacities have broadened and deepened individually and we encourage every composer to write for each individual in the group, rather than for a generic voice part. Just as important, the music making is fully collaborative, often conductor-less, decidedly democratic.[9]

Other notable contemporary vocal ensembles, including Grammy-nominated Seraphic Fire, Ekmeles, Trident, Ensemble Signal, and others, are displaying the value and reemerging prevalence of vocal chamber music. It is technically and artistically challenging and professionally fulfilling, and it builds important collaborative networks. It also increases professional visibility and versatility and brings lesser-performed repertoire to audiences in creative and portable ways. With recognition of its professional viability, how can chamber music be added to curriculums or within studios with maximum educational benefit? How can it be utilized as a teaching tool that becomes as useful and frequent as art songs and arias?

PEDAGOGIC OPPORTUNITIES

The pedagogical value of chamber duets and trios is uniquely outstanding and is discussed in detail in chapter 6. It provides opportunities for experienced and inexperienced singers alike to grow in new technical, artistic, and dramatic dimensions. The ongoing support of collaborative relationships creates safe environments in which singers can respond and make corrections during rehearsals and performances. Learning opportunities also exist for singers who struggle with acting or communicating emotions as they mirror collaborative partners.

Programs with chamber music integration among vocal and instrumental departments create healthy learning environments as students coach with multiple teachers and gain different perspectives. Approaching a chamber work through the lens of an instrumentalist's part during a coaching can directly influence a singer's technique. This may be as a result of modeling a sound or articulation, watching for bow or key strokes, or through observation of body language. Margo Garrett notes:

> One of the main objectives of the greatest singers I have ever known, and one that affords the greatest pleasure in their singing, they say, is the fun of coloring words. Any word, in any language, needs to be colored first by actually feeling the meaning while singing the word; it will actually change vocal color. Then, the ability to darken or change the vowel will color the word further. And this coloring of vowels is learned, in my observation, by imitating string, wind, and brass instruments—and not from any piano. Ah, but once learned, how wonderful when a singer brings that knowledge and skill back to us at the piano![10]

Chamber works written for two (or more) voices and piano present learning opportunities directly related to modeling vocal qualities such as breathing, phrasing, dynamics, vibrato, diction, expression, acting, and gesturing. Teachers can use vocal duets as a means of modeling correct sounds as they sing together with their students. It is an efficient and effective way to demonstrate correct diction, style, and phrasing compared to verbal instruction alone. Chamber music, like solo art song and operatic repertoire, comes in many different styles, languages, and levels of technical and artistic difficulty. Choosing appropriate repertoire for pedagogical growth is at the discretion of the teacher. Acting and generating appropriate facial expressions in response to another singer—or simply reflecting expressions—is another benefit of using chamber music as a pedagogical tool. If teachers feel that singing with their students distracts them from the ability to teach and assess, they can pair students together for similar results. Personal research suggests performing chamber music can lessen performance anxiety in some singers because when the focus is no longer solely on them, it is easier to recover from mistakes. Additionally, when singers feel accountability toward an ensemble, they are less likely to feel stigmatized by errors and increase resiliency.

Chamber music creates variety in recital and concert programming. Sets of art songs and arias can be augmented by chamber music with voices or instruments, and the variation in voice types and instrumentation adds visual, aural, technical, and artistic variety to programs. Chamber repertoire can complement existing sets of art songs, since many singers are surprised to discover that their favorite art song composers also composed exquisite chamber repertoire. A set of songs enhanced by chamber music could introduce additional instrumentalists or vocalists and enrich the program. Like infusing a bold color to a monochromatic painting, the addition of another musician can dramatically stimulate the performer's style, interpretation, and confidence.

Cross-departmental (or cross-studio) collaboration increases a sense of community within music programs and can create an opportunity for a chamber music series or chamber music outreach program. This exciting venture generates entrepreneurial initiative and community engagement as students create new partnerships and gain increased performance opportunities. This initiative can help students better understand the communities and audiences in which they live and how to program music and interact with audiences in meaningful ways.

FINAL THOUGHTS

The benefits of researching, rehearsing, and performing chamber music are impactful, important, and critical to the success of the twenty-first-century musician. Now that some of its benefits have been established, how does one go about performing chamber music?

NOTES

1. "21st-Century Musician (21CM)," DePauw University, music.depauw.edu/21cm/, accessed April 15, 2018.

2. "21st Century Musicianship," Lawrence University, www.lawrence.edu/conservatory/21st-century-musicianship, accessed April 15, 2018.

3. "The Role of the Musician in the 21st Century: Rethinking the Core," Libby Larsen, libbylarsen.com/as_the-role-of-the-musician, accessed April 15, 2018.

4. Patricia Shehan Campbell, David Myers, Ed Sarath, Juan Chattah, Lee Higgins, Victoria Lindsay Levine, David Rudge, and Timothy Rice, "Transforming Music Study from Its Foundations: A Manifesto for Progressive Change in the Undergraduate Preparation of Music Majors," Report of the Task Force on the Undergraduate Music Major November 2014, College Music Society, 44, www.mtosmt.org/issues/mto.16.22.1/manifesto.pdf, accessed April 15, 2018.

5. Margo Garrett, "The Importance of Studying Vocal Chamber Music," *Journal of Singing* 74, no. 1 (2017): 103.

6. Ibid., 100.

7. Bernard Holland, "The 'Call' of Vocal Chamber Music," *New York Times*, Sunday, June 7, 1981, www.nytimes.com/1981/06/07/arts/the-call-of-vocal-chamber-music.html.

8. *Vocal Chamber Music of the Russian Imperial Court*, New York Vocal Arts Ensemble (VOX/Turnabout—TV 34686, 1978), LP.

9. Bradley Wells, e-mail to author, April 15, 2018.

10. Garrett, "The Importance of Studying," 101.

3

HOW TO PROGRAM VOCAL CHAMBER MUSIC

There is a vast array of vocal chamber music repertoire that spans the twelfth through twenty-first centuries in various languages, styles, and combinations of voices and instruments. How does one find a piece that suits one's needs, and how can it complement an otherwise traditional recital of solo art songs and opera arias? Instead of starting with a particular composer or style, one should first consider instrumentation. Is your chamber ensemble strictly vocal? What voice types are available for an ensemble? If you are performing with instrumentalists, how many are involved and what instruments do they play? Is there a keyboardist? What are the individual and collective strengths of the ensemble members?

ENSEMBLE AND INSTRUMENTATION CONSIDERATIONS

In some instances, vocalists will be able to create their vocal chamber ensemble and choose the instrument(s) with which they would like to perform. Other times, the instrumentation will be predetermined, either by educational curricular requirements or as requested by an employer. In either case, these parameters will narrow the field of repertoire options. It may surprise the vocalist to discover that vocal chamber music encompasses a wide range of instrumental and vocal combinations. The indispensable resource *Art of the Song Recital* by Shirlee Emmons and Stanley Sonntag contains two comprehensive appendices devoted to repertoire for voices with other voices and voices with instruments, alphabetized by composer and categorized by voicing and instrument. Corre Berry's *Vocal Chamber Duets: An Annotated Bibliography* specializes its focus on vocal chamber duet literature, with helpful indices that organize repertoire according to voice combinations and poets. Four additional resources for vocal chamber music repertoire with instruments include *Chamber Music for Solo Voice and Instruments, 1960–1989: An Annotated Guide* by Kenneth Klaus; *Art Songs with Obbligato Instruments* compiled by Richard LeSueur, which is categorized by instrument; *Vocal Chamber Music: A Performer's Guide* by Barbara Winchester and Kay Dunlap; and *American Vocal Chamber Music, 1945–1980: An Annotated Bibliography* compiled by Patricia Lust. The last two resources contain entries that are alphabetized by composer and categorized by instrumentation and voicing in their appendices.

In addition to these books, there are wonderful articles in the National Association of Teachers of Singing *Journal of Singing*, including "Singing on the Horn: A Selective Survey of Chamber Music for Voice, Horn and Keyboard" by Laurie S. Shelton; "Airs from the British Isles and Airs from Moravia—Duets Incorporating Diverse Folk Materials" by Corre Berry; and "Music for Voice and Harp" by Shelley Batt Archambo. Since the publication of these resources, many new chamber pieces have been composed that are not yet compiled in a reference source but worth locating and performing. A few examples include *Into the Fire* for mezzo-soprano and string quartet (2012) by Jake Heggie ♪; *Gwendolen's Dream* for soprano, clarinet, and cello (2002) by Jocelyn Hagen ♪; *Three Poems of William Butler Yeats* for high voice, violin, cello, and piano (2009) by Timothy Hoekman ♪; and *Green Sneakers* for baritone, string quartet, and piano (2008) by Ricky Ian Gordon ♪. Other contemporary composers with chamber works include Judith Shatin, André Previn, William Bolcom, Lori Laitman, Jennifer Higdon, John Corigliano, Libby Larsen, John Greer, Ned Rorem, and Dominick Argento, in addition to many more.

Vocal Chamber Music with Instruments

Let us begin our search for vocal chamber music with instruments. It is important to keep in mind the evolution of modern instruments so that one does not expect to find vocal chamber music from the baroque era that includes saxophone or vibraphone. Music of the medieval and Renaissance eras was mostly polyphonic vocal music with the occasional addition of an instrument on the cantus firmus. A useful and comprehensive list of early musical instruments with descriptions can be found in *Chamber Music: An Essential History* by Mark A. Radice.[1] Vocal chamber music of the baroque era expanded its instrumental variety with the birth of the cantata, and obbligato instruments gained equality with the vocal line. The most common instrumental accompaniment was the baroque continuo, composed of keyboard (organ or harpsichord) and cello or violone (double bass). However, cantatas that included additional obbligato instruments became more popular toward the end of the baroque period. Today, it is common to perform baroque music on modern or historical instruments, although period instruments and their players can be more difficult to locate. Baroque obbligato instruments included early versions of the trumpet, horn, bassoon, flute, guitar, oboe, trombone, violin, viola, and cello. The following Renaissance and baroque composers created a large canon of vocal chamber music and would provide an excellent starting place for choosing repertoire:

John Dowland (1563–1626)
Claudio Monteverdi (1567–1643)
Heinrich Schütz (1585–1672)
Alessandro Grandi (1586–1630)
Barbara Strozzi (1619–1677)
Dieterich Buxtehude (1637–1707)
Henry Purcell (1659–1695)
Alessandro Scarlatti (1660–1725)
Francois Couperin (1668–1733)
Antonio Caldara (1670–1736)
Giovanni Bononcini (1670–1747)
Antonio Vivaldi (1678–1741)
George Philipp Telemann (1681–1767)
Jean-Philippe Rameau (1683–1764)

Johann Sebastian Bach (1685–1750)
Domenico Scarlatti (1685–1757)
George Frideric Handel (1685–1759)

Regarding the classical era, Mark Radice explains, "The increasing importance attached to the amateur player accounted in large part for the proliferation of chamber music genres. It also accounted for the characteristic style that came to be associated with chamber music of the mid-eighteenth century, a style that was light, pleasant, and agreeable."[2] Although classical vocal chamber music was not as prevalent as instrumental chamber music, repertoire exists that could be a noteworthy addition to a program. The romantic era was a ripe musical landscape for vocal chamber music, namely because of the development of the modern piano, the birth of *lieder* and *mélodie*, and printed music becoming available for purchase and performance by amateur musicians. Christina Bashford writes, "During the nineteenth century commercial concerts devoted to chamber music became an established part of the musical calendar in many cities, and for most amateur musicians listening to concert performances of chamber music became just as important as—if not more important than—participating in it privately."[3] Composers on the following list wrote a rich array of classical and especially romantic vocal chamber music with instruments.

Franz Joseph Haydn (1732–1809)
Johann Christian Bach (1735–1782)
André Grétry (1741–1813)
Wolfgang Amadeus Mozart (1756–1791)
Ludwig van Beethoven (1770–1827)
Louis Spohr (1784–1859)
Franz Schubert (1797–1828)
Felix Mendelssohn (1809–1847)
Heinrich Proch (1809–1878)
Franz Abt (1819–1885)
Johannes Brahms (1833–1897)
Camille Saint-Saëns (1835–1921)

In the twentieth century, nationalism, the rise of industrialism, and two world wars changed the face of society, politics, personal identity, and music. Vocal chamber music followed suit with increasing harmonic and textural complexity and evolved to become an important vehicle for compositional experimentation. Mark A. Radice writes:

> The expense and logistical challenges involved with rehearsing large ensembles as well as the diversity and novelty of many musical styles cultivated since 1900 have been powerful stimuli for the composition of chamber music. Because tone color has assumed greater importance in music since the time of Debussy, many of these chamber works have unique or distinctively modified instrumentations. Other factors, such as polycultural synthesis, advances in electronic and other technological devices, philosophies, and religious beliefs, have played a role in shaping chamber music composed during approximately the last seventy-five years.[4]

The following composers produced exciting twentieth-century vocal chamber music repertoire:

Jean Sibelius (1865–1957)
Albert Roussel (1869–1937)
Ralph Vaughan Williams (1872–1958)
Maurice Ravel (1875–1937)
Igor Stravinsky (1882–1971)
Anton Webern (1883–1945)
Arthur Honegger (1892–1955)
Paul Hindemith (1895–1963)
Luigi Dallapiccola (1904–1975)
Alan Hovhaness (1911–2000)
Morton Feldman (1926–1987)
George Crumb (b. 1929)
Peter Maxwell Davies (1934–2016)
Libby Larsen (b. 1950)
Ricky Ian Gordon (b. 1956)
Jennifer Higdon (b. 1962)

If vocal chamber music selections are not previously assigned or requested, it can often be a bonding experience for a chamber ensemble to consider options and read repertoire to help inform a decision. This activity is an opportunity for musicians to share opinions about interpretation and practice sight-reading, musical leadership, and nonverbal communication. Additionally, it would be indicative of the ensemble's interpersonal dynamics, which could determine role strengths and the success of future ventures. Although recordings do exist for most pieces, there are plenty of vocal chamber works that have never been recorded, requiring ensembles to sight-read compositions to hear them for the first time. This presents a rare and exciting opportunity for musicians to simultaneously develop an individual and collective musical identity as they read, hear, and interpret new music.

Vocal Chamber Music with Other Voices

As we have learned, vocal chamber music has a wide definition that encompasses voices with instruments *and* exclusively vocal ensembles, which present their own benefits and challenges. No longer are singers balancing timbre, vibrato, and style with other instruments; they are balancing them with other voices. When singers perform duets, trios, or quartets together, it can be a strange experience because it differs from their experiences in choirs. In choral ensembles, singers are often asked to match timbres and phrasing, follow a conductor, sing similar dynamics and words, and create a unified sound and emotion. It can be a challenge to convince vocal chamber ensembles that the technical, musical, and artistic goals have changed. In a vocal chamber ensemble, singers are expected to function as soloists. This involves teaching students how to sing confidently as a soloist, share artistic ideas, and lead physically, vocally, and musically. How is this done, and what repertoire exists for vocal duets, trios, and quartets?

One must consider how to train young singers for success as soloists within a vocal chamber ensemble. This repertoire offers young and experienced singers the opportunity to assert their personality and vocal identity within a group of other voices. There are inherent differences in every personality and voice, and these should be celebrated in the context of a vocal chamber piece. When making repertoire decisions, students should be carefully assigned or given the option of choosing their vocal line (if the piece does not specify voice types). This presents singers a new opportunity to either sing a melody line or sing a harmony line. In an effort to create soloistic equality between vocal lines, singers may need to exchange parts so the lines are balanced. In instances where repertoire indicates soprano, mezzo-soprano, tenor, baritone, or bass, the decisions are obvious.

One of the most interesting aspects of vocal chamber music is how a group of singers interpret the same poetry. Unlike opera, wherein roles and plot are designated by the libretto, vocal chamber music requires two or more singers to share an interpretation of the same poem. This offers a tremendous opportunity for singers to communicate their interpretive ideas to others and to learn how to share and communicate them in the context of performance. At times, there may be discrepancies between interpretative instincts, and this can foster flexibility, mindfulness of different ideas, and problem-solving skills. Musicians may also grow from disagreement and gain a greater appreciation for interpretive possibilities when inspired by peers. Once an interpretation is agreed upon, authentic communication must occur between ensemble members and the audience for an effective performance. This type of active communication is another striking deviation from choral singing. Since they are acting as equal leaders in the ensemble, singers must be musically aware of each other at all times, responding simultaneously to the relationship between each other's texts, notes, phrasing, inhalation, onset, release, intonation, vibrato, diction, dynamics, style, and artistic impulses. This can be a multisensory and demanding activity that challenges singers as soloists and collaborators.

The following lists of repertoire for voices with other voices are suggested according to technical and artistic ability. A more comprehensive list can be found in appendix A and online in PDF form at www.NATS.org.

Beginner

Berlioz, Hector	"Pleure, pauvre Colette" ♪
Carissimi, Giacomo	"Rimanti in pace" from *Duetti da Camera* ♪
Donaudy, Stefano	"Amor s'apprende" ♪
Franck, César	"Soleil," Op. 89, No. 5 ♪
Mendelssohn, Felix	"Ich wollt meine Lieb," Op. 63, No. 1 ♪
Schumann, Robert	"Liebesgarten," Op. 34, No. 1 ♪
Tosti, Francesco	"Venetian Song" ♪
Vaughan Williams, R.	"It Was a Lover and His Lass" ♪

Moderate

Beach, Amy	"A Canadian Boat Song" from *Songs of the Sea*, Op. 10, No. 1 ♪
Brahms, Johannes	"Die Schwestern," Op. 61, No. 1 ♪
Gounod, Charles	"Barcarola" ♪
Massenet, Jules	"Matinée d'Été" ♪
Paladilhe, Émile	"Au bord de l'eau" ♪
Rossini, Gioacchino	"I Gondolieri" ♪
Schubert, Franz	"An die Sonne" D 43 ♪
Tosti, Francesco	Allons voir ♪

Advanced

Cornelius, Peter	"Ich und Du" ♪
Duparc, Henri	La fuite ♪
Fauré, Gabriel	"Tarantelle," Op. 10, No. 2 ♪
Hagen, Jocelyn	"Arise, My Love" from *The Time of Singing Has Come* ♪
Poulenc, Francis	"Colloque" FP 108 ♪
Reger, Max	"Sommernacht," Op. 14, No. 3 ♪
Schubert, Franz	"Gebet" D815 ♪
Viardot, Pauline	"Habanera" ♪

VENUE AND PERFORMANCE SPACE

Performance space is another important condition when forming a chamber ensemble and subsequently choosing repertoire. It is important to research and understand the spaces in which chamber music was originally performed. If chamber music is, by definition, for a small number of performers in intimate spaces, modern recital halls and concert venues can pose both problems and solutions. Balance and ensemble cohesion considerations play an important role in successful performances due to acoustics and a stage's physical size. Smaller spaces with dry acoustics create minimal reverberation and expose precise performances. Live acoustics with greater reverberation can make aural awareness more difficult and weaken musical accuracy. In other instances, contemporary chamber ensemble music may require electronic equipment like amplification, and appropriate equipment must be available in a performance space. One must also be mindful when choosing repertoire for particular venues. If a chamber group is asked to perform for the opening of an intimate art gallery, choosing repertoire for voice, trumpet, piccolo, and snare drum may not match the ambience of the performance space or the mood of its event. A chamber ensemble must be aware if a piano, fortepiano, or harpsichord is available in the space. If it is not, repertoire options may be further limited, and one must bring a tuning device such as a pitch pipe. Lighting in a performance space is also important and can vary substantially, which may necessitate providing stand lights. Vocalists may need to make a decision to use a black folder or a stand and, if they are not provided, travel with them.

PRACTICAL CONSIDERATIONS

Once the vocal chamber ensemble has been established based on instrumentation and performance space, the selection of music can begin. After instrumentation, chamber music repertoire can be searched by multiple criteria, including composer, time period, topic, poet, and so on, just like solo art song repertoire. After a selection is made, it is necessary to gain access to a full score and individual instrumental parts. At times it can be a challenge to find some vocal chamber repertoire, but overall, many publishers have surprisingly vast libraries. Investing in the purchase of vocal chamber music is an important and necessary aspect of being a responsible performer and musician. Ideally, the vocalist will sing from the score when possible, and it is important that each instrumentalist has access to a score, in addition to their individual part. In many instances, performers will need to tape pages together for transitions or tape together a combination of a part and a score for a successful performance. The distribution of parts *and* scores is important in the event that one member of the ensemble miscounts and needs to find an appropriate reentrance point. It is also important so all chamber members can make the same musical markings in their music like phrasing, dynamics, breathing, and translations. Chamber music can be a study in ensemble communication and musical cohesion. Like any healthy relationship, being aware of the needs of others is paramount. In a musical setting, this includes dynamic variations, breath marks, fingering shifts, specific tuning considerations, and so forth. If one instrumentalist needs to mark something, it is wise to communicate this to the entire ensemble as it may be helpful or necessary for another member. More will be discussed about this in chapter 4.

Determining the musical difficulty is important for oneself and for *all* performers in the ensemble. Oftentimes, musical and technical challenges vary between individual parts or lines. There are instances when a difficult part can even be reinterpreted for other instruments, as decided by the performers or as designated by the composer. Before programming a piece that includes instruments of which you have little knowledge, speak with your chamber music colleagues and make an effort to learn about that instrument. What is the range? What is considered easy or difficult? Asking questions can help provide a strong background for future programming.

Another practical consideration is attire. Many instrumentalists are accustomed to wearing formalwear for orchestral or wind ensemble concerts. In chamber music, this can be a personal choice between members of the ensemble. All performers can wear black, the ensemble can designate a color scheme, or the instrumentalists can wear black and the vocalist can deviate with color for variation. For a piece with multiple vocalists, they can wear matching colors or choose complementary colors. It is simply a decision that must be discussed and that will create a visual representation of your collective preparation, interpretation, and performance.

COMPENSATION FOR COLLABORATION

Within the context of university or curricular requirements, some vocal chamber ensembles will form, rehearse, and perform together for personal growth, professional experience, and sometimes a grade. In this situation, a small token of thanks (monetary or otherwise) would adequately convey gratitude. Other musicians may form professional vocal chamber ensembles to further their knowledge of repertoire, grow as musicians and collaborators, and expand their musical networks for future professional opportunities. These groups may make financial decisions including, but not limited to, income distribution, management fees, marketing and publicity, filing as a tax-exempt organization, fundraising, and seeking institutional or donor support. Regardless of compensation, it is critical to act collegially and professionally at *all* times, provide scores and parts for colleagues, schedule rehearsals efficiently, be respectful of others, and be punctual to rehearsals. More about this will be discussed in detail in chapter 6.

DO YOU NEED A CONDUCTOR?

Vocal chamber music can be an exciting genre because of the leadership, autonomy, and artistic responsibility it offers individual musicians within the context of an ensemble. Unlike a choir, wherein the goal is to actualize the conductor's interpretation of the work, vocal chamber ensembles are self-directed. This can provide a unique opportunity of personal and collective responsibility for the group's performance and shared communication of artistic interpretation without external control. Based on this knowledge and historical performance practice, vocal chamber ensembles rarely have conductors. Instead, musicians lead by aural, kinesthetic, and visual cues that, after practice, replace the need for an external conductor. In many instances, the tapestry of musical and artistic cohesion is more tightly woven *because* there is not a conductor. Ensemble members must learn to trust, communicate, share ownership of the musical interpretation, and take risks together. Because chamber music began as an intimate art form between few musicians in small spaces, one can conclude that the relationship between ensemble members can be musically and artistically intimate. A conductor may become an artistic interloper amid the stable foundation of an intimate musical relationship.

A conductor is welcomed and sometimes musically necessary when chamber ensembles are large, seated in artistic configurations, or performing complex repertoire. For a difficult chamber work like *Le marteau sans maître* for contralto, alto flute, guitar, vibraphone, xylorimba, percussion, and viola by Pierre Boulez, a conductor is expected. In instances of complex vocal chamber music, conductors can be critical for providing cues, leading metric changes, hearing and maintaining a balance of timbres, shaping dynamics, and changing tempi. Ensembles who want guidance in rehearsals but strive for an autonomous performance might see value in inviting a conductor to early rehearsals for help with studying the score and gaining confidence with musically challenging transitions. In summary, although vocal chamber repertoire is traditionally self-directed, composers in the twentieth and twenty-first centuries have provided some exceptions.

CHOOSING REPERTOIRE TO SUIT YOUR VOICE

Technical and Artistic Considerations

When choosing vocal chamber music repertoire, it is appropriate for singers to consider the following questions:

1. What is the range and tessitura of voice(s) and instrument(s)?
2. Is it a complementary relationship between technical and artistic abilities?
3. Does it accentuate my voice?
4. Does the text or poetry inspire me?

With such a wide array of options, let us explore each of these questions and discover what possibilities exist within vocal chamber music repertoire.

Range and Tessitura A singer must consider the range and tessitura of his or her part *and* those of additional singers' lines and/or instruments. Every ensemble participant should examine the entirety of the piece to determine whether it is appropriate for his or her technical ability. Vocalists are accustomed to focusing on their individual lines as soloists, with less opportunity for collaboration. Subsequently, a rewarding aspect of vocal chamber music is expanding one's perspective and awareness of the entire score, recognizing the equality between and intersection of each line. For example, is each musician equally skilled to perform Schoenberg's *Pierrot Lunaire*? (figure 3.1).

If a singer is interested in performing Schubert's *Der Hirt auf dem Felsen* for soprano, clarinet, and piano, the soprano should ask the clarinetist if he or she has the technical facility to perform the ending at an appropriate tempo (figure 3.2).

1. Mondestrunken.

Figure 3.1. Arnold Schoenberg, "Mondestrunken" from *Pierrot Lunaire*, Op. 21, mm. 1–7. *Creative Commons* (CC BY-SA 3.0)

Figure 3.2. Franz Schubert, *Der Hirt auf dem Felsen*, D965, mm. 335–349. *Creative Commons* (CC BY-SA 3.0)

Chamber music provides an incomparable learning experience that will facilitate improved communication and an increased ability to read and understand music written for other voice types and instruments. Consider that the role of a conductor is to understand every instrument in his or her ensemble—its timbres, its technical capabilities, its strengths, its weaknesses—and communicate a sense of understanding and synthesis between multiple musicians. If chamber music is more nuanced due to its intimate nature, and each musician takes an equal role as a conductor and leader, then these responsibilities are shared by each individual. The singer should learn ranges, timbres, and capabilities of other voice types and instruments so that choosing vocal chamber repertoire becomes easier as they invest in understanding their musical colleagues.

Complementary Technique and Artistry In operatic repertoire, *Fach*, artistic and technical demands of the role, and orchestral texture are important considerations that can determine repertoire possibilities. In art song, there is more ambiguity and subjectivity because it often depends on the vocal range, dynamic range, texture of the accompaniment, length of the song, and artistic maturity. Although choosing vocal chamber repertoire is most closely related to choosing solo art song repertoire, a singer must consider the technical and artistic demands they face personally and the technical and artistic demands for the *entire ensemble*. In the beautiful chamber work *Dover Beach* by Samuel Barber, the evocative poetry by Matthew Arnold is rich with descriptive metaphors and symbolism. While it can be a rewarding experience to study and perform this piece, the baritone and string quartet must be competent musicians, collaborators, and poetic interpreters. In one experience I had coaching this piece, I asked the ensemble to explain what was happening in a particular phrase—what did the music in that phrase symbolize? Unfortunately, the singer was the only one able to provide an answer. This suggested a lack of collaboration and artistic vision between the musicians in the group. Based on this experience, the string players began discussing their poetic and musical interpretations, which differed from the singer. What an important discovery! After sharing ideas, the ensemble demonstrated equal musical and artistic ownership, and the cohesion and intensity of the work grew dramatically. They began discussing exciting questions like, "Why did Barber choose that particular chord to highlight that word? Who has the melody? Does my timbre represent a particular emotion?" It was an inspirational moment of growth for the musicians involved.

Accentuating the Voice The question "Does it accentuate my voice?" is an interesting one in vocal chamber music, a genre that simultaneously showcases the collective *and* individual sounds of the group. In ensembles that feature voices with other voices, singers must look through the entire score and consider their timbre in relationship to others. The concept of choral "blend" is undesired more often than not in chamber music, but the voices should be balanced in regard to presence and volume. They should also have an equal ability to technically execute the piece, shape the dynamics and phrasing, and interpret the poetry with correct text inflection and diction. Franz Abt wrote a number of German duets that are strophic, melodically and rhythmically homophonic, and limited in range. These provide an appropriate musical setting for young duet partners so they can reinforce each other's singing through shared diction, phrasing, and dynamics. A very different example is *La fuite* by Duparc, which is grand in dynamic, artistic, and technical scope. The soprano and tenor lines overlap soloistically, the rhythmic and harmonic language is complex, the range is wide, and the French poetry is symbolic. This duet demands advanced singers who feel vocally, musically, and interpretively confident.

Instrumental vocal chamber music that incorporates different timbres can affect balance. Projecting alongside a solo flute in Libby Larsen's delightful *Righty, 1966* or alongside a solo oboe in Vaughan Williams's mesmerizing *Ten Blake Songs* is very different than performing Wolfgang Plagge's *Libera Sequentiarum* with trumpet or Respighi's *Il Tramonto* with string quartet. Light voices in particular will need to consider how well their sound will project beside a loud instrument or within a group of instruments. Are the instrumental sounds sustained against the voice, and if so, in what range are they playing? Will the instrument be playing in its most resonant range and cover the singer in a low part of their range, or is the singer mostly in his or her most resonant range? Are the dynamics balanced between the vocal line and instrumental line? There are certainly accommodations that can help a singer. Careful attention to the direction of a bell or sound source of the instrument is important. Directing the sound away from the singer can help so he or she is not tempted to oversing. It can also be helpful if the instrument's sound is not directed at the audience, which can cause an unanticipated imbalance. Being creative with staging can often be the solution to alleviating balance issues. If a trumpet player standing upstage left of a singer angles the bell downstage left, neither the singer nor the audience will be overwhelmed by the sound. Balance issues with a string quartet can be lessened if the singer stands downstage of the quartet. Being creative with staging can often be the solution to alleviating balance issues.

Poetic Inspiration Being inspired to communicate the text of a work as a solo performer is a powerful desire and an important aspiration. To discover and share a collective interpretation with an ensemble can have an equally profound impact for the performers and the audience. The canon of vocal chamber repertoire is vast and includes settings of a myriad of poets. One recommended resource that organizes repertoire by poet is *American Vocal Chamber Music, 1945–1980: An Annotated Bibliography* compiled by Patricia Lust. It is common to thematically program recital sets around one poem interpreted by multiple composers. This can become even more exciting when one or more of the settings is chamber music. A wonderful example comes in the seven settings of Goethe's *Erlkönig*, edited by Max Friedlaender and Hans Sitt. Among compositions for voice and piano, Spohr's setting with violin is included. Hearing the timbre of a violin set as the character or "voice" of the *Erlkönig* in its high range makes a strong and unsettling impact for some when contrasted with the other "traditional" settings. Another example of a poem found in art song and vocal chamber music is Lewis Carroll's *Jabberwocky*, set by Richard Hundley for voice and piano and William Sydeman for soprano (or tenor), flute, and cello. Singers could unify a set of songs around one poet instead of one poem. A set of Thomas Campion's poetry could include solo art songs by Quilter and Gurney and a chamber piece like Virgil Thomson's *Four Songs to Poems of Thomas Campion* for mezzo-soprano, clarinet, viola, and harp. This particular Thomson set is also of interest because it comes in two versions: one for piano and voice and one for chamber ensemble. When a composer chooses to interpret a poem as solo art song *and* as chamber music (like Dominick Argento's song cycle *Six Elizabethan Songs*), it can be a worthwhile study to see how the coloration, phrasing, dynamics, textures, and interpretation change with the addition of instruments. ♪

Suggested Listening Examples of Vocal Chamber Music with Keyboard (Duets, Trios, and Quartets)

Johann Christian Bach—"Già la notte s'avvicina," Op. 4, No. 1 ♪
Franz Joseph Haydn—"Alles hat seine Zeit" ♪
Felix Mendelssohn—"Maiglöckchen und die Blümelein," Op. 63, No. 6 ♪
Johannes Brahms—"Fragen," Op. 64, No. 3
Max Reger—"Nachts," Op. 14, No. 1 ♪
Robert Schumann—"Es ist verraten" from *Spansiches Liederspiel*, Op. 74, No. 5 ♪
Carl Maria von Weber—"Va, ti consola," Op. 31, No. 2 ♪
Benjamin Britten—"Mother Comfort" from *2 Ballads for 2 Voices and Piano* ♪

Suggested Listening Examples of Vocal Chamber Music with Other Instruments

George Frideric Handel—"Flammende Rose, Zierde der Erden" HWV 210 ♪
Ludwig van Beethoven—"What Shall I Do to Show How Much I Love Her?" WoO 152, No. 6 ♪
Franz Schubert—*Der Hirt auf den Felsen* D965 ♪
Louis Spohr—"Sei still mein Herz," Op. 103, No. 1 ♪
Johannes Brahms—"Gestillte Sehnsucht," Op. 91, No. 1 ♪
Camille Saint-Saëns—"Le bonheur est chose légére" ♪
Gustav Holst—"My Soul Has Nought but Fire and Ice" from *Four Songs for Voice and Violin*, Op. 35 ♪
Ernest Chausson—*Chanson perpétuelle*, Op. 37 ♪
Maurice Ravel—*Chansons madécasses*
Benjamin Britten—"The Stream in the Valley" ♪
Joseph Schwantner—*Sparrows* ♪
John Corigliano—"The Foggy Dew" from *Three Irish Folksong Settings*
Lowell Liebermann—"Die gar traurige Geschichte mit dem Feuerzeug" from *Struwwelpeterlieder*, Op. 51 ♪

André Previn—*The Giraffes Go to Hamburg* ♪
Eric Ewazen—"Everyone Said It Snowed Last Night" from . . . *to Cast a Shadow Again* ♪
Jake Heggie—"My True Love Hath My Heart" ♪

CHOOSING REPERTOIRE TO AUGMENT YOUR PERFORMANCE

Programming Considerations: Variety and Staging

In a *The Washington Post* article from October 30, 2015, mezzo-soprano Anne Sofie von Otter discussed the joy and challenges of navigating a musically diverse and versatile singing career. Not only has she excelled in opera, she also enjoys exploring pop music, vocal symphonic works, and (pertinent to our discussion) vocal chamber music. Anne Midgette wrote:

> For her next album, "For Sixty Cents," [von Otter] is making a foray into contemporary music, which—unlike most classical artists noted for diversity—she has hitherto largely avoided. "Some contemporary music around is not my taste," she says, "but some of it is. I love John Adams. Well, who shall I do it with? A whole orchestra is too expensive, and just piano is not fun." She has decided to look for "a young, cool and hip string quartet," and landed on Brooklyn Rider—one of the most prominent contemporary ensembles.[5]

It is fascinating that such an accomplished mezzo-soprano of this generation describes a chamber ensemble as "young, cool, and hip," and finds the genre to be an important addition to a versatile career in the twenty-first century. Von Otter went on to perform a chamber music recital in November of 2015 at the Library of Congress featuring baroque and contemporary works with harpsichord and theorbo.

Variety At most colleges and universities, recital programming is governed by curricular and/or degree requirements. For most of these recitals, there is an expectation that multiple languages, time periods, and styles will be represented. Vocal chamber music repertoire, which can fulfill these criteria, can be a welcome addition to a collaborative degree recital or a shared junior recital or simply to fulfill a chamber music requirement. As discussed earlier, augmenting a recital program with vocal chamber music can offer aural and visual stimulation to performers and audiences. It may garner a more widespread audience that appreciates the inclusion of instrumental and vocal repertoire. Moreover, it helps singers build a versatile skill set for collaborating within an important network of instrumentalists and ensembles in the future. While standard solo art song sets and operatic arias are important in vocal repertoire, it can be a pleasant surprise to experience a set with an instrument or additional singers. If one wants to perform Brahms's *lieder*, why not consider his *Three Duets*, Op. 20? If a tenor wants to perform a piece without piano, he could explore John Corigliano's *Three Irish Folksong Settings* for high voice and flute. A soprano programming Gounod art songs could add his *Viens, mon Coeur* with cello as an enjoyable addition for the audience. Musicians have a responsibility to communicate with audiences and to offer an entertaining program so they are encouraged to attend future recitals. A simple change in programming that invites aural and visual variety can be stimulating and memorable.

Staging Performing vocal chamber music requires careful consideration about staging and setup. Traditionally, solo instrumentalists stand alongside the singer, unless their instrument requires sitting (cello, string quartet, harp, guitar). Both the singer and instrumentalist will perform using music and stands (although all musicians should have the music memorized and only be using it as a reference). Using music as a reference is traditional performance practice in vocal chamber music and important in the event that one ensemble member makes a mistake and must rejoin. Vocal duets, trios, or quartets share the center of the stage in front of the piano, where a soloist would traditionally stand. If singers are performing a longer cycle, like Robert Schumann's *Spanisches Liederspiel*, which varies voice pairings by movement, they may want to place four chairs stage left of the piano so nonsinging members of the quartet may sit. The ensemble may instead make the decision to remain standing while others sing or choose to enter and exit the stage between songs. The musicians' comfort and overall aesthetic of the performance should inform these decisions. However, allot time for transitions when estimating the length of the program, and detailed information and diagrams should be given to stage managers prior to the performance date.

Staging is often a greater challenge when performing with instrumentalists. The most important arrangement consideration is creating clear sight lines between all performers. A string quartet will traditionally be center stage with the singer in front (figure 3.3).

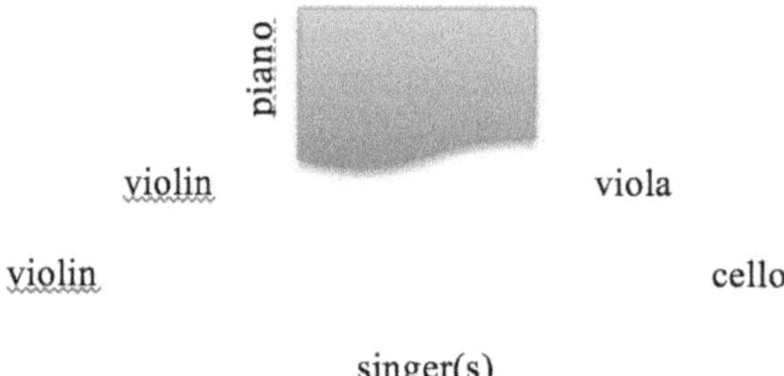

Figure 3.3. Sample Staging with String Quartet. ***Creative Commons*** **(CC BY-SA 3.0)**

Another common arrangement places the singer in the middle of the ensemble (figure 3.4).

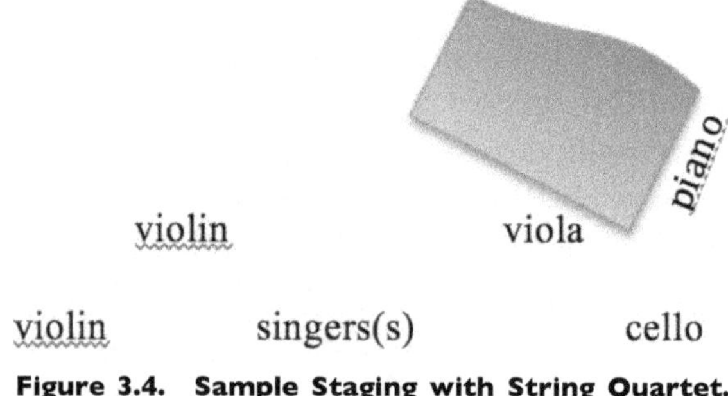

Figure 3.4. Sample Staging with String Quartet. ***Creative Commons*** **(CC BY-SA 3.0)**

An arrangement specific to performances of baroque repertoire with the harpsichord facing upstage in the center of the ensemble is shown (figure 3.5).

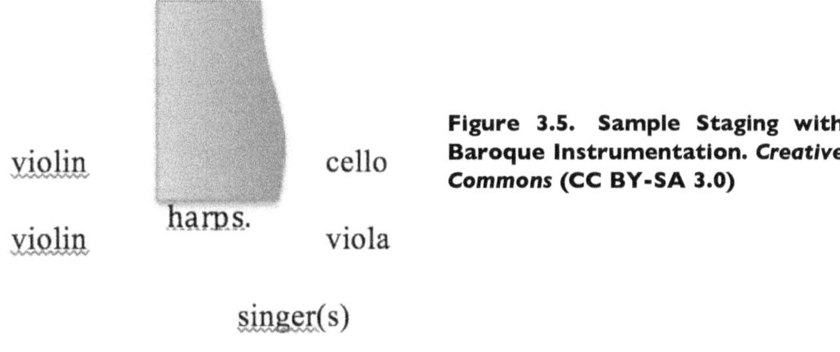

Figure 3.5. Sample Staging with Baroque Instrumentation. *Creative Commons* (CC BY-SA 3.0)

The keyboardist should have a clear sight line to the cellist (or continuo instrument) and the vocalist. The singer must pay careful attention to the string players' bow strokes for onset and release of tone. Instrumentalists must be able to see each other for cues and cut-offs.

In the instance of one vocalist with continuo or one vocalist with keyboard and an instrument, there are two common stagings. Both will allow for important sight lines between all three musicians. The singer will normally be center stage, and the instrumentalist will either stand stage left of the singer (figure 3.6) or be situated stage right of the keyboard (figure 3.7).

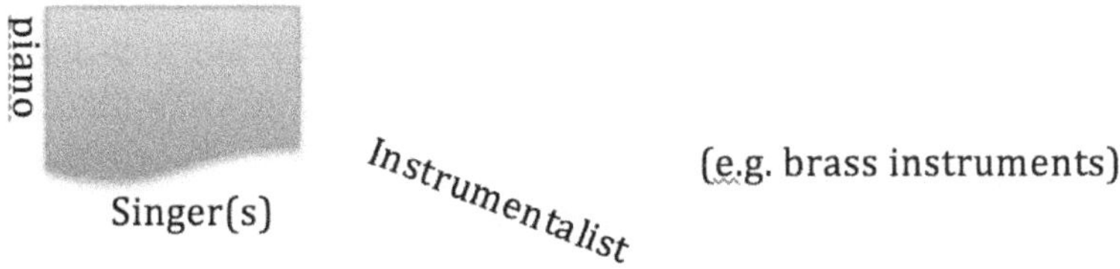

Figure 3.6. Sample Staging with Stage Left Instrumentalist. *Creative Commons* (CC BY-SA 3.0)

The placement of the instrumentalist in relation to the singer and keyboard is critical for the balance of the ensemble. For all brass instruments, the bell should be angled away from the audience and singer, unless there is a need for greater sound. With string instruments, both

Figure 3.7. Sample Staging with Stage Right Instrumentalist. *Creative Commons* (CC BY-SA 3.0)

the keyboardist and the singer should be able to see the bow movement for onsets, phrasing, and cut-offs. With wind instruments, both the keyboardist and the singer should be able to see the inhalatory gesture of the player to create ensemble unity during onsets and releases.

If there are two instruments and two singers, as in Beethoven's *Scottish Songs* for piano, tenor, baritone, viola, and violin, a suggested setup would look like figure 3.8, figure 3.9, or figure 3.10 according to preference, instrumentation, and balance of sound.

It is important to note that while these arrangements are traditional, they are not standardized. Staging decisions should be based on the size of the performing space, lighting, and sight lines. These are essential decisions for a successful chamber music performance.

A final consideration that affects formation and staging is bowing. All music, chairs, and stands should be put onstage prior to the beginning of the piece. This can take a significant amount of time, depending on the number of chairs, stands, lights, or complexity of electronic accommodations, and so on. Be certain to account for setup and teardown time when programming a recital or concert for a particular length. It is

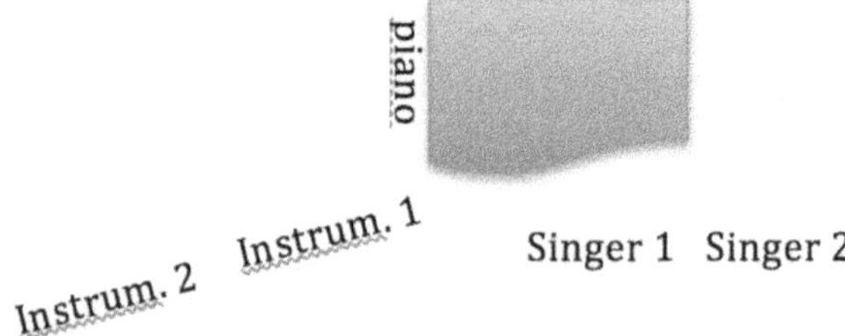

Figure 3.8. Sample Staging with Multiple Singers and Stage Right Instrumentalists. *Creative Commons* (CC BY-SA 3.0)

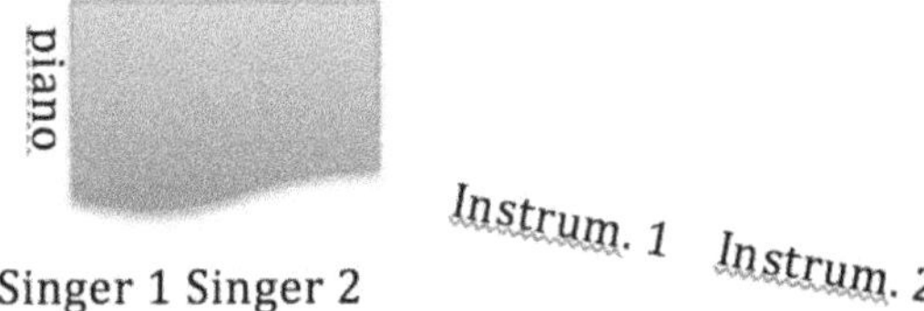

Figure 3.9. Sample Staging with Multiple Singers and Stage Left Instrumentalists. ***Creative Commons*** **(CC BY-SA 3.0)**

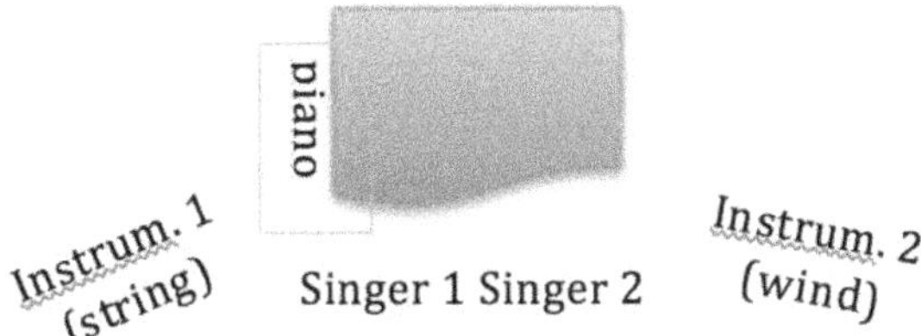

Figure 3.10. Sample Staging with Multiple Singers and Instrumentalists Sharing Center. ***Creative Commons*** **(CC BY-SA 3.0)**

common for musicians to enter the stage in the order in which they are standing and/or seated. On occasion, the instrumentalists will enter first and the singer will enter last. All musicians should remain standing and bow together before and following the performance, graciously thanking the audience for their time and attention. Upon the conclusion of the performance, the singer can exit first with instrumentalists following in succession, or all musicians can walk out in performance order, with the musician closest to the exit leading off. Instrumentalists may carry their instruments offstage with them, and all music should remain on stands. Because setup and teardown can take time and disrupt the flow of a recital, chamber pieces are often programmed at the beginning and ending of recital halves so stage managing can be done before the performance, during intermission, or after the conclusion of the recital.

NOTES

1. Mark A. Radice, *Chamber Music: An Essential History* (Ann Arbor: University of Michigan Press, 2012), 6–7.

2. Ibid., 26.

3. Christina Bashford, "Chamber Music," Oxford Music Online, www.oxfordmusiconline.com/subscriber/article/grove/music/05379, accessed September 14, 2016.

4. Radice, *Chamber Music*, 274.

5. Anne Midgette, "Anne Sofie von Otter Set to Perform in D.C. in November," *The Washington Post*, October 30, 2015.

4

BREATHE WITH THE BOW

Communicating with Instrumentalists

Few things compare to experiencing a finely tuned chamber music performance. The intimate musical dialogue between performers is nuanced, expressive, compelling, and synchronized. Instrumentalists and singers respond to each other's body language, facial expressions, inhalations, and musical interpretation. This can be a result of a collaboration over years, though this level of performance is possible to put together in a short time frame with the use of carefully planned rehearsals.

FORMING AN ENSEMBLE

Initiating conversation between musicians is the first step to performing chamber music. This recognition of a shared passion for chamber music may serendipitously occur over casual conversation but is more often the result of building a strong network of friends and colleagues. This network can connect performers interested in collaborating and foster new relationships with musicians who have mutual interests. If you are interested in performing a chamber work with violin, for example, but do not personally know any violinists, asking for recommendations among friends is a great place to begin. Other options include contacting a violin professor or area private teacher for a recommendation or contacting your local musicians' union. Professional relationships begin with initial correspondence, so respectfully providing the following information will help potential colleagues recognize that you value their expertise and time.

What Repertoire Will Be Performed?

- Has the repertoire been preselected?
- Are there multiple movements or multiple works?
- Does the repertoire selected meet the practical and artistic needs of the event and of the performers involved?
- Is there flexibility regarding repertoire selections?
- If the repertoire is technically demanding, does the musician you are contacting have the ability to perform it at a level that is acceptable to you and your ensemble/teacher/employer?

It is important to use discretion when choosing members of a chamber ensemble because it affects the quality of the performance. Judicious consideration of technical and artistic ability is important, but potential collaborators should also be organized, responsible, and reliable.

When and Where Are the Rehearsals and Performances?

- Is there a dress rehearsal?
- Who is responsible for reserving or renting the rehearsal and performance space?
- Have locations been established, and are they appropriate for the music being performed?
- Is there a fee to use the performance spaces and, if so, who is responsible for payment?
- Will you have an opportunity to rehearse in the performance space to become comfortable with the stage, lighting, space, and piano if it is being used?
- Who is responsible for having the piano tuned?
- Who is responsible for bringing stands and other equipment, such as chairs, amplification speakers, stand lights, and so on?

In a collegiate setting, many of these details are managed by the institution. Even so, an excellent performance and entrepreneurial opportunity may be to perform the same concert in multiple venues within the community. Concert series, residencies, or workshops at churches, retirement homes, or public schools may be appropriate venues. It would be wise to visit the venue, observe the spacing and lighting, discover the quality of the piano, and be mindful of acoustics before committing to a performance. Acoustics can influence the quality of a chamber music performance, particularly when a fast tempo is combined with complex rhythms and musical textures. If there is a cost associated with renting the space or piano, consider grants, free-will donations, and/or private donor funding.

How Many Rehearsals Are Expected?

- Will a rehearsal schedule be provided in advance, or will rehearsals be called as needed?
- Will this ensemble meet regularly and, if so, over how many weeks or months?
- How long will rehearsals last?
- Who will lead rehearsals, and will a coach be present?
- How will rehearsals be efficiently run to maximize time together?

Your ensemble will need to decide the amount of time necessary to prepare for an excellent performance. It is recommended that a new ensemble establish a weekly meeting time and location. Creating a rehearsal plan is paramount to a successful collaboration so that ensemble members can practice and rehearse in an efficient manner. The most common causes leading to a poor rehearsal are lack of preparation and indecision. If one member of the ensemble is technically unprepared to rehearse a section, they become a "weak link" that prevents the ensemble from reaching its full potential. This embarrassment and wasted time can easily be avoided with foresight. Establishing clear expectations for rehearsals and performances creates accountability for everyone involved. A rehearsal plan that is generated on a weekly basis may include sight-reading new music, running multiple movements of a rehearsed piece, giving attention to specific spots, discussing interpretation, or running the entire program to build and establish muscle memory and stamina.

Will There Be Compensation and, If So, How Much?

- Is this an educational or volunteer performance, or are performers expecting compensation? If so, contracts should be created and signed, specifying responsibilities and remuneration.

Creating and comprehending contracts can be a complicated endeavor that may necessitate education and research. Chamber Music America (CMA), a national organization, is a valuable resource with online calendars, links, and business tools. A membership to CMA includes access to a bimonthly magazine, directories, grant applications, and "First Tuesdays" seminars:

> Each workshop in this free series—on practical subjects ranging from contract negotiations to the use of new media—is presented by an expert in the field and recorded for download on CMA's website. Presented monthly, October to June.[1]

It is a highly useful resource for organizations, businesses, students, educators, advocates, ensembles, and professional musicians interested in chamber music.

How and When Will Music Be Provided?

- Are performers expected to provide their own music, or will it be provided for them?
- How will you provide music before the first rehearsal?
- Performers should have individual parts and the full score.
- Number measures before working with instrumentalists.
- Indicate metronome markings in the score.
- Poetic and literal translations should be provided for all foreign languages.
- Will a recording be made available?

One of my earliest experiences working with a chamber ensemble was when I programmed J. S. Bach's cantata BWV 51, *Jauchzet Gott in allen Landen*, for my master's degree recital. I contacted colleagues who were interested in collaborating, established rehearsal and performance dates, purchased the music (included instrumental parts), and reserved spaces. I provided individual parts for the instrumentalists and the harpsichordist and was ready to begin! Before the first downbeat, the first violinist asked for a copy of the full score. I had none. Nor did I have copies of the literal and poetic translations of the German text, which was requested next. These were needs I should have anticipated because they would have helped the ensemble function more musically, emotionally, and cohesively. I learned an important lesson to better understand the needs of all ensemble members as it pertains to music and translations. I also learned if you loan purchased or rented parts (and scores), make a return policy and ask that all pencil markings be erased unless you want them for posterity.

Organizing important details will help provide a successful rehearsal process, enabling a focus on music making instead of wasting valuable time and energy. After an ensemble has been established, it may be worthwhile to designate one person with strong organizational and time management skills as the logistical coordinator. This person may be the contact liaison for the ensemble, sending necessary e-mails and ensuring that rehearsals stay on track and on time. Another member of the ensemble with strong writing skills could be responsible for creating a program. Perhaps a member of the ensemble has an affinity for marketing and could promote the concert using print media (posters or newspapers) or virtual media on websites or social media platforms. Speaking about the program before or during the concert is an excellent way to engage audiences, and a charismatic and dynamic public speaker will make a meaningful impact. Employing musicians as stakeholders promotes a sense of personal investment, responsibility, and pride in the accomplishments of the ensemble.

A VOCABULARY FOR COMMUNICATING WITH INSTRUMENTALISTS

A common concern expressed by many singers interested in performing chamber music is communicating with instrumentalists in a respectful and knowledgeable way. How can singers gain a working knowledge of fundamental aspects concerning different instrumentation, and why is this important? While instrumentalists and singers share many similarities, there are distinct differences. Singers should have a basic vocabulary so that they can (a) respectfully and knowledgeably speak with colleagues about their instruments (period instruments will be discussed in a later chapter); (b) be able to read instrumental lines and understand range and technical challenges; (c) understand transpositions; and (d) have confidence asking for and achieving a desired sound as an ensemble.

The most basic and helpful way to learn about instruments is to speak with instrumentalists about their particular idiosyncrasies as it relates to their field of study. As a student and now a professor, I often ask musicians for a "tour" of their instrument, including clarification about dynamic capabilities, how different articulation markings sound, how vibrato is created, and what is technically challenging for that instrument. For example, I coached a soprano and harpist on John Lambert's *A Song Cycle on the Birth of Jesus* and Louis Vierne's *Quatre poèmes grecs*. Both are multimovement works with significantly different challenges for the harpist. *A Song Cycle on the Birth of Jesus* includes recitative-like movements, shifting meters, and multiple fermatas, which demand clear musical communication and mutual leadership between the vocalist and harpist. The *Quatre poèmes grecs* includes virtuosic tempi markings and unremitting sixteenth note patterns of subdued harmonic shifts. I asked the harpist to demonstrate extreme dynamics (loud and quiet sounds on the harp), had her explain why and when she had to use foot pedals, and questioned whether she could bring out particular accented notes or if that was not possible for her instrument. It was enlightening, and my student gained knowledge about the instrument and its capabilities. This information will be of great value in the future when she chooses repertoire with harp. In coachings, I often encourage students to ask each other questions, balancing both humility in what they do not know and confidence in what they do know, always trusting their musical instincts to inspire the dialogue.

String Instruments

Instruments in the string family include violin, viola, cello, double bass, harp, and guitar. Singers will recall that our sound is produced by a power source (air), vibrator (vocal folds), and resonator (the vocal tract). Other instruments work in the same manner, and identifying these aspects is a great starting point. In the bowed string family, which includes the violin, viola, cello, and double bass, the power source is the plucking of a finger or stroke of a bow, the vibrator is the string, and the resonator is the wooden bridge and body of the instrument. The strings of the violin produce higher pitches, while the viola, cello, and double bass produce lower pitches, respectively. With exceptions, the violin is written in treble clef, viola in alto clef, cello in bass or tenor clef, and double bass in bass clef. Using the left hand, players shorten or lengthen the resonating part of the string to change pitch by pressing a string down on the soundboard. Tuning is achieved by changing the tension of the strings using the tuning pegs or, if the instrument is slightly out of tune, the fine tuners. Tightening the string raises pitch, while loosening the string lowers pitch. Tuning must often be checked because a string instrument's intonation is affected by temperature, humidity, and the intensity of one's own playing.

String musicians can pluck the strings (*pizzicato*) or use a bow (*arco*) to create a connected sound. Singers should have an understanding of bow speed, direction, and force, so they can adjust their onset, breath management, and dynamics for musical synthesis. Downbeats, accents, and agogically strong notes are usually played with a downbow, while upbeats are usually played with an upbow. Many other markings that indicate articulations, effects, or stops should be discussed with instrumentalists as an opportunity to unify musical vision.

String vibrato evolved from a mid-nineteenth-century ornament and became an expressive device during the late romantic era. Stylistically, it should be used sparingly in repertoire composed prior to the mid-1800s. Vibrato speed and quality can influence the authenticity and quality of a performance, so understanding how it works can substantially change the sound of an ensemble. Pitch oscillation on a string instrument can be created by the finger, wrist, or forearm, and a vocalist should share a similar vibrato style when collaborating.

A string quartet, traditionally composed of two violins, viola, and cello, is a standard chamber music ensemble, and many vocal chamber works are written in collaboration with this instrumentation. Popular examples of string quartet and voice repertoire include Samuel Barber's

Dover Beach with baritone, Ralph Vaughan Williams's *On Wenlock Edge* with tenor, Ottorino Respighi's *Il tramonto* ♪ with mezzo-soprano, Arnold Schoenberg's *String Quartet No. 2* with soprano, and Ned Rorem's *Mourning Scene* with tenor. Lesser-known but equally worthwhile works include Geoffrey Bush's *Farewell Earth's Bliss* with baritone, Ildebrando Pizzetti's *Tre Canzoni* with soprano, Virgil Thomson's *Stabat Mater* with soprano, and Ralph Vaughan Williams's *Merciless Beauty* with high voice. Additionally, myriad examples of vocal chamber repertoire exist for solo string instruments and seemingly endless combinations of string instruments. These can be with or without piano or additional wind instruments, percussion, and/or electronic music.

Choosing to perform with a singular string instrument may be based on timbrel preference. It is not a coincidence that many chamber pieces are written for viola and mezzo-soprano voice because the two share timbrel warmth and range. In other instances, decisions may be made based on availability of a particular instrument, and there is no shortage of repertoire options for any combination. John Toms, who sang the American premiere of Britten's *Serenade for Tenor, French Horn, and Strings*, says:

> For the performer, being part of a small ensemble can be a lot of fun; more fun, sometimes, than being part of a small vocal group. And for the teacher, these songs offer new opportunities for training superior students. The problems of balance and ensemble when singing with one solo instrument are quite different from those in which the singer is accompanied only by a piano. . . . When the composition calls for several instruments, there is more to be learned, for the experience is not unlike that of singing with an orchestra, even to a comparable rehearsal routine. Moreover, since few student singers ever get a chance to sing with an orchestra—not excepting those who attend the larger music schools of the country—a gap in their training can easily be filled by using those works which call for a few instruments. In short, by becoming acquainted with this type of vocal literature, and in making a place for it on recitals, both singers and vocal teachers can find ample rewards.[2]

Collaborations with harp, a string instrument of early origin, pose unique challenges due to the difficulty of availability and transportation of the instrumentation, but can be well worth the search. Its soft and ethereal timbre is a wonderful match for all voice types and provides strong harmonic support similar to that of a piano. The modern concert harp has vibrating strings, tuning pegs that adjust pitch through string tension, and a soundboard. Strings are plucked and chromatic shifts are created using foot pedals located at the base of the instrument. In her article "Music for Voice and Harp," Shelley Batt Archambo offers a large list of repertoire for voice and harp, including publishers, voice type, and additional instruments when needed. Most are original compositions, although arrangements are also included. She writes:

> Since biblical days, the harp has provided accompaniment for the voice—even that of King David, a "harper" and a singer. But it was not until the development (c. 1810) and later acceptance (c. 1850) of the double-action pedal harp that the combining of voice and harp became quite widespread. This new harp was easily capable of playing in any key, unlike most of its predecessors. The flexibility of the double-action pedal harp serves to make it an excellent choice in accompaniment for the voice.[3]

The classical guitar lends itself well to vocal collaboration because of its portability and ability to provide harmonic support. Its nylon strings, wide fingerboard, and softer dynamics differentiate it from the acoustic steel string guitar, which is most often heard in popular music. Tablature or standard notation is most often used for classical guitar. "For centuries, the guitar has been associated with song. However, the primitive design of earlier guitars caused composers to reserve their best efforts for more refined instruments—at first, the lute and its Spanish counterpart, the *vihuela,* and later, the piano."[4] In his article "Contemporary Art Songs for Voice and Classical Guitar: A Select Annotated List," James Maroney continues that it was not until the beginning of the romantic period when a large number of original songs were written for voice and guitar, although guitar transcriptions remained popular. Since then, many well-known songs and song cycles for voice and guitar have been written, including Dominick Argento's *Letters from Composers*, Joaquín Rodrigo's *Folias canarias* ♪, William Walton's *Anonymous in Love*, and Benjamin Britten's *Songs from the Chinese*, in addition to other works included in Maroney's article.

Varied repertoire choices exist for voice and string instruments in multiple combinations. Because string players are not dependent on breath for phrasing, instrumentalists and singers must communicate clearly with each other through eye contact or body movement to indicate onsets, releases, *accelerando*, *ritardando*, and phrasing. Clearly marking indications like these (especially breaths) in the vocalist's and the instrumentalist's music is critical. Translating markings in all parts creates a more detailed representation of the composer's intention and musicians' interpretation. It must be reiterated that rehearsal staging should be the same during performance so that previously created sight lines are dependable. Chamber music is ultimately conversational music, and the necessity of eye contact is at its root.

Wind Instruments

Wind instruments can be categorized into two families: woodwinds and brass. Woodwinds include flute, oboe, saxophone, clarinet, English horn, and bassoon. Brass instruments include trumpet, trombone, horn, euphonium, and tuba. There are often additional instruments within these families, such as the saxophone, which includes soprano, alto, tenor, and baritone saxophone. Returning to the foundational understanding of sound production, the power source is air, the vibrators are the lips or reed(s), and the resonator is the instrument itself. Its shape and materials determine its resonant properties and timbre. An *embouchure* is defined as "the position and use of the lips, tongue, and teeth in playing a wind instrument."[5] Tonguing is a method of using the tongue to shape the air based on its position (arch) and location of closure (tip). The *embouchure* and breath support affect the quality of the tone. Similar to the strings family, intonation can be affected by temperature as the resonating material minutely shrinks and expands. Wind players pull out the tuning slide or mouthpiece when they are sharp (lengthening the resonating tube), and push in when they are flat (shortening the resonating tube). Since wind instrumentalists and singers both use air as the power source, they should discuss phrase lengths and breathe accordingly. Breathing together helps unify the ensemble's onsets and releases.

It is important to be aware that some instruments transpose, which means that an instrument's pitch sounds different from the note written on the page. Scores may be written to reflect an instrument's part in concert pitch (sounding) or transposed (what is written). For example, when a B♭ clarinet plays a C, it sounds as a B♭. A transposed part will be evident because the key signature will be different than the vocal line. Transposing instruments include clarinet, saxophone, trumpet, trombone, horn, euphonium, and tuba.

Woodwinds There is a plethora of repertoire for voice and woodwinds. Instruments in this family are capable of melismatic flexibility; they produce softer dynamics, which can result in better balance; and their onsets are clear and easily sounded. Vibrato on woodwind instruments can be achieved diaphragmatically, and articulations are varied. Lips are the vibrators for piccolo and flute, and the rest of the woodwind family use reeds as vibratos. Clarinets and saxophones use single reeds that vibrate against a mouthpiece. Oboes, English horns, and bassoons use double reeds that vibrate against each other. Reeds have different strengths and thicknesses, which contribute to the quality of sound, and they are affected by changes in temperature, humidity, age, and use. Staging that directs the instrumentalist's tone holes upstage can be helpful to find appropriate balance. Singers looking for vocal chamber works with woodwind instruments will exhaust themselves with options. There is an abundance of baroque cantatas, numerous virtuosic works scored for coloratura soprano and flute, and musically varied works in which the voice(s) and woodwind(s) play different narrative roles or are dramatically intertwined. Some unique works from the twentieth and twenty-first centuries include Ralph Vaughan Williams's *Ten Blake Songs* for tenor or soprano and oboe ♪, Lori Laitman's *Living in the Body* for soprano or mezzo-soprano and alto saxophone, Libby Larsen's *Righty, 1966* for soprano and flute, and Igor Stravinsky's *Pastorale* for soprano, clarinet, oboe, English horn, and bassoon ♪.

Brass Instruments Brass instruments can easily be overpowering in a chamber music setting, and choosing repertoire requires knowledge of how a singer's voice will balance the instrument's sound. They change notes using the overtone series, which is how players produce many pitches using only seven valve combinations or slide positions. *Embouchure* and air flow are main contributors to intonation and sound quality. Vibrato on brass instruments can be created diaphragmatically or mechanically, but jaw vibrato is the most commonly used. Similar to voices, range is used to describe low, middle, and high registers. In her comprehensive article, "Singing on the Horn: A Selective Survey of Chamber Music for Voice, Horn, and Keyboard," Laurie S. Shelton describes similarities between the horn and the voice, which are applicable to other brass instruments. She writes:

> Horn players actually require less breath than singers because the throat of a horn mouthpiece is much smaller than a human trachea: overblowing results in cracked notes for both. A balanced lip embouchure is just as critical as balanced laryngeal function, for the lips are the vocal cords of the horn player. The horn itself merely magnifies the sound, just as bone resonance magnifies the sound of a singer. In fact, no two horn players sound exactly alike, as is obviously true of any two singers.[6]

When exploring repertoire, look carefully at the range, dynamic level, register, and overall texture of the work to ensure that the vocal line is not doubled or overpowered. Balancing dynamics can be achieved through technical prowess and by changing the staging so that the instrument's bell is pointed in a different direction to diffuse some sound. As the owner of a light soprano voice who performs in a chamber duo with trumpet, I have often used staging to combat balance issues. I carefully choose repertoire that allows me to sing in a resonant range, avoid repertoire where the trumpet and vocal line double each other, limit vibrato at times for style and pitch acuity, and use strong articulation.

Because many chamber works with brass instruments require a resonant voice to penetrate the timbre, light voices may want to explore the lighter textures of baroque repertoire. Noteworthy works include Lori Laitman's *Captivity* for trumpet and medium voice; Wolfgang Plagge's *Libera Sequentiarum* for soprano and trumpet; Eric Ewazen's *. . . to cast a shadow again* for low (or high) voice, trumpet, and piano; Benjamin Britten's *Canticle III* for tenor, horn, and piano; Franz Schubert's *Auf dem Strom*, Op. 129, for high voice, horn, and piano ♪; Sharon Davis's *Merrie English Love Songs* for trombone and woman's voice with percussion; and Jan Koetsier's *Galgenlieder* for high voice and tuba ♪.

Percussion and Other Instruments

Percussion instruments are pitched or nonpitched. The materials that constitute this family are woods, skins, metals, glass, and others. Pitched percussion instruments include hand bells, steel drums, vibraphone, timpani, and marimba. Nonpitched examples include cymbals, triangles, bongo drums, snare drum, tambourine, and wood block. Percussion can be notated in many different ways, so asking a percussionist about their instrument's notation would be a valuable learning experience. In the same way that singers watch string players' upbows and downbows to prepare inhalation and determine phrasing, singers can watch percussionist's arms, hands, and mallets. There are chamber pieces written for percussion and voice alone such as Virgil Thomson's *Five Phrases from Song of Solomon* ♪ and Jocelyn Hagen's *Dear Theo: Letters from Vincent Van Gogh* ♪, but it is more common to find percussion included in a larger group of instruments as in Arnold Shoenberg's *Nachtwandler* for soprano, piccolo trumpet, snare drum, and piano. Voice and percussion duo Aurora Borealis's web page includes a large list of repertoire for voice, percussion, and additional instruments, including recent commissions. Electronic instruments and recorded sound are also found in twentieth- and twenty-first-century chamber pieces. Markings are varied, so careful attention must be paid to the composer's instructions.

FINAL THOUGHTS: A WORD ON PROFESSIONAL ETIQUETTE

Every communication, rehearsal, and performance is a networking opportunity that can further a musician's career. The more often singers work with instrumentalists, the wider their network becomes, leading to a potential increase in performance opportunities. Instrumentalists often think differently about music than vocalists and can offer insight into interpretation, reading from a score, achieving pitch and rhythmic accuracy, and composers and repertoire. Vocalists can provide similar benefits to instrumentalists, particularly with text settings and translations. For these reasons, maintaining a sense of professionalism and respect for others' time and talent is very important. Showing interest in how an instrument works exhibits seriousness about performing with that, or a different, instrumentalist in the future. Create an excellent reputation with other musicians by communicating in a friendly and respectful manner, organizing time and resources, being punctual to rehearsals and performances, and becoming knowledgeable about their instruments and repertoire.

NOTES

1. "Tools of the Trade," Chamber Music America, www.chamber-music.org/programs/classical/professional-development, accessed December 23, 2017.
2. John Toms, "Chamber Music for Voice," *Journal of Singing* 12, no. 1 (1955): 4.
3. Shelley Batt Archambo, "Music for Voice and Harp," *Journal of Singing* 42, no. 2 (1985): 14.
4. James Maroney, "Contemporary Art Songs for Voice and Classical Guitar—A Select Annotated List," *Journal of Singing* 60, no. 1 (2003): 9.
5. "Embouchure," Merriam-Webster, www.merriam-webster.com/dictionary/embouchure, accessed December 29, 2017.
6. Laurie S. Shelton, "Singing on the Horn: A Selective Survey of Chamber Music for Voice, Horn, and Keyboard," *Journal of Singing* 54, no. 3 (1998): 25.

5

STYLISTIC CONSIDERATIONS

Music has a unique ability to connect performers and listeners to the past, transporting us to a different place and time while connecting us with universal themes and emotions. Singers spend countless hours analyzing notes and rhythms, interpreting markings, and translating texts, serving as the instrument through which composers chose to communicate. Repertoire from different musical eras possesses varying aesthetics, musical and textual emphases, and opportunity for personal interpretation. For performers to be successful, musicians must acquire knowledge of performance practice, otherwise known as the ways in which music was historically performed. Numerous resources on performance practice exist, but how do we apply these concepts to chamber repertoire? How can we gain a synthesized knowledge of both instrumental and vocal performance practice and effectively integrate it during a performance? Are historically accurate performances necessary, or can repertoire be adapted for the twenty-first century and modern instruments?

PERFORMANCE PRACTICE

Numerous factors influence historical performance practices of vocal music, and hundreds of books, journals, and websites are devoted to specific topics in great detail. These resources, which explore the usage and interpretation of specific markings in different eras, should be consulted when researching individual pieces. For the sake of brevity and as a starting point, three overarching themes directly affect the study and performance of chamber music. These include:

1. the development and evolution of instruments used in early, classical, romantic, and modern music;
2. musical aesthetic, influenced by geography, culture, and time period; and
3. the function of music and demands on the performers.

Since chamber music has included a wide array of instrumentation over the course of its long history, gaining a basic understanding of how instruments developed can be useful information. It may help performers create authentic performances or, if they prefer to present works on modern instruments, have a foundational understanding of how the sound quality may have differed during the composer's lifetime. The application of this knowledge can have a significant impact on phrasing, breathing, and articulation for instrumentalists and singers.

My first exposure to a period instrument was at the Eastman School of Music when I heard Beethoven's "Moonlight" sonata (No. 14 in C♯ minor, Op. 27, No. 2) played on a fortepiano during a music history course ♪. Having heard this work performed many times on modern pianos, my ears anticipated a similar timbre and volume. Hearing it performed on an instrument similar to the one Beethoven would have used to compose the work was startling as it exposed me to the fortepiano's expressive dynamic capability and timbral intimacy, which I had never associated with his piano works. That experience gave me greater insight into the sounds and textures Beethoven was inspired by as he made musical decisions in his compositions, which also made me reconsider the works of his contemporaries in the early romantic period.

I tell this story to demonstrate the value of learning about performance practice, given that a significant amount of chamber music heard today is performed on modern instruments. What nuances, strengths, and limitations do period instruments have compared to modern instruments, and how might they affect the markings in the music? How might they affect balance with the voice and its range of dynamic variation? Is it possible to perform on modern instruments while considering performance practice rules? Do stylistic considerations influence repertoire decisions? If collaboration is at the heart of chamber music, we must fully consider the range of vocal and instrumental possibilities as they evolved over hundreds of years and the ways in which they impacted technique and musical aesthetic.

We use words like *baroque*, *classical*, *romantic*, and *modern* to describe and define periods of time that encompassed general musical and stylistic characteristics, but as performers, we often overestimate our audience's familiarity with repertoire. Although we feel like we are representing "early music" when performing a Bach cantata from the baroque era, it may be the first hearing for a modern audience, particularly when interpreting Bach's markings as they would have been in his lifetime. What is historically old now sounds new and exotic in a modern era. In *Early Music*, Thomas Forrest Kelly explains:

> With the passage of time, performing styles change, musical desiderata change, instruments change. With the passage of a great deal of time, those things change a great deal; when an old piece is rediscovered, revived, and played by those much later musicians, and heard by those much later listeners, the result may be very satisfactory indeed, or it may not—but it will probably be different in many respects from how the hypothetical piece sounded when it was new.[1]

Subsequently, the resultant conversation about style has more to do with valuing and interpreting the musical "language" composers used during their lifetimes, likening compositional tools such as embellishments, articulations, and phrase markings to the "grammar" or "vocabulary" within that language. Language, of course, evolves; and as stylistic principles changed, either as reactions to what came before or due to geographic and/or nationalistic trends, so did musical principles. Music of the baroque period demonstrates the ideals of extravagance through the language of polyphony and ornamentation, while music of the classical period demonstrates balance and clarity through a greater emphasis on form. Romanticism witnessed a literary movement that aroused nationalistic allegiances and emphasis on the individual, which promoted new genres like *lied* and *mélodie*. It also supported the careers of solo performers who displayed their individualism through improvisation. Composers responded with virtuosic and large-scale compositions, adding specific markings that indicated clear intention and mood. The reactionary twentieth century was highly influenced by the expansion of technology, rise and fall of empires and governments, and convergence of cultures. The resulting musical soundscape reflected a kaleidoscope of new sounds and styles, exposing the struggle between conformists and nonconformists. Traditional forms were augmented or altered with unconventional combinations of instruments. New compositional means, including serialism, pointillism, and minimalism, offered composers new ways of organizing sound, using extended techniques to present new avenues of expression. This wide and varying array of compositional tools across hundreds of years reflects the nuances of musical language that, on a larger stage, reflect philosophical, cultural, and aesthetic differences. Our job as performers is to be concerned with performance practice not merely as musical archaeologists, but as musical interpreters of different styles through pronunciation, accent, and idiomatic use.

A benefit of working within a chamber ensemble is the potential historical knowledge instrumentalists will contribute based on their scholarship and research, opening a wider dialogue about historically informed decisions and personal interpretation. One of the challenges can be sifting through the large amount of information regarding performance practice, so this chapter will serve to highlight some of the primary considerations.

EARLY MUSIC

Extensive scholarly research on performance practices of early music (referencing pre-baroque and baroque repertoire) using treatises and extant scores is available in various books, journal articles, and websites. However, recordings tend to be a singer's first resource when learning a new work, so we must be cautious about indiscriminately choosing recordings of early music without an understanding of appropriate style. Because much of what we hear on these recordings is ornately improvised, optimistically based on accurate stylistic paradigms, singers are often surprised to discover that original scores are quite empty. In *Sing-*

ing in Style, a text that should be on every singer's shelf, author Martha Elliott notes the following:

> An early baroque score offers only the bare bones of the music, needing the experience and judgment of the performers, combined with their inspiration and spontaneity, to bring it to life. The same is true of a jazz standard, which invites performers to add improvisation, rhythmic alteration, and melodic embellishment in a variety of tempos and moods.[2]

Heavily edited scores, generally from the nineteenth century, are easily accessible in anthologies and on public domain websites but are written in a way that superimposes nineteenth-century grammar with seventeenth-century language. In an attempt to recover composers' original writing, singers should locate scores that are as close as possible to a manuscript, such as Urtext scores:

> The term "Urtext" has been debated ever since it was first used. Yet the idea behind it is simple and easy to understand: the musician is offered a musical text which solely reflects the composer's intentions. One might think that this is self-evident. However, well into the twentieth century the great performers of the day were absolutely convinced that musical texts—especially those of works from the eighteenth century—were incomplete or had suffered from faulty transmission, in particular concerning how they were to be performed. This being the case, they altered the text, made additions and polished it, either at their own discretion or citing eye witnesses or ear witnesses. In so doing they generally did not refer to the original sources but often arranged the first printed version that came along, which itself probably differed from the original. Thus, the original musical text was substantially distorted, sometimes to the extent that it was no longer recognizable.[3]

In their Urtext form, compositions were commonly scored for a melody and a figured bass that was historically played by the lute, viol, theorbo, or harpsichord. If period instrumentalists are unavailable, Elliott writes, "The modern performer has numerous accompaniment alternatives when singing early Baroque secular songs: collaboration with an experienced lutenist or viol player, or finding transcriptions of lute songs for modern guitar. Other options include working with a harpsichordist who is experienced at realizing thoroughbass or finding a suitable realized accompaniment."[4] When modeling an early style on a modern instrument, there are limitations to consider. Due to technological advancements, our best intentions will be hindered because materials used to create early instruments have evolved in ways that support modern demands, including tuning, extended ranges, and greater dynamic contrasts. Kelly explains:

> Problems arise even in those cases where old instruments are valued—particularly among the stringed instruments, where a Stradivarius violin is the *ne plus ultra* of modern violin players. In principle a Strad is a Baroque instrument; but many aspects of string construction have changed over time—pitch (requiring more tension on the string), neck length and angle (to play louder and higher notes, a longer fingerboard is needed, and that requires resetting the neck at a different angle), strings (gut has been replaced with steel), bow (the baroque bow has given way to the Tourte bow, heavier and longer with more hair and more tension)—in search of more virtuosity and more volume. . . . It is not at all evident that Stradivarius would recognize it.[5]

Regardless of the instruments on which it is being played, chamber musicians must have at least a basic understanding of how to realize figured bass, in order to explore harmonies and their textual relationships. This is especially important as it pertains to improvised ornamentation and making decisions about consonances, dissonances, articulation, and dynamics. The optional use of various continuo instruments affected style and sonority:

> Players improvised accompaniments, using the sequence of chords and the rhythm indicated. An organist will "realize" the continuo very different from a lutenist: the organ can sustain a chord indefinitely at the same volume but is not very effective at arpeggiated or rolled chords. Conversely, the lute is soft, and if it plays all the notes of a chord at once it will have a too-sharp attack and the sound will decay, so the player is likely to roll the chords to keep the sound alive (although a short sharp attack might be very useful if the singer were singing a word like "pierce" or "strike"). A harpsichordist will perform from the same bass-line differently from either. There is a great deal for the continuo player to think about, and one of the joys of playing Baroque music is to play continuo, for one is always making the music for the first time, and making every

> effort to respond to the meaning and expression of the melodic line, while taking account of other colleagues playing in the same continuo group.[6]

Much of early chamber music provided improvisatory opportunities for instrumentalists and vocalists alike, based on the interplay between harmony and melody, with an emphasis on text declamation. Chamber groups may enjoy the scholarly exercise of transcribing or composing improvisations that complement text and exploring new forms of ornamentation until they feel able to employ these improvisatory tools during rehearsals or performances. An instrumental resource that provides singers with easily accessible examples that compares the written score with suggested improvisations is Telemann's *12 Sonate Metodiche*, or *Methodical Sonatas* from 1728 and 1732 in figure 5.1.

Figure 5.1. Georg Philipp Telemann, Methodical Sonatas, TWV 41:h3, mm. 1–3. *Creative Commons* (CC BY-SA 3.0)

Cantatas by Carissmi, Buxtehude, Telemann, Bach, and Handel were composed for many different voice types and instruments and are often in recitativo and aria format with figured bass. These serve as an excellent point of departure for singers interested in exploring baroque repertoire. Singers, however, should be aware that instrument terminology can be deceiving, seeing as "throughout the Baroque period; the term 'flauto' on musical scores of this time normally refers to the recorder rather than the transverse flute."[7] Since scores call for particular instruments, how can modern instruments replicate a baroque vernacular? Karl Hochreither goes into extensive detail about the use of continuo instruments in the informative resource *Instrumental-Vocal Works of Johann Sebastian Bach*. He writes:

> Ultimately, [historical performance practice] depends essentially on the players and their technique. Thus, a greatly relativizing component of this

> problem is addressed: present-day instrumentalists unconsciously transfer the sound ideal that they have been taught onto their old or reconstructed instruments. Conversely, however, players of modern instruments can modify their sound with historical playing techniques. Training programs should pay much greater attention to this. Studying historical sound pictures and playing techniques is indispensable: one can always argue about the mode and extent of such translation or transferal.[8]

This quote underscores the importance of style, recognizing baroque music was based on dance forms with accentuation of dissonance and affect. Recalling that original scores allowed for improvisational flexibility, interpretation, and expression, singers must be aware of technical differences if they hope to offer audiences an informed baroque experience. "Articulation must always serve clarity and distinctness. These two concepts—so intellectually historically instructive for the entire Baroque era—were binding for philosophers and artists alike. Ultimately, they are the measure of good performance in general."[9] A way in which singers can derive important information about articulation and phrasing is from collaboration with string players. The baroque bow was distinctly different from the modern bow in size, shape, and quantity and quality of hair. It was lighter than the modern bow, and the frog (closest to the hand) was heavier than the tip. This resulted in a lighter sound (with less hair touching and staying on the strings), less precise articulations, a heavy down bow (albeit lighter than the modern down bow), and a light up bow (also lighter than a modern up bow). The allocation of a singer's breath is directly related to bow speed and weight, so playing and singing with understanding of timbre, weight, and articulation will create a more accurate interpretation of baroque phrasing.

Early music was often performed in small spaces, and the necessity of vocal projection was not a priority, especially since early instruments produced less sound than modern instruments. Pitch centers were lower, A=415 compared to the modern A=440 ♪. Modern singers accustomed to filling large halls with their voice may be tempted to take an operatic approach to singing early music, but if they are concerned with performance practices, they must consider the vast differences in style and preference specific to the region and time period in which the music was composed. In her chapter "National Singing Styles," which explores specific technical approaches to seventeenth-century embellishments, Sally Sanford writes:

> The singer's art was closely aligned with the orator's during the Baroque period. The clear and expressive delivery of a text involved not only proper diction and pronunciation, but also an understanding of the rhetorical structure of the text and an ability to communicate the passion and meaning of the words. How this was achieved differed according to the particular characteristics of the language and culture as well as the musical style.[10]

Generally, singers and instrumentalists can learn from each other's sound quality, seeking to find a synthesis in color, dynamics, phrasing, shaping, articulation, and ornamentation. Vibrato was generally used as an ornament for singers and instrumentalists, alongside various graces and diminutions, that functioned as text painting.[11] Declamation of words was of primary importance for both vocalists and instrumentalists, with dissonance playing a large role in text painting and affect.

Some singers are often intimidated by (or disinterested in) performing early chamber music, but doing so offers exciting opportunities to study lesser-known works, perform with different instrumentalists, explore new ornamental vocal techniques, and improvise in a way that demonstrates uniquely personal expression of texts and harmonies. Many resources exist to explore, study, hear, and see professional and scholarly examples of early music performances. Early Music America (EMA) is a reputable digital platform that offers an extensive list of online score sources.

TRANSITIONING: BAROQUE INTO CLASSICAL

During the transition from the baroque to the classical period, the function and performance of chamber music shifted based on geographical region. For example, the influential Italian cantata, popularized by Scarlatti, Vivaldi, and Handel, had an extensive impact across the European continent, but French cantatas such as Jean-Philippe Rameau's cantata *Les amants trahis* ♪ (figure 5.2) diverged in structure and purpose.

Figure 5.2. Jean-Philippe Rameau, *Les amants trahis, cantata à deux voix avec accompagnement de viole et de clavecin*, Duo mm. 90–111. *Creative Commons* (CC BY-SA 3.0)

"As in Italy, poetic rather than musical innovations stimulated cantata composition, but in France the poetry aimed to educate rather than entrance."[12] As Italy was influenced by operatic idioms of aria, recitative, and ritornello, French cantatas were more structured and notation was to be strictly followed.

> Leaps, step-wise motion, lack of motives and an avoidance of text repetition perpetuated the aesthetic of *douceur*. In airs, melodic fragments articulated prosody instead of structuring musical statements through sequential treatment, as in Italian airs. . . . Extremes of tempo were avoided, *notes inégales* appeared in middle or slow tempos, and *agréments* (embellishments) and cadential gestures, particularly the *cadence fermée*—and

extended appoggiatura on the penultimate tone, a trill and an anticipation of the final tone—remained *de rigueur*.[13]

Some of the largest developments that affected stylistic considerations in classical chamber music included the standardization of vertical harmonic function, notation that ended the improvisatory performance practice of the baroque period, and the continued evolution and standardization of instruments. Beethoven's *26 Irish Songs* ♪, published in 1814 and written for violin, viola, pianoforte, and two voices, is an excellent example of the evolving style (figure 5.3).

Figure 5.3. Ludwig van Beethoven, "Once More I Hail Thee," mm. 1–12 (No. 3 from 25 Irish Songs, WoO 152). *Creative Commons* (CC BY-SA 3.0)

As new language of tonal harmony and improvisatory expectations formed, John Irving summarizes:

> The composer (who in the eighteenth century was so often also the performer) expected his music to be rendered sensible, expressive, meaningful by *being spoken*. The performer (whether or not synonymous with the composer) had a duty to make that music speak by reading the signs it contained (whether notated or not) and applying performance conventions to them that differed widely across Europe and were diversely recorded in vocal and instrumental treatises published through the century in many places and in many languages. All such treatises, though, presumed the same thing: that the performer will afford the music a way of being spoken.[14]

CLASSICAL INTO ROMANTIC

In *Classical and Romantic Performing Practice 1750–1900*, Clive Brown gives extensive detail regarding the treatment of specific accents, articulation, bowing, tempo, embellishment, vibrato, and *portamento*. This resource has a vast array of information and musical examples for those with specific questions or particular interest in the area of performance practice. He writes:

> The present-day musician who wishes to understand the ways in which, with respect to embellishment, eighteenth-and-nineteenth-century performers might have responded to the notation of their day, or the sorts of expectations that composers might have had about the interpretation of their notation, needs to be conscious of a number of important distinctions. At one extreme was the addition of more or less elaborate fiorituras to the given musical text, substantially modifying the melodic line or introducing new material at cadence: at the other was the application of various less obtrusive embellishments, ranging from vibrato portamento, and subtle modifications of rhythm to the interpolation of arpeggiation, trills, turns, and appoggiaturas.[15]

In classical repertoire, and increasingly into the romantic period, composers continued to provide specific information regarding tempo, dynamics, and *rubato*. More technically challenging music emerged

Figure 5.4. Johannes Brahms, "Gestillte Sehnsucht," Op. 91, No. 1, mm. 43–48. *Creative Commons* (CC BY-SA 3.0)

as instruments became capable of performing faster notes and louder sounds in increased ranges, as illustrated by Johannes Brahms's *Zwei Gesänge* ♪ for mezzo-soprano, viola, and piano (figure 5.4).

One of the most significant developments was that of the piano, which evolved from the harpsichord, clavichord, and fortepiano. Due to the materials and mechanistic differences between these instruments, the timbre, articulation, and dynamics make a remarkable difference for the singer.

> Performance techniques on the harpsichord and clavichord differ very considerably from those of the modern piano, and are strongly related to both historical developments and the acoustical and mechanical characteristics of these instruments. Neither instrument has the power of the piano; however, this is offset by their transparency of tone, allowing clarity in part-playing and a wealth of nuances.[16]

The clavichord, the smallest and quietest keyboard instrument, which gained popularity alongside the harpsichord in the sixteenth century, was used mainly for domestic purposes because of its portability. The harpsichord, a plucked-keyboard instrument that was larger in size, louder, and more appropriate for concert halls, became the favored continuo instrument in the baroque and classical eras. Authors Murray Campbell, Clive Greated, and Arnold Myers write, "On the harpsichord it is not possible to colour chords by placing greater emphasis on certain notes, as it is with the clavichord and piano. Different textures and sonorities must therefore be achieved by fine adjustments in the striking and release time of the constituent notes."[17] Common performance practice on the harpsichord involved rolling chords to avoid an overabundance of sound. As composers required more distinctive dynamic contrasts, the fortepiano evolved around 1770 and became the instrument that Mozart, Haydn, and Schubert utilized through the 1820s. The strings were struck (instead of plucked) and could be sustained by hand and knee pedals, thus revolutionizing the mechanics of the piano. The modern piano, with a metal frame and up to an eight-octave range, generates a louder sound, wider range of dynamics, control, articulations, and sustained sound. Technology was used to develop many instruments during the eighteenth and nineteenth centuries, including advancements of the reed, mouthpiece, strings, the addition of valves or tone holes, and stronger materials. Instruments evolved to meet composers' increasing technical demands including volume, range, and expressive dynamic capability.

As singers pursue historically informed performances, choosing instruments that are appropriate to the time period in which a work was composed can make a significant difference to the singing style and ensemble. They are able to reflect the composer's idiomatic writing style and markings. Harpsichords and fortepianos are often available within academic and collegiate programs and may be a wise introductory period instrument. As a result of instrumental development and accessibility, chamber music became popular with the middle class, and a wide range of repertoire could be composed and performed. The cantata was supplemented by duets, trios, and quartets with piano, in addition to vocal works with melodically independent instrumental lines. Chamber music benefited from sophisticated poetry, which inspired composers to synthesize harmonic function, both vocal and instrumental, with expressive interpretation. Large-scale chamber music was also composed as the concert hall increased in popularity, scope, and size, slowly redefining chamber music's paradigm.

MODERN AND NEW MUSIC

The style of twentieth- and twenty-first-century music is difficult to define because of the simultaneous construction and deconstruction of form, tonality, harmony, and genre. This can be equally intimidating and liberating for singers who are eager to explore the vast and varied array of vocal chamber music of this time period. Some repertoire adheres to traditions of the past, offering accessible notation, memorable melodies, and traditional vocal technique. Other pieces require extended singing techniques, such as sirens, *Sprechtstimme* ♪, whispering, microtones, straight tone, and sound effects. Instrumentalists' extended techniques may include flutter tongue, microtones ♪, multiphonics, harmonics, scordatura, bowing on unusual parts of the strings, prepared piano ♪, and the use of electronic instruments or recorded sounds. As singers gain fluency with the musical language in other time periods, interpreting symbols, figured bass, expressive markings, and articulations, repertoire in the twentieth century offers an expanded vocabulary with new syntax. In *New Vocal Repertory*, Jane Manning writes:

> It is unfortunate that an advanced musical idiom has tended to lead the faint-hearted to believe that new music is beyond their capabilities. In fact, many contemporary composers write as mellifluously for the voice as did Handel or Mozart; others may need more concentrated technical work before they lie easily, but are rarely more vocally taxing than Bach. The simplest avant-garde notation may look dauntingly modern on the page but turn out to be the most suitable of all for beginners. Executing so-called "extended vocal techniques" may be less problematic than spinning a series of long legato notes with perfect control. Many new works can make the most modest demands vocally and musically yet give audiences a refreshing surprise.[18]

Audiences are often interested in music that is familiar to them, so familiarizing contemporary audiences with modern chamber music begins with exposure, repetition, and accessibility. Speaking to audiences about some of the extended techniques involved in a piece helps them aurally anticipate not only the sound, but why the composer chose to use those compositional tools to express an idea or soundscape. This is an especially unique opportunity in the genre of chamber music, where ensembles can range from traditional string quartets to ensembles upward of fifteen or more instrumentalists to minimal scorings, such as solo voice and tuba. The options are seemingly endless, giving singers opportunity to perform with small or large ensembles and a myriad of instrumental combinations. Similar to studying the colors and brushstrokes used in abstract art, presenting the composer's technical or artistic blueprint will help performers and audiences understand why the composer chose to use particular sounds, timbres, harmonies, and effects in reimagined ways. When performing the work of a living composer, it is an excellent idea to contact composers for their input and participation in the creative process, gaining new insight into their specific compositional language and intent. At times, a score covered with contemporary notation and markings can seem confusing or overwhelming, but it is simply a roadmap written in a new, modern language that requires deciphering. As Sharon Mabry explains in *Exploring Twentieth-Century Vocal Music: A Practical Guide to Innovations in Performance and Repertoire*:

> Deciphering modern notation can be likened to puzzle solving. One must assume that each notational symbol makes a contribution to the whole work. Each small part must be analyzed for characteristics that help it fill out, or make apparent, the larger musical picture. It is not merely an individual bit or hurdle to overcome on the way to the finale. Therefore, individual notation gestures must be deciphered and mastered for the performer to appreciate the composer's larger aesthetic intent. If the analysis and eventual comprehension of those gestures is not achieved, the singer will never truly feel at ease with the performance outcome. There will always be a shyness or insecurity in the vocalism, due to an intellectual uncertainty about how each gesture should be sung or, in some cases, *uttered*.[19]

Ultimately, performing with style is seeking to understand and represent a composer's intentions using the musical language he or she used.

In some instances, like locating original early instruments, the application of performance practice can be challenging. In other instances, like learning how to improvise in a baroque or contemporary vernacular, it is exciting and collaborative when working with an instrumentalist who brings additional expertise or experience to the performance. Spending time with different musical vocabularies provides a new set of tools that distinguishes era, aesthetic, and zeitgeist in a way that is compelling to performers and audiences alike.

NOTES

1. Thomas Forrest Kelly, *Early Music* (New York: Oxford University Press, 2011), 69.
2. Martha Elliot, *Singing in Style: A Guide to Vocal Performance Practices* (New Haven, CT: Yale University Press, 2006), 7.
3. "What Is 'Urtext,'" Urtext Editions, Henle, last modified February 11, 2018, www.henleusa.com/en/urtext-editions/what-is-urtext.html.
4. Elliot, *Singing in Style*, 12.
5. Kelly, *Early Music*, 72.
6. Ibid., 55.
7. Murray Campbell, Clive Greated, and Arnold Myers, *Musical Instruments: History, Technology, and Performance of Instruments of Western Music* (New York: Oxford University Press, 2004), 122.
8. Karl Hochreither, trans. Melvin Unger, *Performance Practice of the Instrumental-Vocal Works of Johann Sebastian Bach* (Lanham, MD: Scarecrow Press, 2002), 78–79.
9. Ibid., 146.
10. Sally Sanford, "National Singing Styles," in *A Performer's Guide to Seventeenth-Century Music*, ed. Stewart Carter, rev. Jeffrey Kite-Powell (Indiana: Indiana University Press), 3–30, www.jstor.org/stable/j.ctt16gzcwn.8.
11. Elliot, *Singing in Style*, 21.
12. Berta Joncus, "Private Music in Public Spheres: Chamber Cantata and Song," in *The Cambridge History of Eighteenth Century Music*, ed. Simon P. Keene (Cambridge: Cambridge University Press, 2009), 522.
13. Ibid., 523–24.
14. John Irving, "Performance in the Eighteenth Century," in *The Cambridge History of Eighteenth Century Music*, ed. Simon P. Keene (Cambridge: Cambridge University Press, 2009), 435.

15. Clive Brown, *Classical and Romantic Performing Practice 1750–1900* (Oxford: Oxford University Press, 1999), 416.

16. Murray Campbell, Clive Greated, and Arnold Myers, *Musical Instruments: History, Technology, and Performance of Instruments of Western Music* (New York: Oxford University Press, 2004), 342.

17. Campbell et al., *Musical Instruments*, 344.

18. Jane Manning, *New Vocal Repertory* (New York: Oxford University Press, 1986), 2.

19. Sharon Mabry, *Exploring Twentieth-Century Vocal Music: A Practical Guide to Innovations in Performance and Repertoire* (New York: Oxford University Press, 2002), 56.

6

PEDAGOGICAL ADVANTAGES OF USING VOCAL CHAMBER MUSIC IN THE VOICE STUDIO

As a young singer who also studied flute, the most enjoyable part of my weekly private lessons was instrumental duets. It was an exciting experience to sight-read music with my teacher because I heard qualities in the tone that I admired and wished to replicate. I was supported and encouraged to push the limits of my technical and musical abilities. It was exhilarating to be performing alongside a professional musician, teacher, and mentor. More recently, as a college professor, I contemplated singing vocal duets with my students. I wondered if that would bring them the same joy, confidence, and growth opportunity I had experienced as a young instrumentalist and if it could be pedagogically useful for my students. Why do so many instrumental teachers utilize duets pedagogically and vocal teachers traditionally do not?

In the spring of 2016, I conducted a five-week research study at Gettysburg College wherein twelve undergraduate music majors, minors, and nonmajors in my studio were asked to sight-read vocal duets with me at the end of their weekly applied lessons. A different duet was utilized each week based on technical or artistic deficiencies I identified during the student's lesson (e.g., diction, phrasing, breath management, vowel modification). As I accompanied from the piano, the student and I sang together, which provided a unique teaching and learning opportunity based on the pedagogical techniques of modeling and scaffolding. During their last lesson of the semester, students were asked to sight-read a trio with each other. Audio and video rehearsal recordings were collected, and an individual interview with each student was conducted at the end of the five-week study. Students were asked the following questions:

1. What is your past experience with singing duets?
2. How comfortable are you sight-reading?
3. How do you feel your sight-reading has developed as a result of singing duets?
4. How do you feel your musicianship has been affected as a result of singing duets?
5. How has singing duets or trios affected your vocal technique?

These interviews were transcribed, coded, analyzed, and categorized based on themes. Discovered commonalities included (a) improvement in areas of vocal technique such as alignment, breath management, tone quality, registration, vowel modification, diction, phrasing, dynamics, and style; (b) development of collaborative awareness supported by ongoing responsivity to visual and aural cues; and (c) lessened performance anxiety due to a sense of technical and emotional reinforcement that lessened the negative association of making mistakes. I suggest that vocal chamber music can be used as a pedagogical tool in the voice studio and offers a new opportunity to work with students whose learning styles may extend beyond verbal instruction alone. An extensive list of graded vocal chamber repertoire can be found in appendix A as a tool for pedagogical use in the voice studio.

SCAFFOLDING AND MODELING

In this exploration, scaffolding is defined as providing temporary support by an authoritative figure as students develop skill sets and gain independence as learners. Modeling is learning by observation, after which the teacher reinforces a student's reproductions of observed skills. Teachers and/or advanced students paired with developing students can provide provisional structure using duet, trio, or quartet repertoire. In most voice studios, some use of scaffolding and modeling is common because, despite our best attempts to verbally describe tone quality, students aurally recognize the characteristics of a desired tone as demonstrated by a professional musician. Imagine describing the complex physical process of producing a beautiful sound without offering an aural example—either by modeling for your student or listening to a recording of a preferred sound. It would be fruitless without an appropriate aural representation.

This is why we listen to and sing along with many professional recordings, emulating the tone, phrasing, diction, and dynamics of our favorite singers. Why not use vocal chamber music as an additional tool to continue modeling technique and artistry through the process of learning and simultaneously performing music? It is a natural extension for the training of young singers because their music careers, whether in opera, in chamber music, as recitalists, or as pedagogues, will require them to perform alongside other singers in a collaborative and supportive way. Robert H. Woody wrote, "It is assumed that the ability to imitate the expressivity of a high-quality model is prerequisite to incorporating 'original' expressivity into one's own performances."[1] This creates excellent potential for vocal growth in students because every subtle change is being reinforced by the teacher over the span of a song. The teacher simultaneously challenges and supports the individuality of each singer's musicianship and vocalism.

Research suggests that modeling communicates musical concepts more clearly than verbal instruction alone, and several scholars have investigated the value attached to the social construct of modeling and scaffolding and its positive implications on the cooperative learning process.[2] Wiggins wrote:

> In a constructivist music classroom, students would have opportunities to construct their own understanding of the dimensions, multidimensions, and metadimensions of music through interaction with "real-world" music (as opposed to music contrived to teach a particular concept) by performing, creating, and listening. They would have opportunities to solve genuine musical problems (performance problems, creation problems, listening problems that are genuine in that they are problems "real" musicians solve) with the support (scaffolding) of peers and teacher. They would have multiple opportunities to share ideas (musical ideas and ideas about

> music) with peers and teacher and a right to have their ideas respected and valued by all. . . . They would be agents of their own learning, empowered to develop their own musicianship in genuine musical contexts.[3]

Vocal programs and private studios strive to implement educational goals that prepare singers with varying learning styles for a career (or proficiency) in music. These goals include healthy and efficient technique, artistry, knowledge of repertoire and style, musicianship, adaptability, flexibility, collaboration, and communication. A vocal curriculum that effectively integrates modeled vocal chamber music can help to achieve these goals. The inclusion of vocal chamber music augments traditional solo repertoire and verbal instruction by teaching students how to employ critical tools such as enhanced collaborative awareness; the ability to read music with greater speed, scope, and comprehension; and the facility to make subtle technical and musical changes in the moment based on observation. A student commented, "I have definitely gotten better at listening to other people around me. I've gotten better at being aware of my surroundings and what's going on in the music." Modeling duets affords teachers and learners a new perspective that acknowledges experiences, strengths, and areas for growth in teacher-student relationships and student-student relationships within a supportive educational environment.

VOCAL DUETS AND TECHNIQUE

Some singers are hesitant to perform with their teachers, but it is skill that is critical for professional success, musical growth, and personal growth. In an effort to create a positive learning environment that encourages growth and minimizes stigmatization of mistakes, the creation of a curriculum that incorporates chamber music can benefit the individual singer and voice studio, whether private or collegiate. According to Blank and Davidson, performers in small chamber groups create "professional and socio-emotional relationships" that present questions regarding "the nature of leadership, recognition of the existence of conflict, and compromise and strategies to resolve conflict."[4]

Utilizing chamber music as a pedagogical tool in the voice studio presents an opportunity to teach technical and artistic concepts and provide a platform for teaching musicians how to be leaders, convey their opinions, and reconcile discordant ideas while working toward a shared goal of improved performance and communication.

Using historical vocal pedagogy as a model, "duets were a favorite medium of chamber music throughout the baroque era, used both for public performance and for voice teaching. After a singing student's vocal technique was established, a way of learning style and expression was to sing duets with the teacher."[5] The famous Neapolitan composer and teacher Francesco Durante composed *12 Chamber Duets for Learning to Sing*, and singers and teachers who have used Mathilde Marchesi's vocal exercises may be interested to learn that she also composed eight *Vocalises à 3 voice in L'art du Chant*, Op. 22. Marchesi was a German teacher and singer during the second half of the nineteenth century who established a school of singing in Paris in 1881. She taught Nellie Melba and Emma Calvé, among other famous singers.[6] This unique selection of vocalises was dedicated to Marchesi's "À ses trois filles, Teresa, Stella, and Bianca."[7] The trios mirror Marchesi's numerous solo vocalises in variation, length, and difficulty and offer similar pedagogical emphases like dynamic contrast, vowel formation and modification, phrasing, articulation, and so on. This resource provides an excellent point of departure for those interested in using vocal chamber music as a pedagogical tool, particularly because they are methodically organized exercises composed without text. Teachers and/or students can select vowels on which to sing, have freedom of interpretation, and switch vocal lines for increased reading practice.

Performing duets with students presents a convenient way to determine that mistakes will be corrected, the voice will gain technical improvement, interpersonal issues will be navigated, and leadership skills will be gained. When performing teacher-student duets (or establishing student ensembles) with a pedagogical concentration, it is important to consider the following:

1. Carefully choose repertoire that is technically and emotionally appropriate for the student.

2. Establish a musical "road map" before the reading so the student can anticipate any musical, technical, or textual difficulties.
3. Discuss the translation.
4. Encourage scanning of all lines to gather complete information about the poetic/narrative interaction and musical relationship.
5. Engage discussion regarding the poetry and "roles" of varying parts such as motivation for aural and visual communication during reading (cueing, breathing, dynamics, eye contact, gesturing or movements, etc.).
6. Be prepared to stop as necessary to correct errors, model improvements, and reinforce correct concepts through scaffolding.

Choosing an appropriate duet that will help a student grow as a singer can often be challenging, mainly because singers and teachers of voice do not realize how many repertoire options exist. Art song duets range from homophonic settings of simple poetry to those that feel operatic in artistic and technical scope. Choosing vocal chamber repertoire follows the same parameters as choosing solo art song. For example, if a baritone is having difficulty with language while studying Lalo's "Oh! Quand je dors," adding Lalo's duet "Au fond des Halliers" would be a natural extension to increase collaborative awareness and provide a French diction scaffold within the same style. Students studying Mozart art songs could be delighted to learn of chamber duets written by one of his contemporaries, Vincenzo Righini, that offer a similar style, range, and technical challenge. Young or inexperienced singers with basic German diction and musical skills may benefit from scaffolded learning before singing solo *lieder*. Franz Abt wrote numerous duets that can provide instruction through homophonic musical lines, simple harmonies, and the same German text in both lines. Obtaining vocal chamber duets and organizing them according to pedagogical use may prove to be an excellent resource for studios of any level and aid in the technical development of all singers.

Sample lists are provided with suggested duets for technical growth in the areas of agility and sostenuto. Similar to solo art songs, there are multiple technical challenges inherent to each duet, but my hope is that the following lists present a starting place for musicians and teachers who are unfamiliar with vocal chamber music.

Duets to Reinforce Vocal Agility

Francesco Durante (1684–1755)—Alfin m'ucciderete
George Frideric Handel (1685–1759)—Tanti strali al sen mi scocchi, HWV 197
Vincenzo Righini (1756–1812)—L'Eco, Op. 8, No. 8
Vincenzo Righini (1756–1812)—L'Ambasciata, Op. 8, No. 6
Carl Maria von Weber (1786–1826)—3 Duetti, Op. 31
Gioacchino Rossini (1792–1868)—La Regata Veneziana from *Soirées musicales*, No. 9
Gioacchino Rossini (1792–1868)—La Pesca from *Soirées musicales*, No. 10
Hector Berlioz (1803–1869)—Le Trébuchet, Op. 13, No. 3
Friedrich Curschmann (1805–1841)—Der Wald, Op. 17
Maria Malibran (1808–1836)—Belle, viens à moi
Édouard Lalo (1823–1892)—Dansons!
Anton Rubinstein (1829–1894)—Sang das Vögelein, Op. 48, No. 2
Gabriel Fauré (1845–1924)—Tarantelle, 2 Duets, Op. 10, No. 2
Ned Rorem (b.1923)—Cadenza from Gloria

Duets to Reinforce Vocal Sostenuto

Gioacchino Rossini (1792–1868)—La Serenata from *Soirées musicales*, No. 11
Franz Schubert (1797–1828)—Licht und Liebe
Robert Schumann (1810–1856)—In der Nacht, Op. 74, No. 4
Robert Schumann (1810–1856)—Spruch from *Drei Lieder*, Op. 114, No. 3
Robert Schumann (1810–1856)—Er und Sie, Op. 78, No. 2
Robert Schumann (1810–1856)—Ich bin dein Baum, o Gärtner, Op. 101, No. 3
Isidor Dannström (1812–1897)—Wåren och Glädjen, Op. 15, No. 6
Ludvig Norman (1831–1885)—Vexelsång, Op. 17, No. 4
Camille Saint-Saëns (1835–1921)—Le soir
Pyotr Tchaikovsky (1840–1893)—Nicht Leidenschaft from *Sechs Duette für zwei Singstimmen*, Op. 46
Jules Massenet (1842–1912)—Horace et Lydie

VOCAL DUETS (AND TRIOS AND QUARTETS) AND COLLABORATION

We have explored *why* chamber music is beneficial for singers, but *how* do we teach them to collaborate? The first way is to form teacher-student groups who perform duets during the lesson time at the discretion of the teacher. Verbal instruction is often the main medium of communication in the voice studio. Duets offer the teacher (or scaffold) the opportunity to utilize singing as a form of instruction, using visual and aural cues to model musical or technical concepts. Students employ sensitive listening, observational, and critical thinking skills as they observe, recognize, and respond with technical progress in areas that include alignment, breath management, tone quality, registration, diction, phrasing, dynamics, and style. A student noted, "Being in a group encourages people to be their best self, so to speak. It encourages us to sing with our best qualities and put 110 percent in. I use more breath support, try to make my sound as resonant as possible, and I try not to shy away from higher notes or lower notes." They also develop leadership skills as they share responsibility for conveying changes in emotion due to textual or musical changes, entrances and cut-offs, shaping phrases, and physical interaction. Teachers can quickly and authoritatively address issues in the student's collaborative responses, technical problems, or artistic weaknesses. Rehearsing teacher-student duets also transforms the relationship between teacher and student to one of professional musician and aspiring professional musician, inspiring confidence and motivation.

Teaching students how to collaborate by forming student chamber groups is also of benefit. Teachers of singing can create groups that couple stronger singers with less experienced singers or voice types that complement each other technically or expressively. A student commented, "I have noticed that in order to hear my notes as they relate to everything else, I have to sing out more." By initially coaching the chamber group and attending rehearsals, teachers can guide singers on how to navigate a rehearsal by encouraging them to speak respectfully but honestly about their opinions regarding the music and text. Many students hold back during chamber music rehearsals for fear of expressing an "incorrect" opinion, feeling "pushy," or offending a colleague or because they feel like opinions have been dismissed or invalidated by a peer. Finding the balance between mediating rehearsals and supporting autonomy will become self-evident.

Teaching students how to verbally communicate about music and expression is one of the most important aspects of training young singers in chamber music. The addition of aural and visual stimuli become important extensions of this verbal communication, increasing the depth of understanding between musicians. Creating visual reinforcement between an expressive singer and one who struggles with showing emotion facially or vocally can benefit from this arrangement. One student reported, "I'm a visual learner, so it was very beneficial for me to watch another person sing and then imitate correct physical habits in my own way." Students should be encouraged to make eye contact when indicating onsets and releases and during musically dramatic moments. Experienced singers can model appropriate times to smile, frown, gesture, or take an expressive breath. Partners can reproduce similar effects until they learn to do them autonomously. Research about mirror neurons is beginning to help us understand why humans instinctively mirror or reflect movements and expressions and how it can benefit learning and empathy processes. In the NATS *Journal of Singing*, Lynn Helding discusses research studies on the human mirror neuron system and speculates that mirror neurons may help singers improve the ability to practice, perform, empathize, and act through external or self-observation.[8] In their article, "Being Together in Time: Musical Experience and the Mirror Neuron System," coauthors Katie Overy and Istvan Molnar-Szakacs theorize:

> Thus, what is exciting about the discovery of mirror neurons, and a homologous system in the human brain, is the idea that the brain does not function as an isolated stimulus-response perception-action machine. Firstly, the brain's functioning is intimately connected with the body, and secondly, the brain has evolved to interact with and to understand other brains. Properties of the human MNS thus allow us to consider social communication, and more specifically musical communication in a new light—less in terms of pitch/timbre/rhythmic patterns—and more in terms of action sequencing, goals/intentions, prediction, and shared representations.[9]

The implications for studying duets and modeling healthy technique and communicative artistry are intriguing. When tasked with achievement of similar goals by means of scaffolding and modeling, students must respond to each other visually and aurally to match phrasing, tone quality, dynamic variability, articulation of diction, expression, and gestures. A student said, "I found myself making subtle changes, really small adjustments in my Italian." Another affirmed, "With duets, you get more support and more freedom with singing. It's really fun." Students who excel in these areas can provide a strong model for less experienced students, encourage them through positive reinforcement, and support peer growth while gaining leadership skills.

PERFORMANCE ANXIETY

An unexpected result from my study was the positive effect performing duets had on alleviating performance anxiety. Numerous students reflected that supporting another singer in an ensemble created a sense of technical and emotional reinforcement that lessened the negative association of making mistakes. One of them expressed, "There's a communal feeling that we're all trying to figure this out and so, by not being alone, it takes a little bit of the pressure off. When you're alone, you tend to think, 'What are they thinking about me?' and 'I can't mess up.' You're not so understanding with yourself, but you are when there are other people involved. Having that in mind, it takes off that social pressure so I could really think about the music." Chamber music can inspire increased concentration on musical elements, stronger initial performances, and increased enjoyment while singing.

Many musicians suffer from performance anxiety and often need coping strategies to mitigate its myriad causes and effects. Christopher Arneson writes: "Psychological stress is intrinsic to performance. Depending on the particular survey, percentages of performers suffering from significant performance anxiety can range from twenty to ninety."[10]

It is a notable discovery that vocal chamber music could be a potential avenue to lessen performance anxiety. Students may experience less anxiety in performance and faster technical and/or artistic growth within supportive peer groups because mistakes become relabeled as growth opportunities. These growth opportunities are born from musical accountability because, in a chamber ensemble, the music will continue despite one person's mistake. The focus should be less on self and more on the ensemble. A student observed, "I really need to cue into what my partner is doing and let that make my sound better. There is musical accountability when another person is involved." Subsequently, students assimilate resilience to continue after making mistakes, improve concentration so they can rejoin the ensemble at an appropriate moment, and feel that errors are less stigmatizing when the focus is not exclusively on them.

Conversely, not all students will experience lessened performance anxiety in chamber ensembles. Some students have described increased anxiety when performing in peer groups and a lack of focus on their own technique. These singers are often susceptible to "blending" with other singers instead of employing a soloistic approach to technique and artistry and shy away from asserting their personal artistic interpretations. As voice teachers, we must carefully guide and mentor students through musical experiences that challenge interpersonal skills. Our charge is to help students successfully navigate a new experience and recognize when the student is overwhelmed or not benefiting from the experience. Gwendolyn Walker and Cody Commander warn: "Though students can learn from watching others, comparing themselves unfavorably leads them away from finding their own unique expressiveness. Similarly, if students merely imitate other performers, they undervalue their own unique skill set, which is what makes them individual and interesting in the first place."[11]

PERFORMING VOCAL CHAMBER MUSIC CONCERTS

After students have sight-read and studied duets, trios, and quartets in applied lessons or in a private studio, how can their hard work be utilized in a performance context? An obvious answer, as discussed in chapter 3, is to program vocal chamber music on a solo recital. Chamber music can stimulate performers and audiences with a new aural and visual landscape. Many art song and opera composers have written exquisite chamber pieces that are rarely performed, not for lack of quality or quantity but for lack of exposure and perhaps accessibility. Imagine the appeal of recital sets with the following inclusions:

Das Veilchen	Wolfgang Amadeus Mozart (1756–1791)
Das Veilchen	Fanny Mendelssohn-Hensel (1805–1847)
Das Veilchen (for two sopranos and tenor)	Friedrich Curschmann (1805–1841)

Sleep	Ivor Gurney (1890–1937)
Selige Nacht	Joseph Marx (1882–1964)
Après un rêve	Gabriel Fauré (1845–1924)
La Nuit (for two voices)	Ernest Chausson (1855–1899)

Ah! Love But A Day	Amy Beach (1867–1944)
Take, O Take Those Lips Away	
A Canadian Boat Song (for soprano and baritone) from Songs of the Sea, Op. 10	

American Lullaby	Gladys Rich (1904–1994)
Wiegenlied (for soprano and tenor), Op. 78, No. 4	Robert Schumann (1810–1856)
Wiegenlied	Johannes Brahms (1833–1897)
A Slumber Song of the Madonna	Samuel Barber (1910–1981)

Walpurgisnacht, Op. 2, No. 3	Johann Karl Gottfried Loewe (1796–1869)
Walpurgisnacht (for two sopranos), Op. 75, No. 4	Johannes Brahms (1833–1897)

(Neapolitan Dialect)	
La conocchia from Nuits d'été à Pausilippe	Gaetano Donizetti (1797–1848)
'A vucchella	Paolo Tosti (1846–1916)
Tre bote sì e pono (for two voices)	Francesco Florimo (1800–1888)
Tarantella Sorrentina (for female and male voices)	Vincenzo Valente (1855–1921)

Other possibilities exist that could make more advantageous use of the wealth of vocal chamber music and its ability to unite students' technical and collaborative capabilities with audience appeal. Studio recitals, departmental recitals, or a recital series dedicated to vocal chamber music are excellent avenues for young students who may not be prepared to perform a full solo recital but are looking for performance opportunities. It also offers an opportunity to showcase numerous students' individual strengths in a collaborative context. Collegiate programs could consider adding a chamber music requirement to the curriculum if one does not already exist, including vocalists in what is often a requirement for instrumentalists. Many institutions structure their curriculum to guide students on repertoire, rehearsal technique, and collaborative communication through the scheduling of coachings and performance opportunities. This can be a valuable curricular component that increases young musicians' marketability by widening their skill set and augmenting the breadth of knowledge of repertoire.

Vocal chamber music could be used as outreach or recruitment in local high schools or middle schools. It is accessible for young listeners, is appealing to young singers who are already familiar with small ensemble context because of choir, and would require no sets, props, or costumes, making it cost-efficient and audience-friendly. Singers could also offer to coach small ensembles of adolescent students, using skills developed in their studios to maximize leadership and educational opportunities.

A final idea that is central to chamber music's genesis is the creation of a *Hausmusik* (household music) concert series. Instead of performing chamber music on recital stages, concerts can be performed in intimate venues like local homes, libraries, art museums, hospitals, or retirement homes. *Hausmusik* concerts are common around the world and bring chamber music back into the home and community, renewing a musical conversation over shared values that brings people closer to the music and each other. A series such as this could also involve a community-based objective, like raising money for scholarships, charities, or other worthy causes. An example of such a series is described below, serving the community with music:

> "If Music Be the Food . . ." is a series of benefit concerts whose mission is to increase awareness and support, through the sharing of great music, for people in the local community who are struggling with food insecurity, and to teach music students about the importance of utilizing their art for service in their communities. All participants in every aspect of the endeavor volunteer their services and pay their own costs, so that all proceeds can go directly to the hungry. No tickets are sold for the concerts, rather, audience members are invited to bring non-perishable food items or monetary donations for the partnering food bank as the price of

admission. Created by violist Carol Rodland in Rochester, New York, in 2009, "If Music Be the Food . . ." is rapidly becoming a national musicians' movement.[12]

For centuries, chamber music has appealed to audiences, performers, and pedagogues because it is similar to a private conversation: personal, meaningful, and authentic. With repertoire options for singers of every skill level, it offers an unsurpassed learning, performance, professional, and collaborative opportunity.

NOTES

1. Robert H. Woody, "The Relationship between Explicit Planning and Expressive Performance of Dynamic Variations in an Aural Modeling Task," *Journal of Research in Music Education* 47, no. 4 (1999): 331–42.

2. See Penny L. Beed, E. Marie Hawkins, and Cathy M. Roller, "Moving Learners toward Independence: The Power of Scaffolded Instruction," *The Reading Teacher* 44, no. 9 (1991): 648–55; Marc R. Dickey, "A Comparison of Verbal Instruction and Nonverbal Teacher-Student Modeling in Instrumental Ensembles," *Journal of Research in Music Education* 39, no. 2 (1991): 132–42 and "A Review of Research on Modeling in Music Teaching and Learning," *Bulletin of the Council for Research in Music Education* 113 (1992): 27–40; Warren Haston, "Teacher Modeling as an Effective Teaching Strategy," *Music Educators Journal* 93, no. 4 (2007): 26–30; Kelly A. Parkes and Mathias Wexler, "The Nature of Applied Music Teaching Expertise: Common Elements Observed in the Lessons of Three Applied Teachers," *Bulletin of the Council for Research in Music Education* 193 (2012): 45–62; R. K. Rosenthal, "The Relative Effects of Guided Model, Model Only, Guide Only, and Practice Only Treatments on the Accuracy of Advanced Instrumentalists' Musical Performance," *Journal of Research in Music Education* 32, no. 4 (1984): 265–73; R. C. Sang, "A Study of the Relationship Between Instrumental Music Teachers' Modeling Skills and Pupil Performance Behaviors," *Bulletin of the Council for Research in Music Education* 91 (1987): 155–59; Woody, "The Relationship between Explicit Planning and Expressive Performance," 331–42.

3. Jackie Wiggins, "Authentic Practice and Process in Music Teacher Education," *Music Educators Journal* 93, no. 3 (2007): 36–42.

4. Marilyn Blank and Jane Davidson. "An Exploration of the Effects of Musical and Social Factors in Piano Duo Collaborations," *Psychology of Music* (2007): 231–48.

5. John Glenn Paton, *Gateway to Italian Art Songs: An Anthology of Italian Song and Interpretation* (Van Nuys, CA: Alfred Publ. Co., 2004).

6. Elizabeth Forbes, "Marchesi Family," Oxford Music Online, www.oxfordmusiconline.com/grovemusic/view/10.1093/gmo/9781561592630.001.0001/omo-9781561592630-e-0000017730, accessed May 22, 2017.

7. Mathilde Marchesi, *L'Art du Chant, 8 Vocalises à 3 voix, Op. 22*, imslp.org/wiki/8_Vocalises_%C3%A0_3_voix,_Op.22_(Marchesi,_Mathilde), accessed May 22, 2017.

8. Lynn Helding, "The Mind's Mirrors," *Journal of Singing* 66, no. 5 (2010): 585–89.

9. K. Overy and I. Molnar-Szakacs, "Being Together in Time: Musical Experience and the Mirror Neuron System," *Music Perception* 26, no. 5 (2009): 489–504.

10. Christopher Arneson, "Performance Anxiety: A Twenty-First Century Perspective," *Journal of Singing* 66, no. 5 (2010): 537–46.

11. Gwendolyn Walker and Cody Commander, "The Emotionally Prepared Singer," *Journal of Singing* 73, no. 3 (2017): 261–68.

12. "Our Mission," If Music Be the Food, www.ifmusicbethefood.com/, accessed May 20, 2017.

7

SINGING AND VOICE SCIENCE

Scott McCoy

This chapter presents a concise overview of how the voice functions as a biomechanical, acoustic instrument. We will be dealing with elements of anatomy, physiology, acoustics, and resonance. But don't panic: the things you need to know are easily accessible, even if it has been many years since you last set foot in a science or math class!

All musical instruments, including the human voice, have at least four things in common, consisting of a power source, sound source (vibrator), resonator, and a system for articulation. In most cases, the person who plays the instrument provides power by pressing a key, plucking a string, or blowing into a horn. This power is used to set the sound source in motion, which creates vibrations in the air that we perceive as sound. Musical vibrators come in many forms, including strings, reeds, and human lips. The sound produced by the vibrator, however, needs a lot of help before it becomes beautiful music—we might think of it as raw material, like a lump of clay that a potter turns into a vase. Musical instruments use resonance to enhance and strengthen the sound of the vibrator, transforming it into sounds we identify as a piano, trumpet, or guitar. Finally, instruments must have a means of articulation to create the nuanced sounds of music. Let's see how these four elements are used to create the sounds of singing.

PULMONARY SYSTEM: THE POWER SOURCE OF YOUR VOICE

The human voice has a lot in common with a trumpet: both use flaps of tissue as a sound source, both use hollow tubes as resonators, and both rely on the respiratory (pulmonary) system for power. If you stop to think about it, you quickly realize why breathing is so important for singing. First and foremost, it keeps us alive through the exchange of blood gases—oxygen in, carbon dioxide out. But it also serves as the storage depot for the air we use to produce sound. Most singers rarely encounter situations in which these two functions are in conflict, but if you are required to sustain an extremely long phrase, you could find yourself in need of fresh oxygen before your lungs are totally empty.

Misconceptions about breathing for singing are rampant. Fortunately, most are easily dispelled. We must start with a brief foray into the world of physics in the guise of Boyle's Law. Some of you no doubt remember this principle: the pressure of a gas within a container changes inversely with changes of volume. If the quantity of a gas is constant and its container is made smaller, pressure rises. But if we make the container bigger, pressure goes down. Boyle's law explains everything that happens when we breathe, especially when we combine it with another physical law: nature abhors a vacuum. If one location has reduced pressure, air flows from an area of higher pressure to equalize the two, and vice versa. So if we can create a zone of reduced air pressure by expanding our lungs, air automatically flows in to restore balance. When air pressure in the lungs is increased, it has no choice but to flow outward.

As we all know, the air we breathe goes in and out of our lungs. Each lung contains millions and millions of tiny air sacs called alveoli, where gases are exchanged. The alveoli also function like ultra-miniature versions of the bladder for a bag pipe, storing the air that will be used to set the vocal folds into vibration. To get the air in and out of them, all we need to do is make the lungs larger for inhalation and smaller for exhalation. Always remember this relationship between cause and effect during breathing: we inhale because we make ourselves large; we exhale because we make ourselves smaller. Unfortunately, the lungs are organs, not muscles, and have no ability on their own to accomplish this feat. For this reason, your bodies came from the factory with special muscles designed to enlarge and compress your entire thorax (rib cage), while simultaneously moving your lungs. We can classify these muscles in two main categories: any muscle that has the ability to increase the volume capacity of the thorax serves an inspiratory function; any muscle that has the ability to decrease the volume capacity of the thorax serves an expiratory function.

Your largest muscle of inspiration is called the diaphragm (figure 7.1). This dome-shaped muscle originates from the bottom of your sternum (breastbone) and completely fills the area from that point around your ribs to your spine. It's the second-largest muscle in your body, but you probably have no conscious awareness of it or ability to directly control

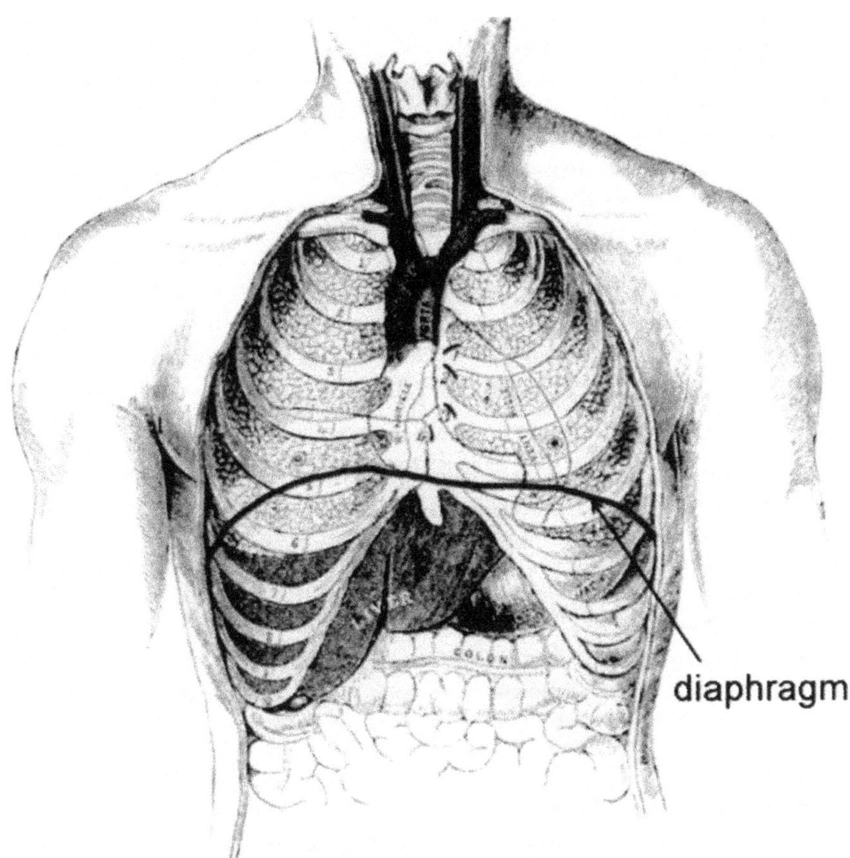

Figure 7.1. Location of diaphragm. ***Courtesy of Scott McCoy***

it. When we take a deep breath, the diaphragm contracts and the central portion flattens out and drops downward a couple inches into your abdomen, pressing against all of your internal organs. If you release tension from your abdominal muscles as you inhale, you will feel a gentle bulge in your upper or lower belly, or perhaps in your back, resulting from the displacement of your innards by the diaphragm. This is a good thing and can be used to let you know you have taken a good inhalation.

The diaphragm is important, but we must remember that it cannot function in isolation. After you inhale, it relaxes and gently returns to its resting position through an action called elastic recoil. This movement, however, is entirely passive and makes no significant contribution to generating the pressure required to sustain phonation. Therefore, it makes no sense at all to try to "sing from your diaphragm"—unless you intend to sing while you inhale, not exhale!

Eleven pairs of muscles assist the diaphragm in its inhalatory efforts, which are called the external intercostal muscles (figure 7.2). These muscles start from ribs one through eleven and connect at a slight angle downward to ribs two through twelve. When they contract, the entire thorax moves up and out, somewhat like moving a bucket handle. With the diaphragm and intercostals working together, you are able to increase the capacity of your lungs by about three to six liters, depending on your gender and overall physical stature; thus, we have quite a lot of air available to power our voices.

Eleven additional pairs of muscles are located directly under the external intercostals, which, not surprisingly, are called the internal intercostals (figure 7.2). These muscles start from ribs two through twelve and connect upward to ribs one through eleven. When they contract, they induce the opposite action of their external partners: the thorax is made smaller, inducing exhalation. Four additional pairs of expiratory muscles are located in the abdomen, beginning with the rectus (figure 7.2). The two rectus abdominis muscles run from your pubic bone to your sternum and are divided into four separate portions, called bellies of the muscle (lots of muscles have multiple bellies; it is coincidental that the bellies of the rectus are found in the location we colloquially refer to as our belly). Definition of these bellies results in the so-called ripped abdomen or six-pack of body builders and others who are especially fit.

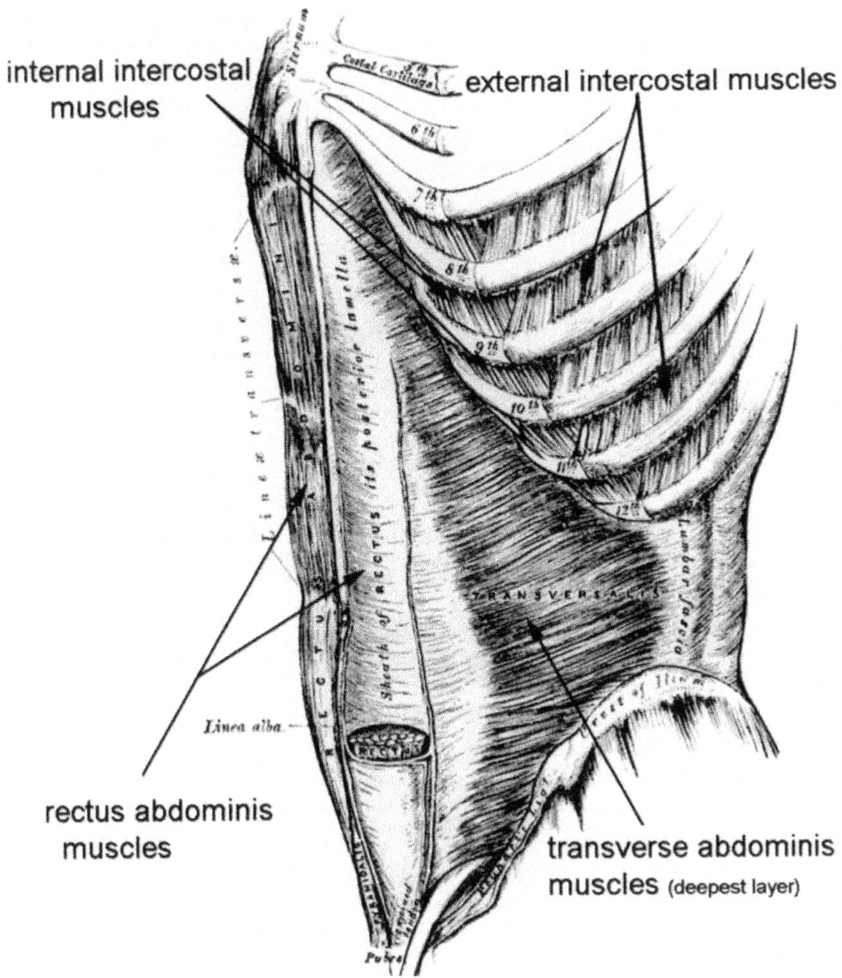

Figure 7.2. Intercostal and abdominal muscles. *Courtesy of Scott McCoy*

The largest muscles of the abdomen are called the external obliques (figure 7.3), which run at a downward angle from the sides of the rectus, covering the lower portion of the thorax, and extend all the way to the spine. The internal obliques lie immediately below, oriented at an angle that crisscrosses the external muscles. They are slightly smaller, beginning at the bottom of the thorax, rather than extending over it. The deepest muscle layer is the transverse abdominis (figure 7.2), which is oriented with fibers that run horizontally. These four muscle pairs

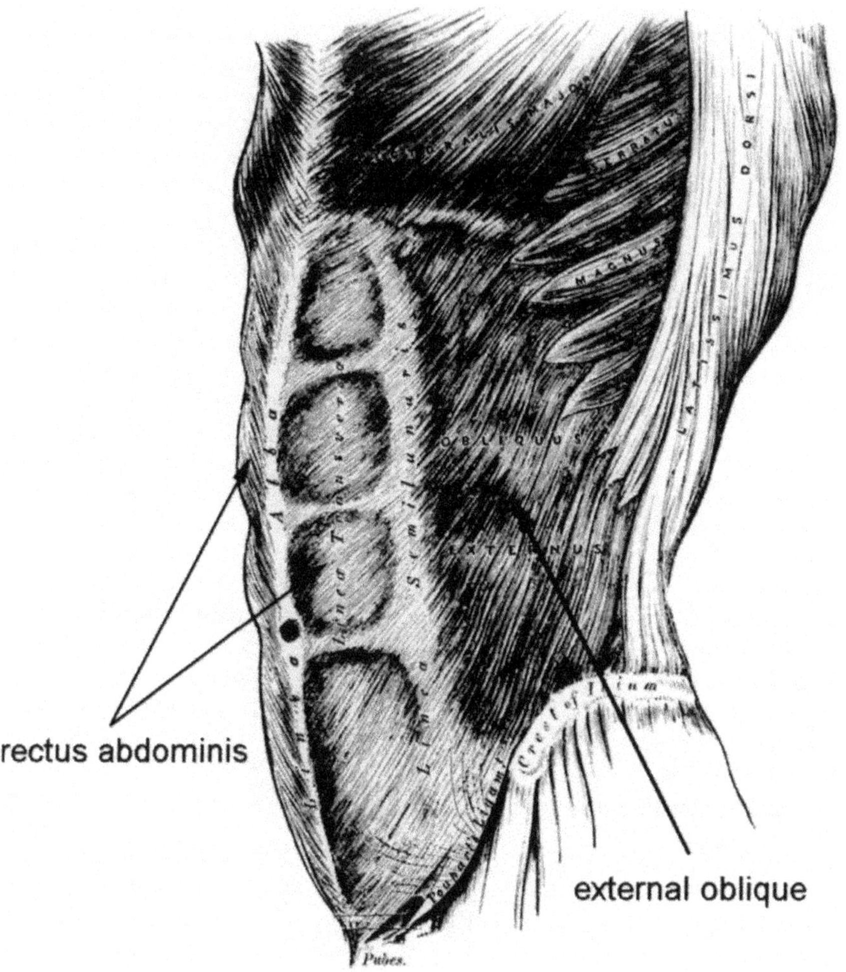

Figure 7.3. External oblique and rectus abdominis muscles. ***Courtesy of Scott McCoy***

completely encase the abdominal region, holding your organs and digestive system in place while simultaneously helping you breathe.

Your expiratory muscles are quite large and can produce a great deal of pulmonary or air pressure. In fact, they easily can overpower the larynx. Healthy adults generally can generate more than twice the pressure that is required to produce even the loudest sounds; therefore, singers must develop a system for moderating and controlling airflow and breath pressure. This practice goes by many names, including breath support, breath control, and breath management, all of which rely on the principle of muscular antagonism. Muscles are said to have an antagonistic relationship when they work in opposing directions, usually pulling on a common point of attachment, for the sake of increasing stability or motor control. You can see a clear example of muscular antagonism in the relationship between your biceps (flexors) and triceps (extensors) when you hold out your arm. In breathing for singing, we activate inspiratory muscles (e.g., diaphragm and external intercostals) during exhalation to help control respiratory pressure and the rate at which air is expelled from the lungs.

One of the things you will notice when watching a variety of singers is that they tend to breathe in many different ways. You might think that voice teachers and scientists, who have been teaching and studying singing for hundreds, if not thousands of years, would have come to agreement on the best possible breathing technique. But for many reasons, this is not the case. For one, different musical and vocal styles place varying demands on breathing. For another, humans have a huge variety of body types, sizes, and morphologies. A breathing strategy that is successful for a tall, slender woman might be completely ineffective in a short, robust man. Our bodies actually contain a large number of muscles beyond those we've already discussed that are capable of assisting with respiration. For an example, consider your latissimi dorsi muscles. These large muscles of the arm enable us to do pull-ups (or pull-downs, depending on which exercise you perform) at the fitness center. But because they wrap around a large portion of the thorax, they also exert an expiratory force. We have at least two dozen such muscles that have secondary respiratory functions, some for exhalation and some for inhalation. When we consider all these possibilities, it is no surprise at all that there are many ways to breathe that can produce beautiful singing. Just remember to practice some muscular antagonism—maintaining a degree of inhalation posture during exhalation—and you should do well.

LARYNX: THE VIBRATOR OF YOUR VOICE

The larynx, sometimes known as the voice box or Adam's apple, is a complex physiologic structure made of cartilage, muscle, and tissue. Biologically, it serves as a sphincter valve, closing off the airway to prevent foreign objects from entering the lungs. When firmly closed, it also is used to increase abdominal pressure to assist with lifting heavy objects, childbirth, and defecation. But if we gently close this valve while we exhale, tissue in the larynx begins to vibrate and produce the sounds that become speech and singing.

The human larynx is a remarkably small instrument, typically ranging from the size of a pecan to a walnut for women and men, respectively. Sound is produced at a location called the glottis, which is formed by two flaps of tissue called the vocal folds (aka vocal cords). In women, the glottis is about the size of a dime; in men, it can approach the diameter of a quarter. The two folds are always attached together at their front point but open in the shape of the letter V during normal breathing, an action called abduction. To phonate, we must close the V while we exhale, an action called adduction (just like the machines you use at the fitness center to exercise your thigh and chest muscles).

Phonation only is possible because of the unique multilayer structure of the vocal folds (figure 7.4). The core of each fold is formed by muscle, which is surrounded by a layer of gelatinous material called the lamina propria. The vocal ligament also runs through the lamina propria, which helps to prevent injury by limiting how far the folds can be stretched for high pitches. A thin, hairless epithelial layer that is constantly kept moist with mucus secreted by the throat, larynx, and trachea surrounds all of this. During phonation, the outer layer of the fold glides independently over the inner layer in a wavelike motion, without which phonation is impossible.

We can use a simple demonstration to better understand the independence of the inner and outer portions of the folds. Explore the palm of your hand with your other index finger. Note that the skin is attached quite firmly to the flesh beneath it. If you poke at your palm, that flesh acts as padding, protecting the underlying bone. Now explore the back of your hand. You will observe that the skin is attached quite loosely—you easily can move it around with your finger. And if you poke at the back of your hand, it is likely to hurt; there is very little padding between the skin and your bones. Your vocal folds combine the best attributes of both sides of your hand. They provide sufficient padding to help reduce impact stress, while permitting the outer layer to slip like the skin on

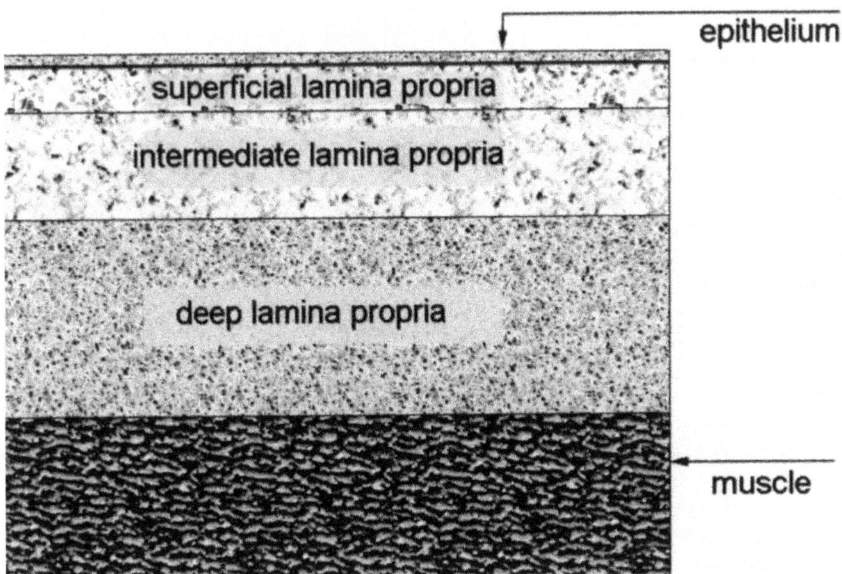

Figure 7.4. Layered structure of the vocal fold. ***Courtesy of Scott McCoy***

the back of your hand, enabling phonation to occur. When you are sick with laryngitis and lose your voice (a condition called aphonia), inflammation in the vocal folds couples the layers of the folds tightly together. The outer layer no longer can move independently over the inner, and phonation becomes difficult or impossible.

The vocal folds are located within the five cartilaginous structures of the larynx (figure 7.5). The largest is called the thyroid cartilage, which is shaped like a small shield. The thyroid connects to the cricoid cartilage below it, which is shaped like a signet ring—broad in the back and narrow in the front. Two cartilages that are shaped like squashed pyramids sit atop the cricoid, called the arytenoids. Each vocal fold runs from the thyroid cartilage in front to one of the arytenoids at the back. Finally, the epiglottis is located at the top of the larynx, flipping backward each time we swallow to prevent food and liquid from entering our lungs. Muscles connect between the various cartilages to open and close the glottis and to lengthen and shorten the vocal folds for ascending and descending pitch, respectively. Because they sometimes are used to identify vocal function, it is a good idea to know the names of the muscles that control the length of the folds. We've already mentioned that

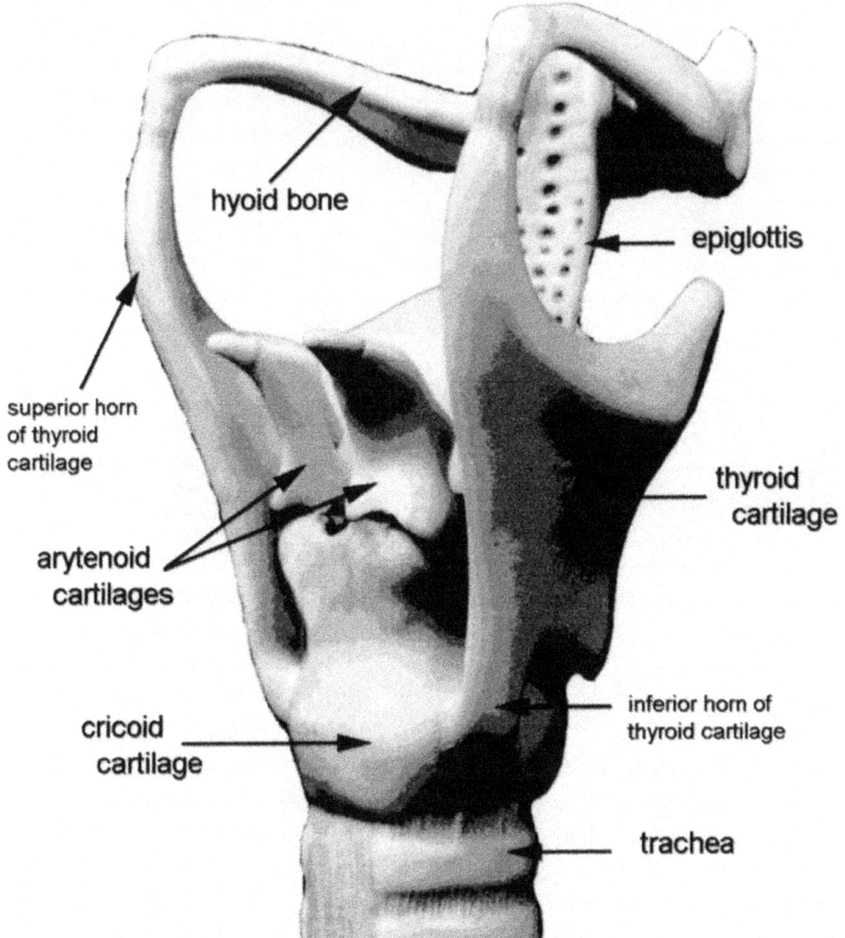

Figure 7.5. Cartilages of the larynx, viewed at an angle from the back. ***Courtesy of Scott McCoy***

a muscle forms the core of each fold. Because it runs between the thyroid cartilage and an arytenoid, it is named the thyroarytenoid muscle (formerly known as the vocalis muscle). When the thyroarytenoid, or TA muscle, contracts, the fold is shortened and pitch goes down. The folds are elongated through the action of the cricothyroid, or CT muscles, which run from the thyroid to cricoid cartilage.

Vocal color (timbre) is created by the combined effects of the sound produced by the vocal folds and the resonance provided by the vocal tract. While these elements can never be completely separated, it is useful to consider the two primary modes of vocal fold vibration and their resulting sound qualities. The main differences are related to the relative thickness of the folds and their cross-sectional shape (figure 7.6). The first option depends on short, thick folds that come together with nearly square-shaped edges. Vibration in this configuration is given a variety of names, including mode 1, thyroarytenoid (TA) dominant, chest mode, or modal voice. The alternate configuration uses longer, thinner folds that only make contact at their upper margins. Common names include mode 2, cricothyroid (CT) dominant, falsetto mode, or loft voice. Singers vary the vibrational mode of the folds according to the quality of sound they wish to produce.

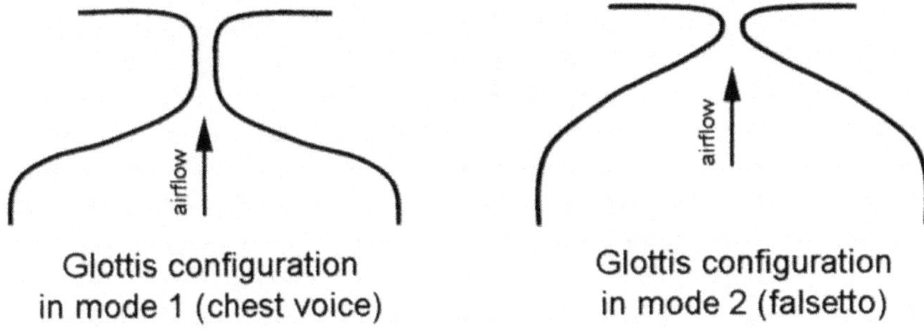

Figure 7.6. Primary modes of vocal fold vibration. ***Courtesy of Scott McCoy***

Before we move on to a discussion of resonance, we must consider the quality of the sound that is produced by the larynx. At the level of the glottis, we create a sound not unlike the annoying buzz of a duck call. That buzz, however, contains all the raw material we need to create speech and singing. Vocal or glottal sound is considered to be complex, meaning it consists of many simultaneously sounding frequencies (pitches). The lowest frequency within any tone is called the fundamental, which corresponds to its named pitch in the musical scale. Orchestras tune to a pitch called A-440, which means it has a frequency of 440 vibrations per second, or 440 Hertz (abbreviated Hz). Additional frequencies are included above the fundamental, which are called overtones. Overtones in the glottal sound are quieter than the fundamental. In voices, the overtones usually are whole number multiples of the fundamental, creating a pattern called the harmonic series (e.g., 100 Hz,

200 Hz, 300 Hz, 400 Hz, 500 Hz, etc. or G2, G3, D4, G4, B4—note that pitches are named by the international system in which the lowest C of the piano keyboard is C1; middle-C therefore becomes C4, the fourth C of the keyboard) (figure 7.7).

Singers who choose to make coarse or rough sounds as might be appropriate for rock or blues often add overtones that are inharmonic, or not part of the standard numerical sequence. Inharmonic overtones also are common in singers with damaged or pathological voices.

Under most circumstances, we are completely unaware of the presence of overtones—they simply contribute to the overall timbre of a voice. In some vocal styles, however, harmonics become a dominant feature. This is especially true in throat singing or overtone singing, as is found in places like Tuva. Throat singers tune their vocal tracts so precisely that single harmonics are highlighted within the harmonic spectrum as a separate, whistle-like tone. These singers sustain a low-pitched drone and then create a melody by moving from tone to tone within the natural harmonic series. You can learn to do this too. Sustain a comfortable pitch in your range and slowly morph between the vowels /i/ and /u/. If you listen carefully, you will hear individual harmonics pop out of your sound.

The mode of vocal fold vibration has a strong impact on the overtones that are produced. In mode 1, high-frequency harmonics are relatively strong; in mode 2, they are much weaker. As a result, mode 1 tends to yield a much brighter, brassier sound.

VOCAL TRACT: YOUR SOURCE OF RESONANCE

Resonance typically is defined as the amplification and enhancement (or enrichment) of musical sound through supplemental vibration. What does this really mean? In layman's terms, we could say that resonance makes instruments louder and more beautiful by reinforcing the original vibrations of the sound source. This enhancement occurs in two primary ways, which are known as forced and free resonance (there is nothing pejorative in these terms: free resonance is not superior to forced resonance). Any object that is physically connected to a vibrator can serve as a forced resonator. For a piano, the resonator is the soundboard (on the

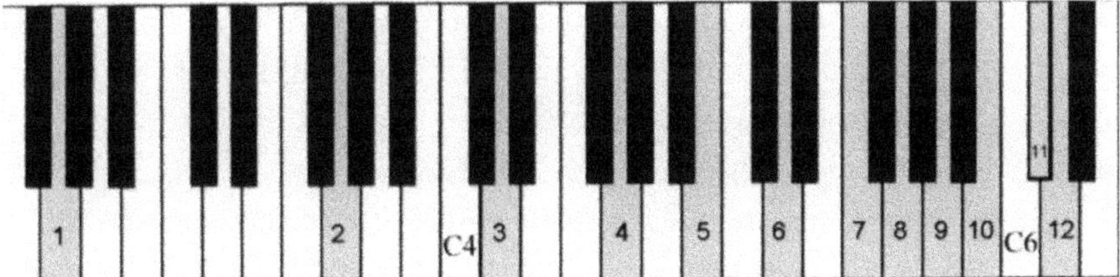

Figure 7.7. Natural harmonic series, beginning at G2. ***Courtesy of Scott McCoy***

underside of a grand or on the back of an upright); the vibrations of the strings are transmitted directly to the soundboard through a structure known as the bridge, which also is found on violins and guitars. Forced resonance also plays a role in voice production. Place your hand on your chest and say /a/ at a low pitch. You almost certainly felt the vibrations of forced resonance. In singing, this might best be considered your private resonance; you can feel it and it might impact your self-perception of sound, but nobody else can hear it. To understand why this is true, imagine what a violin would sound like if it were encased in a thick layer of foam rubber. The vibrations of the string would be damped out, muting the instrument. Your skin, muscles, and other tissues do the same thing to the vibrations of your vocal folds.

By contrast, free resonance occurs when sound travels through a hollow space, such as the inside of a trumpet, an organ pipe, or your vocal tract, which consists of the pharynx (throat), oral cavity (mouth), and nasal cavity (nose). As sound travels through these regions, a complex pattern of echoes is created; every time sound encounters a change in the shape of the vocal tract, some of its energy is reflected backward, much like an echo in a canyon. If these echoes arrive back at the glottis at the precise moment a new pulse of sound is created, the two elements synchronize, resulting in a significant increase in intensity. All of this happens very quickly—remember that sound is traveling through your vocal tract at more than seven hundred miles per hour.

Whenever this synchronization of the vocal tract and sound source occurs, we say that the system is in resonance. The phenomenon occurs at specific frequencies (pitches), which can be varied by changing the position of the tongue, lips, jaw, palate, and larynx. These resonant frequencies, or areas in which strong amplification occurs, are called formants. Formants provide the specific amplification that changes the raw, buzzing sound produced by your vocal folds into speech and singing. The vocal tract is capable of producing many formants, which are labeled sequentially by ascending pitch. The first two, F1 and F2, are used to create vowels; higher formants contribute to the overall timbre and individual characteristics of a voice. In some singers, especially those who train to sing in opera, formants three through five are clustered together to form a super formant, eponymously called the singer's formant, which creates a ringing sound and enables a voice to be heard in a large theater without electronic amplification.

Formants are vitally important in singing, but they can be a bit intimidating to understand. An analogy that works really well for me is to think of formants like the wind. You cannot see the wind, but you know it is present when you see leaves rustling in a tree or feel a breeze on your face. Formants work in the same manner. They are completely invisible and directly inaudible. But just as we see the rustling leaf, we can hear, and perhaps even feel, the action of formants through how they change our sound. Try a little experiment. Sing an ascending scale beginning at B♭3, sustaining the vowel /i/. As you approach the D♮ or E♭ of the scale, you likely will feel (and hear) that your sound becomes a bit stronger and easier to produce. This occurs because the scale tone and formant are on the same pitch, providing additional amplification. If you change to an /u/ vowel, you will feel the same thing at about the same place in the scale. If you sing to an /o/ or /e/ and continue up the scale, you'll feel a bloom in the sound somewhere around C5 (an octave above middle C); /a/ is likely to come into its best focus at about G5.

To remember the approximate pitches of the first formants for the main vowels, /i-e-a-o-u/, just think of a C-major triad in first inversion, open position, starting at E4: /i/ = E4, /e/ = C5, /a/ = G5, /o/ = C5, and /u/ = E4 (figure 7.8). If your music theory isn't strong, you could use the mnemonic "every child gets candy eagerly." These pitches might vary by as much as a minor third higher and lower but no farther: once a formant changes by more than that interval, the vowel that is produced must change.

Formants have absolutely no preference for what they amplify—they are indiscriminate lovers, just as happy to bond with the first harmonic as the fifth. When men or women sing low pitches, there almost always

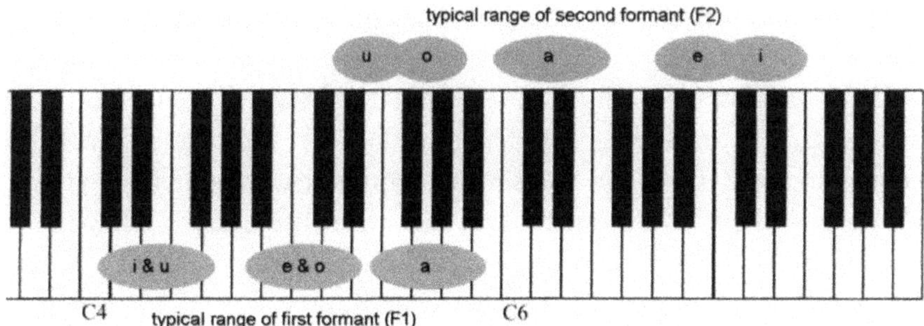

Figure 7.8. Typical range of first and second formants for primary vowels. ***Courtesy of Scott McCoy***

will be at least one harmonic that comes close enough to a formant to produce a clear vowel sound. The same is not true for women with high voices, especially sopranos, who routinely must sing pitches that have a fundamental frequency higher than the first formant of many vowels. Imagine what happens if she must sing the phrase "and I'll leave you forever," with the word "leave" set on a very high, climactic note. The audience won't be able to tell if she is singing "leave" or "love"; the two will sound identical. This happens because the formant that is required to identify the vowel /i/ is too far below the pitch being sung. Even if she tries to sing "leave," the sound that comes out of her mouth will be heard as some variation of /a/.

Fortunately, this kind of mismatch between formants and musical pitches rarely causes problems for anyone but opera singers, choir sopranos, and perhaps ingénues in classic music theater shows. Almost everyone else generally sings low enough in their respective voice ranges to produce easily identifiable vowels.

Second formants also can be important, but more so for opera singers than everyone else. They are much higher in pitch, tracking the pattern /u/ = E5, /o/ = G5, /a/ = D6, /e/ = B6, /i/ = D7 (you can use the mnemonic "every good dad buys diapers" to remember these pitches) (figure 7.8). Because they can extend so high, into the top octave of the piano keyboard for /i/, they interact primarily with higher tones in the natural harmonic series. Unless you are striving to produce the loudest unamplified sound possible, you probably never need to worry about the second formant; it will steadfastly do its job of helping to produce vowel sounds without any conscious thought or manipulation on your part.

If you are interested in discovering more about resonance and how it impacts your voice, you might want to install a spectrum analyzer on your computer. Free (or inexpensive) programs are readily available for download over the Internet that will work with either a PC or Mac computer. You don't need any specialized hardware—if you can use Skype or FaceTime, you already have everything you need. Once you've installed something, simply start playing with it. Experiment with your voice to see exactly how the analysis signal changes when you change the way your voice sounds. You'll be able to see how harmonics change in intensity as they interact with your formants. If you sing with vibrato, you'll see how consistently you produce your variations in pitch and amplitude. You'll even be able to see if your tone is excessively nasal for the kind of singing you want to do. Other programs are available that will help you improve your intonation (how well you sing in tune) or enhance your basic musicianship skills. Technology truly has advanced sufficiently to help us sing more beautifully.

MOUTH, LIPS, AND TONGUE: YOUR ARTICULATORS

The articulatory life of a singer is not easy, especially when compared to the demands placed on other musicians. Like a pianist or brass player, we must be able to produce the entire spectrum of musical articulation, including dynamic levels from hushed pianissimos to thunderous fortes, short notes, long notes, accents, crescendos, diminuendos, and so on. We produce most of these articulations the same way instrumentalists do, which is by varying our power supply. But singers have another layer of articulation that makes everything much more complicated; we must produce these musical gestures while simultaneously singing words.

As we learned in our brief examination of formants, altering the resonance characteristics of the vocal tract creates the vowel sounds of language. We do this by changing the position of our tongue, jaw, lips, and sometimes palate. Slowly say the vowel pattern /i-e-a-o-u/. Can you feel how your tongue moves in your mouth? For /i/, it is high in the front and low in the back, but it takes the opposite position for /u/. Now slowly say the word "Tuesday," noting all the places your tongue comes into contact with your teeth and palate and how it changes shape as you produce the vowels and diphthongs. There is a lot going on in there—no wonder it takes so long for babies to learn to speak!

Our articulatory anatomy is extraordinarily complex, in large part because our bodies use the same passageway for food, water, air, and sound. As a result, our tongue, larynx, throat, jaw, and palate are all interconnected with common physical and neurologic points of attachment. Our anatomical Union Station in this regard is a small structure called the hyoid bone. The hyoid is one of only three bones in your entire body that do not connect to other bones via a joint (the other two are your patellae, or kneecaps). This little bone is suspended below your jaw, freely floating up and down every time your swallow. It is a busy place, serving as the upper suspension point for the larynx, the connection for the root of the tongue, and the primary location of the muscles that open your mouth by dropping your jaw.

Good singing—in any genre—requires a high degree of independence in all these articulatory structures. Unfortunately, nature conspires against us to make this difficult to accomplish. From the time we were born, our bodies have relied on a reflex reaction to elevate the palate and raise the larynx each time we swallow. This action becomes habitual: palate goes up, larynx also lifts. But depending on the style of music we are singing, we might need to keep the larynx down while the palate goes up (opera and classical) or palate down with the larynx up (country and bluegrass). As we all know, habits can be very hard to change, which is one of the reasons that it can take a lot of study and practice to become an excellent singer. Understanding your body's natural reflexive habits can make some of this work a bit easier.

There is one more significant pitfall to the close proximity of all these articulators: tension in one area is easily passed along to another. If your jaw muscles are too tight while you sing, that hyperactivity will likely be transferred to the larynx and tongue—remember, they all are interconnected through the hyoid bone. It can be tricky to determine the primary offender in this kind of chain reaction of tension. A tight tongue could just as easily be making your jaw stiff, or an elevated, rigid larynx could make both tongue and jaw suffer.

Neurology complicates matters even further. You have sixteen muscles in your tongue, fourteen in your larynx, twenty-two in your throat and palate, and another sixteen that control your jaw. Many of these are very small and lie directly adjacent to each other, and you often are required to contract one quite strongly while its next-door neighbor must remain totally relaxed. Our brains need to develop laser-like control, sending signals at the right moment with the right intensity to the precise spot where they are needed. When we first start singing, these brain signals come more like a blast from a shotgun, spreading the neurologic impulse over a broad area to multiple muscles, not all of which are the intended target. Again, with practice and training, we learn to refine our control, enabling us to use only those muscles that will help, while disengaging those that would get in the way of our best singing.

FINAL THOUGHTS

This brief chapter has only scratched the surface of the huge field of voice science. To learn more, you might visit the websites of the National Association of Teachers of Singing (NATS), the Voice Foundation (TVF), or the National Center for Voice and Speech (NCVS). You can easily locate the appropriate addresses through any Internet search engine. Remember: knowledge is power. Occasionally, people are afraid that if they know more about the science of how they sing, they will become so analytical that all spontaneity will be lost or they will become paralyzed by too much information and thought. In my forty-plus years as a singer and teacher, I've never encountered somebody who actually suffered this fate. To the contrary, the more we know, the easier—and more joyful—singing becomes. ♪

8

VOCAL HEALTH FOR THE CHAMBER MUSIC SINGER

Wendy LeBorgne

GENERAL PHYSICAL WELL-BEING

All singers, regardless of genre, should consider themselves as "vocal athletes." The physical, emotional, and performance demands necessary for optimal output require that the artist consider training and maintaining their instrument as an athlete trains for an event. With increased vocal and performance demands, it is unlikely that a vocal athlete will have an entire performing career completely injury free. This may not be the fault of the singer, as many injuries occur due to circumstances beyond the singer's control such as singing through an illness or being on a new medication seemingly unrelated to the voice. ♪

Vocal injury has often been considered taboo to talk about in the performing world as it has been considered to be the result of faulty technique or poor vocal habits. In actuality, the majority of vocal injuries presenting in the elite performing population tend to be overuse and/or acute injury. From a clinical perspective over the past seventeen years, younger, less experienced singers with fewer years of training (who tend to be quite talented) generally are the ones who present with issues related to technique or phonotrauma (nodules, edema, contact ulcers), while more mature singers with professional performing careers tend to present with acute injuries (hemorrhage) or overuse and misuse injuries (muscle tension dysphonia, edema, GERD) or injuries following an illness. There are no current studies documenting use and training in correlation to laryngeal pathologies. However, there are studies that document that somewhere between 35 percent and 100 percent of professional vocal athletes have abnormal vocal fold findings on stroboscopic evaluation. Many times these "abnormalities" are in singers who have no vocal complaints or symptoms of vocal problems. From a performance perspective, uniqueness in vocal quality often gets hired and perhaps a slight aberration in the way a given larynx functions may become quite marketable. Regardless of what the vocal folds may look like, the most integral part of performance is that the singer must maintain agility, flexibility, stamina, power, and inherent beauty (genre appropriate) for their current level of performance taking into account physical, vocal, and emotional demands.

Unlike sports medicine and the exercise physiology literature where much is known about the types and nature of given sports injuries, there is no common parallel for the vocal athlete model. However, because the vocal athlete utilizes the body systems of alignment, respiration, phonation, and resonance with some similarities to physical athletes, a parallel protocol for vocal wellness may be implemented/considered for vocal athletes to maximize injury prevention knowledge for both the singer and teacher. This chapter aims to provide information on vocal wellness and injury prevention for the vocal athlete.

CONSIDERATIONS FOR WHOLE BODY WELLNESS

Nutrition

You have no doubt heard the saying "You are what you eat." Eating is a social and psychological event. For many people, food associations and eating have an emotional basis resulting in either overeating or being malnourished. Eating disorders in performers and body image issues may have major implications and consequences for the performer on both ends of the spectrum (obesity and anorexia). Singers should be encouraged to reprogram the brain and body to consider food as fuel. You want to use high-octane gas in your engine, as pouring water in your car's gas tank won't get you very far. Eating a poor diet or a diet that lacks appropriate nutritional value will have negative physical and vocal effects on the singer. Effects of poor dietary choices for the vocal athlete may result in physical and vocal effects ranging from fatigue to life-threatening disease over the course of a lifetime. Encouraging and engaging in healthy eating habits from a young age will potentially prevent long-term negative effects from poor nutritional choices. It is beyond the scope of this chapter to provide a complete overview of all the dietary guidelines for pediatrics, adolescents, adults, and the mature adult; however, a listing of additional references to help guide your food and beverage choices for making good nutritional choices can be found online at websites such as Dietary Guidelines for Americans, Nutrition .gov Guidelines for Tweens and Teens, and Fruits and Veggies Matter. See the online companion web page on the NATS website for links to these and other resources. ♪

Hydration

"Sing wet, pee pale." This phrase was echoed in the studio of Van Lawrence regarding how his students would know if they were well hydrated. Generally, this rule of pale urine during your waking hours is a good indicator that you are well hydrated. Medications, vitamins, and certain foods may alter urine color despite adequate hydration. Due to the varying levels of physical and vocal activity of many performers, in order to maintain adequate oral hydration, the use of a hydration calculator based on activity level may be a better choice. These hydration calculators are easily accessible online and take into account the amount and level of activity the performer engages in on a daily basis. In a recent study of the vocal habits of musical theater performers, one of the findings indicated a significantly underhydrated group of performers.[1]

Laryngeal and pharyngeal dryness as well as "thick, sticky mucus" are often complaints of singers. Combating these concerns and maintaining an adequate viscosity of mucus for performance has resulted in some research. As a reminder of laryngeal and swallowing anatomy, nothing that is swallowed (or gargled) goes over or touches the vocal folds directly (or one would choke). Therefore, nothing that a singer eats or drinks ever touches the vocal folds, and in order to adequately hydrate the mucous membranes of the vocal folds, one must consume enough fluids for the body to produce a thin mucus. Therefore, any "vocal" effects from swallowed products are limited to potential pharyngeal and oral changes, not the vocal folds themselves.

The effects of systemic hydration are well documented in the literature. There is evidence to suggest that adequate hydration will provide some protection of the laryngeal mucosal membranes when they are placed under increased collision forces as well as reducing the amount of effort (phonation threshold pressure) to produce voice. This is important for the singer because it means that with adequate hydration and consistency of mucus, the effort to produce voice is less and your vocal folds are better protected from injury. Imagine the friction and heat produced when two dry hands rub together and then what happens if you put lotion on your hands. The mechanisms in the larynx to provide appropriate mucus production are not fully understood, but there is enough evidence at this time to support oral hydration as a vital component of every singer's vocal health regime to maintain appropriate mucosal viscosity.

Although very rare, overhydration (hyperhidrosis) can result in dehydration and even illness or death. An overindulgence of fluids essentially makes the kidneys work "overtime" and flushes too much water out of the body. This excessive fluid loss in a rapid manner can be detrimental to the body.

In addition to drinking water to systemically monitor hydration, there are many nonregulated products on the market for performers that lay claim to improving the laryngeal environment (e.g., Entertainer's Secret, Throat Coat Tea, Greathers Pastilles, Slippery Elm, etc.). Although there may be little detriment in using these products, quantitative research documenting change in laryngeal mucosa is sparse. One study suggests that the use of Throat Coat when compared to a placebo treatment for pharyngitis did show a significant difference in decreasing the perception of sore throat.[2] Another study compared the use of Entertainer's Secret to two other nebulized agents and its effect on phonation threshold pressure (PTP).[3] There was no positive benefit in decreasing PTP with Entertainer's Secret.

Many singers use personal steam inhalers and/or room humidification to supplement oral hydration and aid in combating laryngeal dryness. There are several considerations for singers who choose to use external means of adding moisture to the air they breathe. Personal steam inhalers are portable and can often be used backstage or in the hotel room for the traveling performer. Typically, water is placed in the steamer and the face is placed over the steam for inhalation. Because the mucus membranes of the larynx are composed of a saltwater solution, one study looked at the use of nebulized saline in comparison to plain water and its potential effects on effort or ease to sound production in classically trained sopranos.[4] Data suggested that perceived effort to produce voice was less in the saline group than the plain water group. This indicated that the singers who used the saltwater solution reported less effort to sing after breathing in the saltwater than singers who used plain water. The researchers hypothesized that because the body's mucus is not plain water (rather it is a saltwater—think about your tears), when you use plain water for steam inhalation, it may actually draw the salt from your own saliva, resulting in a dehydrating effect.

In addition to personal steamers, other options for air humidification come in varying sizes of humidifiers from room size to whole house humidifiers. When choosing between a warm air or cool mist humidifier, considerations include both personal preference and needs. One of the primary reasons warm mist humidifiers are not recommended for young children is due to the risk of burns from the heating element. Both the warm mist and cool air humidifiers act similarly in adding moisture to the environmental air. External air humidification may be beneficial and provide a level of comfort for many singers. Regular cleaning of the humidifier is vital to prevent bacteria and mold buildup. Also, depending on the hardness of the water, it is important to avoid mineral buildup on the device and distilled water may be recommended for some humidifiers.

For traveling performers who often stay in hotels, fly on airplanes, or are generally exposed to other dry-air environments, there are products on the market designed to help minimize drying effects. One such device is called a Humidflyer, which is a face mask designed with a filter to recycle the moisture of a person's own breath and replenish moisture on each breath cycle.

For dry nasal passages or to clear sinuses, many singers use Neti pots. Many singers use this homeopathic flushing of the nasal passages regularly. Research supports the use of a Neti pot as a part of allergy relief and chronic rhinosinusitis control when utilized properly, sometimes in combination with medical management.[5] Conversely, long-term use of nasal irrigation (without taking intermittent breaks from daily use) may result in washing out the "good" mucus of the nasal passages, which naturally help to rid the nose of infections. A study presented at the 2009 American College of Allergy, Asthma, and Immunology (ACAAI) annual scientific meeting reported that when a group of individuals who were using twice-daily nasal irrigation for one year discontinued using it, they had an increase in acute rhinosinusitis.[6]

Tea, Honey, and Gargle to Keep the Throat Healthy

Regarding the use of general teas (which many singers combine with honey or lemon), there is likely no harm in the use of decaffeinated tea (caffeine may cause systemic dryness). The warmth of the tea may provide a soothing sensation to the pharynx and the act of swallowing can be relaxing for the muscles of the throat. Honey has shown promising results as an effective cough suppressant in the pediatric population.[7] The dose of honey given to the children in the study was two teaspoons. Gargling with salt or apple cider vinegar and water are also popular home remedies for many singers with the uses being from soothing the throat to curing reflux. Gargling plain water has been shown to be efficacious in reducing the risk of contracting upper respiratory infections. I suggest that when gargling, the singer only "bubble" the water with air and avoid engaging the vocal folds in sound production. Saltwater as a gargle has long been touted as a sore throat remedy and can be traced back to 2700 BCE in China for treating gum disease. The science behind a saltwater rinse for everything from oral hygiene to sore throat is that salt (sodium chloride) may act as a natural analgesic (pain killer) and may also kill bacteria. Similar to the effects that not enough salt in the water may have on drawing the salt out of the tissue in the steam inhalation, if you oversaturate the water solution with excess salt and gargle it, it may act to draw water out of the oral mucosa, thus reducing inflammation.

Another popular home remedy reported by singers is the use of apple cider vinegar to help with everything from acid reflux to sore throats. Dating back to 3300 BCE, apple cider vinegar was reported as a medicinal remedy, and it became popular in the 1970s as a weight loss diet cocktail. Popular media reports apple cider vinegar can improve conditions from acne and arthritis to nosebleeds and varicose veins. Specific efficacy data regarding the beneficial nature of apple cider vinegar for the purpose of sore throat, pharyngeal inflammation, and/or reflux have not been reported in the literature at this time. Of the peer-reviewed studies found in the literature, one discussed possible esophageal erosion and inconsistency of actual product in tablet form.[8] Therefore, at this time, strong evidence supporting the use of apple cider vinegar is not published.

Medications and the Voice

Medications (over the counter, prescription, and herbal) may have resultant drying effects on the body and often the laryngeal mucosa. General classes of drugs with potential drying effects include: antidepressants, antihypertensives, diuretics, ADD/ADHD medications, some oral acne medications, hormones, allergy drugs, and vitamin C in high doses. The National Center for Voice and Speech (NCVS) provides a listing of some common medications with potential voice side effects including laryngeal dryness. This listing does not take into account all medications, so singers should always ask their pharmacist of the potential side effects of a given medication. Due to the significant number of drugs on the market, it is safe to say that most pharmacists will not be acutely aware of "vocal side effects," but if dryness is listed as a potential side effect of the drug, you may assume that all body systems could be affected. Under no circumstances should you stop taking a prescribed medication without consulting your physician first. As every person has a different body chemistry and reaction to medication, just because a medication lists dryness as a potential side effect, it does not necessarily mean you will experience that side effect. Conversely, if you begin a new medication and notice physical or vocal changes that are unexpected, you should consult with your physician. Ultimately, the goal of medical management for any condition is to achieve the most benefits with the least side effects. Please see the companion page on the NATS website for a list of possible resources for the singer regarding prescription drugs and herbs. ♪

In contrast to medications that tend to dry, there are medications formulated to increase saliva production or alter the viscosity of mucus.

Medically, these drugs are often used to treat patients who have had a loss of saliva production due to surgery or radiation. Mucolytic agents are used to thin secretions as needed. As a singer, if you feel that you need to use a mucolytic agent on a consistent basis, it may be worth considering getting to the root of the laryngeal dryness symptom and seeking a professional opinion from an otolaryngologist.

Reflux and the Voice

Gastroesophageal reflux (GERD) and/or laryngopharyngeal reflux (LPR) can have a devastating impact on the singer if not recognized and treated appropriately. Although GERD and LPR are related, they are considered as slightly different diseases. GERD (Latin root meaning "flowing back") is the reflux of digestive enzymes, acids, and other stomach contents into the esophagus (food pipe). If this backflow is propelled through the upper esophagus and into the throat (larynx and pharynx), it is referred to as LPR. It is not uncommon to have both GERD and LPR, but they can occur independently.

More frequently, people with GERD have decreased esophageal clearing. Esophagitis, or inflammation of the esophagus, is also associated with GERD. People with GERD often feel heartburn. LPR symptoms are often "silent" and do not include heartburn. Specific symptoms of LPR may include some or all of the following: lump in the throat sensation, feeling of constant need to clear the throat/postnasal drip, longer vocal warm-up time, quicker vocal fatigue, loss of high frequency range, worse voice in the morning, sore throat, and bitter/raw/brackish taste in the mouth. If you experience these symptoms on a regular basis, it is advised that you consider a medical consultation for your symptoms. Prolonged, untreated GERD or LPR can lead to permanent changes in both the esophagus and/or larynx. Untreated LPR also provides a laryngeal environment that is conducive for vocal fold lesions to occur as it inhibits normal healing mechanisms.

Treatments of LPR and GERD generally include both dietary and lifestyle modifications in addition to medical management. Some of the dietary recommendations include: elimination of caffeinated and carbonated beverages, smoking cessation, no alcohol use, and limiting tomatoes, acidic foods and drinks, and raw onions or peppers, to name a few. Also, avoidance of high-fat foods is recommended. From a lifestyle perspective, suggested changes include not eating within three hours of lying down, eating small meals frequently (instead of large meals), elevating the head of your bed, avoiding tight clothing around the belly, and not bending over or exercising too soon after you eat.

Reflux medications fall in three general categories: antacids, H2 blockers, and proton pump inhibitors (PPI). There are now combination drugs that include both an H2 blocker and proton pump inhibitor. Every medication has both associated risks and benefits, and singers should be aware of the possible benefits and side effects of the medications they take. In general terms, antacids (e.g., Tums, Mylanta, Gaviscon) neutralize stomach acid. H2 (histamine) blockers, such as Axid (nizatidine),Tagamet (cimetidine), Pepcid (famotidine), and Zantac (ranitidine), work to decrease acid production in the stomach by preventing histamine from triggering the H2 receptors to produce more acid. Then there are the PPIs: Nexium (esomeprazole), Prevacid (lansoprazole), Protonix (pantoprazole), AcipHex (rabeprazole), Prilosec (omeprazole), and Dexilant (dexlansoprazole). PPIs act as a last line of defense to decrease acid production by blocking the last step in gastric juice secretion. Some of the most recent drugs to combat GERD/LPR are combination drugs (e.g., Zegrid [sodium bicarbonate plus omeprazole]), which provide a short-acting response (sodium bicarbonate) and a long release (omeprazole). Because some singers prefer a holistic approach to reflux management, strict dietary and lifestyle compliance is recommended and consultation with both your primary care physician and naturopath are warranted in that situation. Efficacy data on non-regulated herbs, vitamins, and supplements are limited, but some data do exist.

Physical Exercise

Vocal athletes, like other physical athletes, should consider how and what they do to maintain both cardiovascular fitness and muscular strength. In today's performance culture, it is rare that a performer stands still and sings, unless in a recital or choral setting. The range of physical activity can vary from light movement to high-intensity choreography with acrobatics. As performers are being required to increase their on-stage physical activity level from the operatic stage to the pop-star arena, overall physical fitness is imperative to avoid compromise in the vocal system. Breathlessness will result in compensation by the larynx, which is now attempting to regulate the air. Compensatory vocal behaviors over time may result in a change in vocal performance. The health benefits of both cardiovascular training and strength training are well documented for physical athletes but relatively rare in the literature for vocal performers.

Mental Wellness

Vocal performers must maintain a mental focus during performance and a mental toughness during auditioning and training. Rarely during vocal performance training programs is this important aspect of performance addressed, and it is often left to the individual performer to develop their own strategy or coping mechanism. Yet, many performers are on antianxiety or antidepressant drugs (which may be the direct result of performance-related issues). If the sports world is again used as a parallel for mental toughness, there are no elite-level athletes (and few junior-level athletes) who don't utilize the services of a performance/sports psychologist to maximize focus and performance. I recommend that performers consider the potential benefits of a performance psychologist to help maximize vocal performance. Several references that may be of interest to the singer include: Joanna Cazden's *Visualization for Singers* (Joanna Cazden, 1992) and Shirlee Emmons and Alma Thomas's *Power Performance for Singers: Transcending the Barriers* (Oxford, 1998). ♪

Unlike instrumentalists, whose performance is dependent on accurate playing of an external musical instrument, the singer's instrument is uniquely intact and subject to the emotional confines of the brain and body in which it is housed. Musical performance anxiety (MPA) can be career threatening for all musicians, but perhaps the vocal athlete is more severely impacted. The majority of literature on MPA is dedicated to instrumentalists, but the basis of definition, performance effects, and treatment options can be considered for vocal athletes. Fear is a natural reaction to a stressful situation, and there is a fine line between emotional excitation and perceived threat (real or imagined). The job of a performer is to convey to an audience through vocal production, physical gestures, and facial expression a most heightened state of emotion. Otherwise, why would audience members pay top dollar to sit for two or three hours for a mundane experience? Not only is there the emotional conveyance of the performance but also the internal turmoil often experienced by the singers themselves in preparation for elite performance. It is well documented in the literature that even the most elite performers have experienced debilitating performance anxiety. MPA is defined on a continuum with anxiety levels ranging from low to high and has been reported to comprise four distinct components: affect, cognition, behavior, and physiology. Affect comprises feelings (e.g., doom, panic, anxiety). Affected cognition will result in altered levels of concentration, while the behavior component results in postural shifts, quivering, and trembling. Finally physiologically the body's autonomic nervous system (ANS) will activate, resulting in the "fight or flight" response.

In recent years, researchers have been able to define two distinct neurological pathways for MPA. The first pathway happens quickly and without conscious input (ANS), resulting in the same fear stimulus as if a person were put into an emergent, life-threatening situation. In those situations, the brain releases adrenaline, resulting in physical changes of increased heart rate, increased respiration, shaking, pale skin, dilated pupils, slowed digestion, bladder relaxation, dry mouth, and dry eyes, all of which severely affect vocal performance. The second pathway that has been identified results in a conscious identification of the fear/threat and a much slower physiologic response. With the second neuromotor response, the performer has a chance to recognize the fear, process how to deal with the fear, and respond accordingly.

Treatment modalities to address MPA include psycho-behavioral therapy (including biofeedback) and drug therapies. Elite physical performance athletes have been shown to benefit from visualization techniques and psychological readiness training, yet within the performing arts community, stage fright may be considered a weakness or character flaw precluding readiness for professional performance. On the contrary, vocal athletes, like physical athletes, should mentally prepare themselves for optimal competition (auditions) and performance. Learning to convey emotion without eliciting an internal emotional response by the vocal athlete may take the skill of an experienced psychologist to help change ingrained neural pathways. Ultimately, control and understanding of MPA will enhance performance and prepare the vocal athlete for the most intense performance demands without vocal compromise.

VOCAL WELLNESS: INJURY PREVENTION

In order to prevent vocal injury and understand vocal wellness in the singer, general knowledge of common causes of voice disorders is imperative. One common cause of voice disorders is vocally abusive behaviors or misuse of the voice to include phonotraumatic behaviors such as yelling, screaming, loud talking, talking over noise, throat clearing, coughing, harsh sneezing, and boisterous laughing. Chronic or less than optimal vocal properties such as poor breathing techniques, inappropriate phonatory habits during conversational speech (glottal fry, hard glottal attacks), inapt pitch, loudness, rate of speech, and/or hyperfunctional laryngeal-area muscle tone may also negatively impact vocal function. Medically related etiologies, which also have the potential to impact vocal function, range from untreated chronic allergies and sinusitis to endocrine dysfunction and hormonal imbalance. Direct trauma, such as a blow to the neck or the risk of vocal fold damage during intubation, can impact optimal performance in vocal athletes depending on the nature and extent of the trauma. Finally, external irritants ranging from cigarette smoke to reflux directly impact the laryngeal mucosa and ultimately can lead to laryngeal pathology.

Vocal hygiene education and compliance may be one of the primary essential components for maintaining the voice throughout a career. This section will provide the singer with information on prevention of vocal injury. However, just like a professional sports athlete, it is unlikely that a professional vocal athlete will go through an entire career without some compromise in vocal function. This may be a common upper respiratory infection that creates vocal fold swelling for a short time, or it may be a "vocal accident" that is career threatening. Regardless, the knowledge of how to take care of your voice is essential for any vocal athlete.

Train Like an Athlete for Vocal Longevity

Performers seek instant gratification in performance sometimes at the cost of gradual vocal building for a lifetime of healthy singing. Historically, voice pedagogues required their students to perform vocalises exclusively for up to two years before beginning any song literature. Singers gradually built their voices by ingraining appropriate muscle memory and neuromotor patterns through development of aesthetically pleasing tones, onsets, breath management, and support. There was an intensive master-apprentice relationship and rigorous vocal guidelines to maintain a place within a given studio. Time off was taken if a vocal injury ensued or careers potentially were ended, and students were asked to leave a given singing studio if their voices were unable to withstand the rigors of training. Training vocal athletes today has evolved and appears driven to create a "product" quickly, perhaps at the expense of the longevity of the singer. Pop stars emerging well before puberty are doing international concert tours, yet many young artist programs in the classical arena do not consider singers for their programs until they are in their mid- to late twenties.

Each vocal genre presents with different standards and vocal demands. Therefore, the amount and degree of vocal training are varied. Some would argue that performing extensively without adequate vocal training and development is ill-advised, yet singers today are thrust onto the stage at very young ages. Dancers, instrumentalists, and physical athletes all spend many hours per day developing muscle strength, memory, and proper technique for their craft. The more advanced the artist or athlete, generally the more specific the training protocol becomes. Consideration of training vocal athletes in this same fashion is recommended. One would generally not begin a young, inexperienced singer on a Wagner aria without previous vocal training. Similarly, in non-classical vocal music, there are easy, moderate, and difficult pieces to consider pending level of vocal development and training.

Basic pedagogical training of alignment, breathing, voice production, and resonance are essential building blocks for development of good voice production. Muscle memory and development of appropriate muscle patterns happen slowly over time with appropriate repetitive practice. Doing too much, too soon for any athlete (physical or vocal) will result in an increased risk for injury. When the singer is being asked to do "vocal gymnastics," they must be sure to have a solid basis of strength and stamina in the appropriate muscle groups to perform consistently with minimal risk of injury.

Vocal Fitness Program

One generally does not get out of bed first thing in the morning and try to do a split. Yet many singers go directly into a practice session or audition without proper warm-up. Think of your larynx like your knee, made up of cartilages, ligaments, and muscles. Vocal health is dependent upon appropriate warm-ups (to get things moving), drills for technique, and then cooldowns (at the end of your day). Consider vocal warm-ups a "gentle stretch." Depending on the needs of the singer, warm-ups should include physical stretching; postural alignment self-checks; breathing exercises to promote rib cage, abdominal, and back expansion; vocal stretches (glides up to stretch the vocal folds and glides down to contract the vocal folds); articulatory stretches (yawning, facial stretches); and mental warm-ups (to provide focus for the task at hand). Vocalises, in my opinion, are designed as exercises to go beyond warm-ups and prepare the body and voice for the technical and vocal challenges of the music they sing. They are varied and address the technical level and genre of the singer to maximize performance and vocal growth. Cooldowns are a part of most athletes' workouts. However, singers often do not use cooldowns (physical, mental, and vocal) at the end of a performance. A recent study looked specifically at the benefits of vocal cooldowns in singers and found that singers who used a vocal cooldown had decreased effort to produce voice the next day.[9]

Systemic hydration as a means to keep the vocal folds adequately lubricated for the amount of impact and friction that they will undergo has been previously discussed in this chapter. Compliance with adequate oral hydration recommendations is important and subsequently so is the minimization of agents that could potentially dry the membranes (e.g., caffeine, medications, dry air). The body produces approximately two quarts of mucus per day. If not adequately hydrated, the mucus tends to be thick and sticky. Poor hydration is similar to not putting enough oil in the car engine. Frankly, if the gears do not work as well, there is increased friction and heat, and the engine is not efficient.

Speak Well, Sing Well

Optimize the speaking voice utilizing ideal frequency range, breath, intensity, rate, and resonance. Singers generally are vocally enthusiastic individuals who talk a lot and often talk loudly. During typical conversation, the average fundamental speaking frequency (times per second the vocal folds are impacting) for a male varies from 100 to 150 Hz and 180 to 230 Hz for women. Because of the delicate structure of the vocal folds and the importance of the layered microstructure vibrating efficiently and effectively to produce voice, vocal behaviors or outside factors that compromise the integrity of the vibration patterns of the vocal folds may be considered phonotrauma.

Phonotraumatic behaviors can include yelling, screaming, loud talking, harsh sneezing, and harsh laughing. Elimination of phonotraumatic behaviors is essential for good vocal health. The louder one speaks, the farther apart the vocal folds move from midline, the harder they impact, and the longer they stay closed. A tangible example would be to take your hands, move them only six inches apart, and clap as hard and as loudly as you can for ten seconds. Now, move your hands two feet apart and clap as hard, loudly, and quickly as possible for ten seconds. The farther apart your hands are, the more air you move and the louder the clap, and the skin on the hands becomes red and ultimately swollen (if you do it long enough and hard enough). This is what happens to the vocal folds with repeated impact at increased vocal intensities. The vocal folds are approximately 17 mm in length and vibrate at 220 times per second on A3, 440 on A4, 880 on A5, and more than 1,000 per second when singing a high C. That is a lot of impact for little muscles. Consider this fact when singing loudly or in a high tessitura for prolonged periods of time. It becomes easy to see why women are more prone than men to laryngeal impact injuries due to the frequency range of the voice alone.

In addition to the amount of cycles per second (cps) the vocal folds are impacting, singers need to be aware of their vocal intensity (volume). One should be aware of the volume of the speaking and singing voice and consider using a distance of three to five feet (about an arm's-length distance) as a gauge for how loud to be in general conversation. Using cell phones and speaking on a Bluetooth device in a car generally results in greater vocal intensity than normal, and singers are advised to minimize unnecessary use of these devices.

Singers should be encouraged to take "vocal naps" during their day. A vocal nap would be a short period of time (five minutes to an hour) of complete silence. Although the vocal folds are rarely completely still (because they move when you swallow and breathe), a vocal nap minimizes impact and vibration for a short window of time. A physical nap can also be refreshing for the singer mentally and physically.

Avoid Environmental Irritants: Alcohol, Smoking, Drugs

Arming singers with information on the actual effects of environmental irritants so that they can make informed choices on engaging in exposure to these potential toxins is essential. The glamour that continues to be associated with smoking, drinking, and drugs can be tempered with the deaths of popular stars such as Amy Winehouse and Cory Monteith who engaged in life-ending choices. There is extensive documentation about the long-term effects of toxic and carcinogenic substances, but here are a few key facts to consider when choosing whether to partake.

Alcohol, although it does not go over the vocal folds directly, does have a systemic drying effect. Due to the acidity in alcohol, it may increase the likelihood of reflux, resulting in hoarseness and other laryngeal pathologies. Consuming alcohol generally decreases one's inhibitions, and therefore you are more likely to sing and do things that you would not typically do under the influence of alcohol.

Beyond the carcinogens in nicotine and tobacco, the heat at which a cigarette burns is well above the boiling temperature of water (water boils at 212 degrees F; cigarettes burn at over 1,400 degrees F). No one would consider pouring a pot of boiling water on their hand, and yet the burning temperature for a cigarette results in significant heat over the oral mucosa and vocal folds. The heat alone can create a deterioration in the lining, resulting in polypoid degeneration. Obviously, cigarette smoking has been well documented as a cause for laryngeal cancer.

Marijuana and other street drugs are not only addictive but can cause permanent mucosal lining changes depending on the drug used and the method of delivery. If you or one of your singer colleagues is experiencing a drug or alcohol problem, research or provide information and support on getting appropriate counseling and help.

SMART PRACTICE STRATEGIES FOR SKILL DEVELOPMENT AND VOICE CONSERVATION

Daily practice and drills for skill acquisition are an important part of any singer's training. However, overpracticing or inefficient practicing may be detrimental to the voice. Consider practice sessions of athletes: they may practice four to eight hours per day broken into one- to two-hour training sessions with a period of rest and recovery in between sessions. Although we cannot parallel the sports model without adequate evidence in the vocal athlete, the premise of short, intense, focused practice sessions is logical for the singer. Similar to physical exercise, it is suggested that practice sessions do not have to be all "singing." Rather, structuring sessions so that one-third of the session is spent on warm-up; one-third on vocalises, text work, rhythms, character development, and so on; and one-third on repertoire will allow the singer to function in a more efficient vocal manner. Building the amount of time per practice session—increasing duration by five minutes per week, building to sixty to ninety minutes—may be effective (e.g., Week 1: twenty minutes three times per day; Week 2: twenty-five minutes three times per day, etc.).

Vary the "vocal workout" during your week. For example, if you do the same physical exercise in the same way day after day with the same intensity and pattern, you will likely experience repetitive strain–type injuries. However, cross-training or varying the type and level of exercise aids in injury prevention. So when planning your practice sessions for a given week (or rehearsal process for a given role), consider varying your vocal intensity, tessitura, and exercises to maximize your training sessions, building stamina, muscle memory, and skill acquisition. For example, one day you may spend more time on learning rhythms and translation and the next day you spend thirty minutes performing coloratura exercises to prepare for a specific role. Take one day a week off from vocal training and give your voice a break. This does not mean complete vocal rest (although some singers find this beneficial) but rather a day without singing and limited talking.

Practice Your Mental Focus

Mental wellness and stress management are equally as important as vocal training for vocal athletes. Addressing any mental health issues is paramount to developing the vocal artist. This may include anything from daily mental exercises/meditation/focus to overcoming performance anxiety to more serious mental health issues/illness. Every person can benefit from improved focus and mental acuity.

ADDITIONAL VOCAL WELLNESS TIPS

When working with singers across all genres, the most common presentation in my voice clinic relates to vocal fatigue, acute vocal injury, and loss of high-frequency range. Vocal fatigue complaints are generally related to the duration of their rehearsals, recording sessions, "meet and greets," performances, vocal gymnastics, general lack of sleep, and the vocal requirements to traverse their entire range (and occasionally outside of physiological comfort range). Depending on the genre performed, singing includes a high vocal load with the associated risk of repetitive strain and increased collision force injuries. Acute vocal injuries within this population include phonotraumtic lesions (hemorrhages, vocal fold polyps, vocal fold nodules, reflux, and general vocal fold edema/erythema). Often these are not injuries related to problematic vocal technique but rather due to "vocal accidents" and/or overuse (due to required performance/contract demands). Virtually all singers are required to connect with the audience from a vocal and emotional standpoint. Physical performance demands may be extreme and at times highly cardiovascular and/or acrobatic. Both physical and vocal fitness should be foremost in the minds of any vocal performer, and these singers should be physically and vocally in shape to meet the necessary performance demands.

The advanced and professional singer must possess a flexible, agile, and dynamic instrument and have appropriate stamina. Singers must have a good command of their instrument as well as exceptional underlying intention to what they are singing as it is about relaying a message, characteristic sound, and connecting with the audience. Singers must reflect the mood and intent of the composer requiring dynamic control, vocal control/power, and an emotional connection to the text.

Commercial music singers use microphones and personal amplification to their maximal capacity. If used correctly, amplification can be used to maximize vocal health by allowing the singer to produce voice in an efficient manner while the sound engineer is effectively able to mix, amplify, and add effects to the voice. Understanding both the utility and limits of a given microphone and sound system is essential for the singer both for live and studio performances. Using an appropriate microphone can not only enhance the singer's performance but also reduce vocal load. Emotional extremes (intimacy and exultation) can be enhanced by appropriate microphone choice, placement, and acoustical mixing, thus saving the singer's voice.

Not everything a singer does is "vocally healthy," sometimes because the emotional expression may be so intense it results in vocal collision forces that are extreme. Even if the singer does not have formal vocal training, the concept of "vocal cross-training"—which can mean singing in both high and low registers with varying intensities and resonance options—before and after practice sessions and services is likely a vital component to minimizing vocal injury.

FINAL THOUGHTS

Ultimately, the singer must learn to provide the most output with the least "cost" to the system. Taking care of the physical instrument through daily physical exercise, adequate nutrition and hydration, and focused attention on performance will provide a necessary basis for vocal health during performance. Small doses of high-intensity singing (or speaking) will limit impact stress on the vocal folds. Finally, attention to the mind, body, and voice will provide the singer with an awareness when something is wrong. This awareness and knowledge of when to rest or seek help will promote vocal well-being for the singer throughout his or her career.

NOTES

1. W. LeBorgne et al., "Prevalence of Vocal Pathology in Incoming Freshman Musical Theatre Majors: A 10-year Retrospective Study," Fall Voice Conference, New York, 2012.

2. J. Brinckmann et al., "Safety and Efficacy of a Traditional Herbal Medicine (Throat Coat) in Symptomatic Temporary Relief of Pain in Patients with Acute Pharyngitis: A Multicenter, Prospective, Randomized, Double-Blinded, Placebo-Controlled Study," *Journal of Alternative and Complementary Medicine* 9, no. 2 (2003): 285–298.

3. N. Roy et al., "An Evaluation of the Effects of Three Laryngeal Lubricants on Phonation Threshold Pressure (PTP)," *Journal of Voice* 17, no. 3 (2003): 331–342.

4. K. Tanner et al., "Nebulized Isotonic Saline versus Water Following a Laryngeal Desiccation Challenge in Classically Trained Sopranos," *Journal of Speech, Language, and Hearing Research* 53, no. 6 (2010): 1555–1566.

5. C. Brown and S. Graham, "Nasal Irrigations: Good or Bad?" *Current Opinion in Otolaryngology, Head and Neck Surgery* 12, no. 1 (2004): 9–13.

6. T. Nsouli, "Long-Term Use of Nasal Saline Irrigation: Harmful or Helpful?" American College of Allergy, Asthma and Immunology Annual Scientific Meeting, Abstract 32, 2009.

7. M. Shadkam et al. "A Comparison of the Effect of Honey, Dextromethorphan, and Diphenhydramine on Nightly Cough and Sleep Quality in Children and Their Parents," *Journal of Alternative and Complementary Medicine* 16, no. 7 (2010): 787–793.

8. L. Hill et al., "Esophageal Injury by Apple Cider Vinegar Tablets and Subsequent Evaluation of Products," *Journal of the American Dietetic Association* 105, no. 7 (2005): 1141–1144.

9. R. O. Gottliebson, "The Efficacy of Cool-Down Exercises in the Practice Regimen of Elite Singers," PhD dissertation, University of Cincinnati, 2011.

APPENDIX A

Introductory List of Art Song Duets, Trios, and Quartets for Pedagogical Use in the Applied Voice Curriculum (does not include duet arrangements)

Beginner	Mostly homophonic, strophic, simple accompaniment, tonal, basic rhythms, accessible range and tessitura, simple poetic interpretation		
COMPOSER	*TITLE*	*VOICES*	*SOURCE*
Abt, Franz	*Abschied*, Op. 316, No. 7	2 voices	imslp.org
Abt, Franz	*Heimweh*, Op. 184, No. 9	2 voices	imslp.org
Abt, Franz	*O, wie wunderschön ist die Frühlingszeit!* Op. 132, No. 4	2 voices	imslp.org
Abt, Franz	*Siehst du dort die Bergeshöhen from 4 Duette*, Op. 407	2 voices	imslp.org
Abt, Franz	*Sternlein am Himmel*, Op. 316, No. 10	2 voices	imslp.org
Abt, Franz	*Le Dimanche en mer*	2 voices	imslp.org
Berlioz, Hector	*Pleure, pauvre Colette*	SS or TT	Bärenreiter
Carissimi, Giacomo	*Rimanti in pace from Duetti da Camera*	2 high v	Master Music Publications, Inc.
Cornelius, Peter	*Am Meer*	S and Bar	Breitkopf & Härtel
Cornelius, Peter	*Heimatgedenken*, Op. 16, No. 1	S and Bass	CVR
Cornelius, Peter	*Komm herbei, Tod!* (1847 version)	SS	CVR
Cornelius, Peter	*Liebesprobe*	SBar	CVR
Cornelius, Peter	*Scheiden und Meiden*	SS (or T)	Breitkopf & Härtel
Cornelius, Peter	*Zu den Bergen hebet sich ein Augenpaar*	SBar	Breitkopf & Härtel
Delibes, Léo	*Les Trois Oiseaux*	SS	Note Roehr
Donaudy, Stefano	*Amor S'apprende*	2 voices	Ricordi
Duncan, Martha Hill	*Roadside Flowers*	SS	Graphite Publishing
Dvořák, Antonín	*Fliege, Vöglein . . . from Moravian Duets*, Op. 32, No. 2	2 voices	Boosey
Florimo, Francesco	*Tre bote sì e po no (Neapolitan Dialect)*	2 voices	imslp.org
Franck, César	*L'Ange Gardien*, 6 Duos, No. 1	SA	LudwigMasters Publications
Franck, César	*Aux petits enfants*, 6 Duos, No. 2	SA	LudwigMasters Publications
Franck, César	*La vierge à la crèche*, 6 Duos, No. 3	SA	LudwigMasters Publications

Franck, César	*Soleil from 6 Duos*, No. 5	SA	LudwigMasters Publications
Gounod, Charles	*Par une belle nuit!*	SA	CVR
Hahn, Reynaldo	*En vous disant adieu from Chansons et Madrigaux*, No. 4	SATB	Heugel & Cie
Hahn, Reynaldo	*Pleurez avec moi! from Chansons et Madrigaux*, No. 3	SATB	Heugel & Cie
Hahn, Reynaldo	*Vivons, Mignarde! from Chansons et Madrigaux*, No. 2	SATB	Heugel & Cie
Lassen, Eduard	*Der Frühling und die Liebe from 5 Lieder*, Op. 46, No. 5	2 voices	imslp.org
Marchesi, Mathilde	*L'Art du chant: Huit Vocalise à trois voix*	3 voices	imslp.org
Massenet, Jules	*La danse des rameaux*	SA	imslp.org
Massenet, Jules	*Prélude from Le poème des fleurs*, No. 1	SSA	imslp.org
Mendelssohn, Felix	*6 Duets, Op. 63*	2 voices	Peters
Purcell, Henry	*Lost is my quiet*	S and A/Bar	Novello & Co.
Quilter, Roger	*The Passing Bell*	SA	Boosey & Hawkes
Quilter, Roger	*Weep You No More*	2 voices	Boosey & Hawkes
Righini, Vincenzo	*Il Bacio, from Dodici Duetti da Camera*, Op. 8, No. 4		Southern Music Co
Righini, Vincenzo	*Il Ciglio Nero, from Dodici Duetti da Camera*, Op. 8, No. 3	2 voices	Southern Music Co.
Righini, Vincenzo	*La Speranza Delusa from Dodici Duetti da Camera*, Op. 8, No. 9	2 voices	Southern Music Co.
Righini, Vincenzo	*La Sera Estiva from Dodici Duetti da Camera*, Op. 8, No. 12	2 voices	Southern Music Co.
Rubinstein, Anton	*Volkslied from Zweistimmige Lieder*, Op. 48	2 voices	Peters
Saint-Saëns, Camille	*Pastorale*	SBar	CVR
Saint-Saëns, Camille	*Viens*	SBar	CVR
Schubert, Franz	*Das Abendroth, D236*	3 voices	Breitkopf & Härtel
Schumann, Robert	*3 Lieder für 3 Frauenstimmenm*, Op. 114	SSA	Breitkopf & Härtel
Schumann, Robert	*Sommerruh, Serie 14*, No. 5	2 voices	Peters
Tosti, Francesco	*Canti popolari abruzzesi* (15 duets)	2 voices	Ricordi
Tosti, Francesco	*Venetian Song*	2 voices	Ricordi
Vaughan Williams, R.	*It Was a Lover and His Lass*	2 voices	Boosey & Hawkes

Moderate	Melodic independence with repeated material, advanced accompaniment, tonal and metric challenges, polymeter, moderate range and tessitura		
Abt, Franz	*Frühlingsleben*, Op. 132, No. 9	2 voices	imslp.org
Abt, Franz	*Die Matrosen*, Op. 78	BarB	imslp.org
Abt, Franz	*Nach der Alpe*, Op. 316, No. 9	2 voices	imslp.org
Abt, Franz	*Surre, surre, Käferlein*, Op. 132, No. 6	2 voices	imslp.org
Abt, Franz	*Waldfrieden*, Op. 184, No. 3	2 voices	imslp.org
Abt, Franz	*Waldabend*, Op. 316, No. 8	2 voices	imslp.org
Abt, Franz	*Wanderlust*, Op. 316, No. 6	2 voices	imslp.org
Arditi, Luigi	*Una notte d'amore*	2 voices	imslp.org
Beach, Amy	*A Canadian Boat Song* from Songs of the Sea, Op. 10	SBar	CVR
Berlioz, Hector	*Canon libre à la quinte*	SBar	Breitkopf & Härtel
Berlioz, Hector	*Le Chant des Bretons*, First Version	TTBB	Breitkopf & Härtel
Berlioz, Hector	*Le Chant des Bretons*, Second Version	TTBB	Breitkopf & Härtel
Berlioz, Hector	*Le Trébuchet*	SA	Bärenreiter
Bordèse, Luigi	*Les pifferari*	SA	imslp.org
Brahms, Johannes	*4 Duets*, Op. 61	SA	Peters
Brahms, Johannes	*Fünf Duette*, Op. 66	SA	Peters
Chausson, Ernest	*La Nuit*	2 voices	Alfred
Cornelius, Peter	*Der beste Liebesbrief*	SBar	CVR
Cornelius, Peter	*Brennende Liebe*, Op. 16, No. 2	S and Bass	CVR
Cornelius, Peter	*Ein Wort der Liebe*	SBar	CVR
Cornelius, Peter	*Komm herbei, Tod!* Op. 16, No. 3 (1866 version)	S and Bass	CVR
Cornelius, Peter	*Scheiden*, Op. 16, No. 4	S and Bass	CVR
Cornelius, Peter	*Verratene Liebe*	SS (or T)	Breitkopf & Härtel
Curschmann, Friedrich	*Blumengruss*	SSS	imslp.org
Curschmann, Friedrich	*Das Veilchen*	SST	imslp.org
Curschmann, Friedrich	*Morgenlied*	SSS	imslp.org
Curschmann, Friedrich	*Der Wald*, Op. 17	ST	imslp.org
Dannström, Isidor	*Wåren och Glädjen*, 6 Songs, Op. 15, No. 6 (Swedish)	SA	imslp.org
Donizetti, Gaetano	*Che vuoi di piú*	2 voices	Alfred
Durante, Francesco	*Alfin m'ucciderete*	2 voices	Alfred

Dvořák, Antonín	*Ich schwimm; dir davon . . .* from Moravian Duets, Op. 32, No. 1	2 voices	Boosey & Hawkes
Fauré, Gabriel	*Puisqu'ici-bas toute* âme, Op. 10, No. 1	2 voices	CVR
Franck, César	*La Chanson du Vannier*, 6 Duos, No. 6	SA	CVR
Franck, César	*Les Danses de Lormont*, 6 Duos, No. 4	SA	CVR
Gounod, Charles	*Barcarola*	SBar	CVR
Gounod, Charles	*La siesta*	SS	CVR
Hahn, Reynaldo	*Comment se peut-il faire ainsi?* from Chansons et Madrigaux, No. 5	SAT	Heugel & Cie
Hahn, Reynaldo	*Un loyal Coeur*, from Chansons et Madrigaux, No. 1	STB	Heugel & Cie
Hall, Juliana	*Music like a Curve of Gold*	SA	E.C. Schirmer Music Company, Inc.
Haydn, Joseph	*Guarda qui, che lo vedrai* Hob.XXVa:1	2 voices	Doblinger Music Publishers
Haydn, Joseph	*Saper vorrei se m'ami* Hob.XXVa:2	2 voices	Doblinger Music Publishers
Haydn, Joseph	*An den Vetter* Hob.XXVb:1	3 voices	Bärenreiter
Haydn, Joseph	*Daphnens einziger Fehler* Hob.XXVb:2	3 voices	Bärenreiter
Haydn, Joseph	*Betrachtung des Todes* Hob.XXVb:2	3 voices	Bärenreiter
Haydn, Joseph	*An die Frauen* Hob.XXVb:4	3 voices	Bärenreiter
Haydn, Joseph	*Der Augenblick* Hob.XXVc:1	4 voices	Bärenreiter
Haydn, Joseph	*Die Harmonie in der Ehe* Hob.XXVc:2	4 voices	Bärenreiter
Haydn, Joseph	*Alles hat seine Zeit* Hob.XXVc:3	4 voices	Bärenreiter
Haydn, Joseph	*Die Beredsamkeit* Hob.XXVc:4	4 voices	Bärenreiter
Haydn, Joseph	*Der Greis* Hob.XXVc:5	4 voices	Bärenreiter
Haydn, Joseph	*Die Warnung* Hob.XXVc:6	4 voices	Bärenreiter
Haydn, Joseph	*Wider den Übermut* Hob.XXVc:7	4 voices	Bärenreiter
Haydn, Joseph	*Aus dem Danklied zu Gott* Hob.XXVc:8	4 voices	Bärenreiter
Haydn, Joseph	*Abendlied zu Gott* Hob.XXVc:9	4 voices	Bärenreiter
Lachner, Franz	*6 Duetten*, Op. 106	SA	imslp.org
Lalo, Edouard	*Au fond des Halliers*	ABar	Kalmus
Lalo, Edouard	*O Salutaris*	SAA	Kalmus
Lassen, Eduard	*Frühlingslied* from 5 Lieder, Opus 46, No. 1	2 voices	Easy Classical Duets, Hal Leonard
Loewe, Carl	*Gesang der Geister* über *den Wassern*, Op. 88	SATB	Breitkopf & Härtel
Malibran, Maria	*Belle, viens à moi*	2 voices	Alfred
Malibran, Maria	*Le Prisonnier*	2 voices	Alfred
Massenet, Jules	*Les Fleurs*	ABar or ST	Heugel

(continued)

Massenet, Jules	*La Gavotte de Puyjoli*	SBar	Heugel
Massenet, Jules	*Joie!* from 3 Mélodies, deux duos et un trio, Op. 2, No. 5	2 voices	Heugel
Massenet, Jules	*Marine* from 3 Mélodies, deux duos et un trio, Op. 2, No. 4	2 voices	Heugel
Massenet, Jules	*Matinée d'Été* from 3 Mélodies, deux duos et un trio, Op. 2, No. 6	SSS	Heugel
Massenet, Jules	*Oh! ne finis jamaise* from Poëme d'amour, No. 6	SBar	Heugel
Paladilhe, Émile	*Au bord de l'eau*	SA	CVR
Pessard, Emile	*Les Deux Normands (Duo de Salon)*	2 male voices	imslp.org
Quilter, Roger	*It Was a Lover and His Lass*	ST	Boosey & Hawkes
Righini, Vincenzo	*L'Ambasciata,* from *Dodici Duetti da Camera*, Op. 8, No. 6	2 voices	Southern Music Co.
Righini, Vincenzo	*L'Eco,* from *Dodici Duetti da Camera*, Op. 8, No. 8	2 voices	Southern Music Co.
Righini, Vincenzo	*L'Amor, Necessità,* from *Dodici Duetti da Camera*, Op. 8, No. 11	2 voices	Southern Music Co.
Rossini, Gioacchino	*I Gondolieri*	SATB	Ricordi
Rubinstein, Anton	*Zweistimmige Lieder*, Op. 48 and 67	2 voices	Peters
Saint-Saëns, Camille	*Le Soir*	ATen	CVR
Saint-Saëns, Camille	*Pastorale*	SB	CVR
Savioni, Mario	*Fugga Amor/Segua Amor*	2 voices	Alfred
Schubert, Franz	*An die Sonne,* D439	SATB	Bärenreiter
Schubert, Franz	*Licht und Liebe*	ST	Bärenreiter
Schubert, Franz	*Mignon und der Harfner* from Gesänge aus Wilhelm Meister, Op. 62, No. 1	ST	Bärenreiter
Schumann, Robert	*Vier Duette für Sopran und Tenor*, Op. 34	ST	Peters
Tosti, Francesco	*Allons voir*	2 voices	Ricordi
Tosti, Francesco	*Aimez quand on vous aime!*	2 voices	Ricordi
Valente, Vincenzo	*'O Scrivano* (Neapolitan Dialect)	2 voices—male and female	imslp.org
Valente, Vincenzo	*Tarantella Sorrentina* (Neapolitan Dialect)	2 voices—male and female	imslp.org
Vaughan Williams, Ralph	*It was a lover*	2 voices	CVR
Viardot, Pauline	*Séparation*	2 voices	Alfred
Walker, Gwyneth	*As a Branch in May*	SS	E.C. Schirmer Music Company, Inc.
Weber, Carl Maria von	*3 Duetti*, Op. 31	SS	imslp.org

Advanced	Melodic independence; difficult accompaniment; tonal, rhythmic, and metric complexity; wide range and high tessitura; sophisticated poetry; language		
Brahms, Johannes	*Liebeslieder*, Op. 52, Nos. 1–18 (4-hand piano)	SATB	Peters
Brahms, Johannes	*Neue Liebeslieder*, Op. 65, Nos. 1–15 (4-hand piano)	SATB	Peters
Chausson, Ernest	*Réveil*, Op. 11, No. 2	2 high vcs	Leduc
Cornelius, Peter	*Der Tod des Verräters*	TBarB	Breitkopf & Härtel
Cornelius, Peter	*Ich und du*	S and B/A	Breitkopf & Härtel
Dannström, Isidor	*Wåren och Glädjen*, 6 Songs, Op. 15, No. 6 (Swedish)	SA	imslp.org
Duparc, Henri	*La fuite*	ST	CVR
Fauré, Gabriel	*Tarantelle*, Op. 10, No. 2	SS/ST	CVR
Greer, John	*Liebeslied-Lieder* (4-hand piano)	SATB	CMC
Hagen, Jocelyn	*The Time of Singing Has Come*	ST	Graphite Publishing
Hüe, Georges	*L'éternelle Sérénade*	SATB	Heugel
Laitman, Lori	*Fresh Patterns*	SS	Enchanted Knickers Music
Laitman, Lori	*I Am in Need of Music*	SA	Enchanted Knickers Music
Lalo, Edouard	*Dansons!*	2 voices	Kalmus
Lehmann, Liza	*Nonsense Songs from "Alice in Wonderland": A Song-Cycle for Four Voices* (includes solos, duet, and quartets)	SATB	Chappell
Ludvig, Norman	*5 Songs—Sånger*, Op. 17 (Swedish)	SS (ST No. 4)	imslp.org
Massenet, Jules	*Dialogue Nocturne*	ST	Heugel
Netzel, Laura	*3 Duets*, Op. 39 (Swedish)	SS or SA	imslp.org
Pessard, Emile	*Pendant le bal (Duo-Valse)*	Female and male voice	imslp.org
Poulenc, Francis	*Colloque*, FP 108	SBar	Salabert
Reger, Max	*Fünf Duette*, Op. 14	SA	Schott
Rorem, Ned	*Gloria* for two voices and piano	2 voices	Boosey & Hawkes
Rossini, Gioacchino	*La Pesca* from *Notturno a due voci* from *Soirées musicales*, No. 10		CVR
Rossini, Gioacchino	*La Regata Veneziana* from *Notturno a due voci* from *Soirées musicales*, No. 9		CVR
Schubert, Franz	*Gebet*, D815	SATB	Bärenreiter
Schumann, Robert	*Spanische Liebes-Lieder*, Op. 138 (4-hand piano)	SATB	Peters
Tchaikovsky, Pyotr Ilyich	*Sechs Duette für zwei Singstimmen*, Op. 46	SA(1, 3–6), SB (2)	CVR
Viardot, Pauline	*Habanera*	2 voices	Alfred

APPENDIX B

Contemporary Art Songs for Voice and Classical Guitar—A Select Annotated List

James Maroney

The last century witnessed a significant number of art songs composed with accompaniments other than the piano. An instrument of particular note is the classical guitar. Hundreds of modern art songs feature guitar, many written by some of music's finest composers, including Benjamin Britten, Dominick Argento, Joaquin Rodrigo, Thea Musgrave, Elliot Carter, William Walton, Mario Castelnuovo-Tedesco, John Rutter, Michael Tippett, Daniel Pinkham, and Peter Maxwell-Davies. Works range from short, simple pieces to challenging, substantial song cycles. They employ numerous compositional styles and performance techniques, with texts in more than twenty languages. The modern literature for classical voice and guitar is a rich body of works that should be avidly explored by singers and guitarists.

Renowned guitarist/lutenist Julian Bream once stated that the guitar "is *the* most beautiful accompaniment to the voice. The guitar has an evocative sound, lending support to the singer. One gives luster to the other."[1] The classical guitar indeed is well suited to vocal music. Like the piano, it can play both melodically and harmonically. Further, it is capable of easily displaying a wide variety of sounds, such as harmonics, *tamburo*,[2] and portamento. The key of a piece often can readily be changed through the use of a capo.[3] While not a loud instrument, the classical guitar has a full, rich sound and excellent projection, allowing it to be heard well with most singers. Yet its somewhat softer sound helps to create an intimate environment, making it quite suitable for smaller concert venues. Finally, its portability means that instrument availability or quality is not a concern when choosing a place to perform.

A BRIEF HISTORICAL OVERVIEW

For centuries, the guitar has been associated with song. However, the primitive design of earlier guitars caused composers to reserve their best efforts for more refined instruments—at first, the lute and its Spanish counterpart, the *vihuela*, and later the piano. In fifteenth-century southern Europe, where the guitar's presence is first well documented, the instrument was relatively small and had only four courses.[4] It possessed a rather thin timbre and limited pitch range, so its music was restricted to simple chordal accompaniments. Later, in mid-sixteenth-century Spain, an extra set of double strings was added. The new five-course instrument became known as the *guitarra española*. While somewhat more versatile than its predecessor, this instrument was viewed as most appropriate for the general populace—an accessible alternative to the *vihuela*, whose compositions were far more sophisticated and difficult. Thus, as was true for the earlier four-course guitar, music for the *guittarra española* was rather simplistic.[5]

By the last decades of the 1700s, the transition was made to an instrument with six single-string courses (yet smaller than the modern guitar), and the initial half of the nineteenth century saw the first period wherein a significant number of original songs for voice and guitar was composed. Interest during this time was most evident in Vienna, due largely to performer Mauro Giuliani, who, as one of the first truly accomplished guitarists, gave some of the earliest concerts highlighting the instrument in a solo capacity.[6] He wrote a vast amount of music for guitar, including 174 songs in three languages.[7] Giuliani and his Viennese guitar school influenced many composers, including Franz Schubert and Carl Maria von Weber. Schubert wrote many songs with guitar, and approximately twenty of them were published during his lifetime.[8] Weber played the guitar and composed around ninety songs for it; he also featured the guitar in arias from several operas.[9] The popularity of the guitar in Vienna prompted numerous transcriptions, including songs by Beethoven and Haydn.[10]

The guitar also was gaining greater acceptance elsewhere in Europe, as well as in the United States. Rossini used it in certain operas, as did Verdi.[11] Songs with guitar were so popular in England that many early nineteenth-century English ballads were transcribed from their original piano or orchestral accompaniments.[12] American Stephen Foster took nineteen of his songs originally scored with piano and arranged the accompaniments for guitar.[13] Holdings of mid-1800s American music in the Library of Congress reveal a large quantity for voice and guitar that consist of transcriptions of popular songs with piano.

The late 1800s witnessed the guitar's evolution to its larger, standardized contemporary design. Not coincidentally, the development of its modern playing technique began in the same era. As the twentieth century progressed, substantive original literature for the guitar grew dramatically, aided in no small part by composers who were not guitarists. This trend ran contrary to the long-standing tradition of guitarist-composers, resulting in works unconstrained by former notions of the guitar's capabilities. However, this new repertoire for guitar was largely devoid of ensemble compositions, especially songs. Given the often subservient accompanimental status accorded the instrument in previous eras, it seems logical that, in order to elevate its standing, the guitar's new repertoire would have to be markedly dissociated from its past. Only then could the instrument be allowed to reach its full potential.

By the second half of the twentieth century, composers and performers felt that this potential was being realized. Since 1945, there has been much renewed interest in the medium of voice and guitar, with hundreds of compositions written by many renowned composers. Many seek to exploit the full potential of both instruments and are strikingly original and musically satisfying.

CONTEMPORARY ART SONGS FOR VOICE AND CLASSICAL GUITAR

Following is a select annotated list of published contemporary works for the duo of solo voice and classical guitar. They are in alphabetical order by composer, in the following format:

Composer
Title of work (Publisher name and catalog number)
Language
Voice type (Pitch range/tessitura)
Difficulty level
Cycle, group or collection, and number of songs (duration)
Titles of individual songs
Comments

Further Explanations

Publisher: An index of publishers is provided at the end of the article.
Language: Additional singing versions other than the original language are noted in parentheses.
Voice type: Specific classifications (e.g., soprano, tenor, male, female, etc.) are indicated only when information in the score is explicit. Otherwise, the voice type is identified by the music's tessitura as high, medium, or low.
Pitch range/tessitura: The first specifies the lowest and highest notes of the voice part, while the second indicates the predominant range. When the voice type is high, medium, or low, the pitch range and tessitura are given for a female singer; the male singer's pitches would be an octave lower.
Difficulty level: This is judged primarily by the singer's music. However, significant differences in difficulty between the voice and guitar parts are noted in the comments. Considerations include the work's length and degree of tonality, along with its use of melodic motion, pitch range, rhythm, and dynamics.

Easy—contains few technical challenges and therefore generally is intended for beginning singers.

Medium difficult—poses some moderate challenges and likely would be appropriate for singers with one to three years of vocal instruction.

Difficult—significant technical and musical demands are placed on the performer. This music is best suited to more advanced singers, such as those on the upper undergraduate or graduate levels of vocal performance.

Very difficult—refers to highly challenging works that frequently require extreme technical demands and that are usually reserved for singers on the graduate or professional levels.

Cycle, group, or collection: "Cycle" denotes a set of songs specifically intended to be performed together in a particular sequence. "Group" refers to a collectively titled set of songs by one composer, linked by a common theme, compositional style, or opus number, which need not be performed together or in a given order. A "collection" is a set of songs in which each work was composed independently. They are not linked by any trait except perhaps that of composer and are not expected to be performed together. If none of these terms appears, then the work is a single song.

Duration: The time is usually rounded to the nearest minute, unless a more precise timing is provided in the score. For single songs, the duration is listed in the comments only if it exceeds six minutes.

Comments: The text's author and source are provided when known, followed by important aspects of the piece. Technical concerns crucial when selecting a work for study and performance are mentioned; these may include the degree of tonality, extended techniques, and characteristics of the voice part, such as its use of pitch, rhythm, dynamics, and text. Although each work is discussed largely from a vocal perspective, brief comments about the guitar part often are included. Other aspects contributing to the work's distinction also are mentioned.

Acuña, Luis Gustavo

Ayer, yo fui feliz (Margaux—em 5101)
Spanish
Medium voice (B3–F5/B3–F5)
Medium difficult

Utilizing traits of traditional Spanish music, this song features repetitive melodies of lively descending stepwise phrases balanced by wide upward leaps to sustained notes. The guitar accompaniment is varied yet uncomplicated.

Alemann, Eduardo A.
Pompas Fúnebres (Ricordi S.A.—BA 13294)
Spanish
Soprano (G3–B5/B3–G5)
Very difficult
Described as a cantata, this fifteen-minute composition consisting of eight untitled movements is based on a poem by Antonio Espina. The work is atonal, with numerous disjunct, fragmented vocal lines. The musical settings of the movements vary greatly, aided by the use of many nontraditional techniques for both players, such as *Sprechstimne*, glissando, *tamburo*, vocal tremolo, string scraping, and quarter tones. The guitar part, while rather demanding, is generally chordal in design.

Angelis, Ugalberto de
Tre Canti (Sonzogno-2901)
Italian
High voice (C4–A5/F♯4–F♯5)
Very difficult
Group of three songs (7')
O pura, o cara
Fili d 'erba
Andromaca
Giorgio Vigolo wrote the poems used in this piece. The songs are atonal with extensive chromaticism and dissonance, as well as very intricate, unusual rhythms in often changing meters. The vocal lines are quite disjunct, especially in "O pura, o cara," which contains many unusual chromatic intervals. Tempi are rather slow; the first and last songs are set to *lento* and *molto lento*, while "Fili d'erba" is *andante*. Extreme changes in dynamics are common and integral to the music. The guitar part requires many harmonic and percussive sound effects.

Apivor, Denis
Seis Canciones (Bèrben—E. 1640 B.)
Spanish
High voice (B3–A♭5/E4–E5)
Difficult
Group of six songs (23')
La Guitarra
La Niña del Bello Rostro
Canción de Jinete
Pueblo
Virgen con Miriñaque
Raíz Amarga
With texts by Federico Garcia Lorca, these songs possess a distinctive Spanish folk flavor—most feature melodic ornamentation and other musical traits typical of that style. Meter and tempo changes are common. Many moods are utilized, including very emotional, dramatic sections, such as in "La Guitarra," "Canción de Jinete," and "Raíz Amarga." The guitar is quite prominent and features many distinctive solo passages.

Argento, Dominick
Letters from Composers (Boosey—BH BK 686)
English
High voice (A3–A5/E4–G5)
Difficult
Group of seven songs (25')
Frédéric Chopin (to a friend)
Wolfgang Amadeus Mozart (to his father)
Franz Schubert (to a friend)
Johann Sebastian Bach (to the Town Council)
Claude Debussy (to a friend)
Giacomo Puccini (to a friend)
Robert Schumann (to his fiancée)
As the work's title implies, the texts are taken from the written correspondence of composers. The songs are generally tonal yet with much chromaticism. There is a great deal of stylistic contrast among the pieces, as many utilize musical mannerisms associated with each composer. Also quite varied are the songs' moods. "Franz Schubert"

is slow and somber, revealing the composer in a state of utter despair. The amorous letter in "Robert Schumann" was written to Klara shortly before their marriage and is set to long, lyrical phrases. In the very fast and humorous "Giacomo Puccini," the composer notes his passionate dislike for Paris and Parisians. The music for the guitar is very expressive and well written; many of the songs feature demanding solo passages.

Azpiazu Iriarte, José de
Cinco Canciones Populares Españolas (UME—UMG19403)
Spanish
High voice (D4–A5/E4–E5)
Medium difficult
Group of five songs (12')
El Marabú
El Pajarillo
Tirana del Zarandillo
El Paño Moruno
Los Pastores
The composer has provided new accompaniments for these traditional Spanish folk songs. The melodies are straightforward, requiring little stylistic ornamentation from the singer, and the songs are consistently lively and lighthearted. The first song, "El Marabú," concludes with an exuberant glissando from A4 to A5, ending on the word "Ay!" The guitar accompaniment differs in each song yet is not difficult.

Azpiazu Iriarte, José de
Noche de San Juan (UME—UMG19985)
Spanish
High voice (E4–A5/A4–F♯5)
Medium difficult
This piece would be a worthy introduction to Spanish folk music for inexperienced performers. The repetition of the melody allows the singer to focus on the stylistic trills and ornamentation within. The guitar part, save for several brief solo passages, is accompanimental in design, consisting almost exclusively of chords.

Azpiazu Iriarte, José de
Recuerdo (UME—UMGI 9886)
Spanish
High voice (C4–G5/E4–E5)
Medium difficult
Written in the Spanish style, this work features an appealing melody and attractive guitar harmonies set to alternating measures of 6/8 and 3/4. The song concludes with an octave glissando up to E5, which then must be sustained considerably while diminishing to pianissimo. The uncomplicated yet varied guitar accompaniment includes pizzicato and harmonics.

Babbitt, Milton
Four Cavalier Settings (Peters—P67533)
English
Tenor (B2–A4/D3–A♭4)
Very difficult
Cycle of four songs (12')
To Electra
A Song
Anacreontic
To Sycamores
This cycle is performed with no interruption; each section flows seamlessly into the next. It is atonal, with fragmented, highly disjunct chromatic phrases in both parts. The rhythms are very challenging due to intricate subdivisions in diverse meters. The dynamics change constantly and are often at extreme levels. The relative lack of chordal material in the guitar lends sparseness to the work's musical texture.

Baxter, Garth
From the Heart: Three American Women—Volume One: Three from Sara (Columbia—CO 345A)
English
High or medium voice (B3–E♭5/C4–D5)
Medium difficult
Cycle of three songs (9')
There Will Come Soft Rains

The Inn of Earth
February Twilight
The cycle features texts by American poet Sara Teasdale, who enjoyed popularity and critical acclaim in the 1920s. The songs are tonal with ample chromaticism; the second song, "The Inn of Earth," is the most challenging in that regard. Different musical settings correspond to the poems' varied moods; the first two songs are satirical, while the last, "February Twilight," is pastoral. Although written for soprano, the pitch range is best suited for a mezzo-soprano or baritone. The colorful guitar accompaniment is important in establishing the musical impression of each song.

Baxter, Garth
From the Heart: Three American Women—Volume Two: Two Remembrances (Columbia—CO 34513)
English
High or medium voice (B3–G5/C4–E♭5)
Medium difficult
Group of two songs (5')
August
Gone With the Wind
Susan Laura Logo wrote the words for these songs in the late 1960s. The group is tonal with long, uncomplicated chromatic melodies set to slow, relaxed tempi. The first song, "August," is written in a "bluesy style" (the composer's words). The accessible guitar part is often texturally sparse, helping to reinforce the songs' simple, intimate nostalgia.

Baxter, Garth
From the Heart: Three American Women—Volume Three: Willa (Columbia—CO 345C)
English
High or medium voice (C4–F♯5/E4–D5)
Difficult
Cycle of four songs (12')
The Tavern
The Hawthorn Tree

L'Envoi
Spanish Johnny
With texts by Willa Cather, the first three songs contain introspective lyrics, while the fourth, "Spanish Johnny," tells of the early American frontier. The cycle is tonal, with lyrical vocal passages made somewhat challenging by the liberal use of chromaticism and changing meters. The richly varied guitar part is perhaps most prominent in the last song, which displays long, Spanish-style solos.

Behrend, Siegfried
Impressionen einer Spanischen Reise (Suite espagnola No. 6) (Sikorski—H.S.3730)
Spanish
High voice (C4–F5/E4–F5)
Medium difficult
Suite of three songs (10')
Malagueña
Murciana
El Vito
This suite contains three well-known Spanish folk songs. The accompaniments have been revised to reflect the capabilities of modern guitar playing while preserving the music's traditional flavor. Each song features distinctive traits of the Spanish style: "Malagueña" requires brief yet rapid vocal ornamentations; "Murciana" alternates between 6/8 and 3/4; "El Vito" demands a powerful, declamatory vocal delivery. The guitar part features many rapid passages in the first and last pieces, much of it in flamenco style.

Behrend, Siegfried
Yo Lo Vi (Modern—M 1608 E)
Spanish
High voice (B♭3–E♭6/E4–B5)
Very difficult
Cycle of five songs (10')
Non te Escaparas
Dios lo Perdone y era su Madre
Yo Lo Vi

Porque fue Sensibile
Ya es Hora
This atonal cycle features texts by Francesco de Goya. The rhythms are uncomplicated, save for the constant yet unmarked meter changes in "Dios lo Perdone y era su Madre." The melodies vary greatly in difficulty; "Non te Escaparas" and "Porque fue Sensibile" are fairly simple, but the others use unusual intervals exceeding an octave, often in the extreme upper pitch range. The guitar part requires the use of many nontraditional performance techniques yet is not excessively demanding.

Benedict, Robert
Alleluia (in a Neo-Baroque style) (Waterloo Music)
English
High or medium voice (B3–F♯5/E4–C♯5)
Medium difficult
This animated song begins with a simple melody set to three verses of contemporary sacred text written by the composer, followed by many short, accessible melismas on the word "Alleluia." The accompaniment is contrapuntal yet not complicated and may be played on the piano (a separate, somewhat different part is supplied). Although the title page states "for soprano," the work is suitable for many voices of either gender.

Beraldo, Primo
Intorno ad una Fonte (Zanibon—G. 5964 Z.)
Italian
Medium voice (E4–F♯5/G4–E5)
Difficult
The song's text is taken from the poems of Giovanni Boccaccio. The work is chromatic yet tonal, with lyrical vocal melodies interspersed with more declamatory phrases. The rhythms are uncomplicated despite frequent changes in meter and subtle variations in its overall *adagio* tempo. There are brief sections of speaking and *Sprechstimme*. The guitar part is not difficult, yet a wide variety of tone colors is called for.

Berkeley, Lennox
Songs of the Half-Light (Chester—JWC 4066)
English

High voice (D4–A5/G4–G5)
Difficult
Cycle of five songs (13')
Rachel
Full Moon
All that's past
The Moth
The Fleeting
This cycle, featuring texts by Walter de la Mare, was commissioned by Peter Pears, who premiered it with Julian Bream at the 1965 Aldeburgh Festival. The work is tonal with much chromaticism. Meter changes are common, yet the rhythms are uncomplicated. The melodic approach differs for each song, depending on the mood of the poetry. Particularly notable is the musical setting of "The Moth," with the guitar's incessant thirty-second-note patterns aptly depicting the insect's movements. The guitar part is both substantial and demanding.

Biberian, Gilbert
Epigrams (Bèrben—E. 2079 B.)
French
High voice (E♭4–C6/F4–F♯5)
Difficult
Cycle of four songs (8')
Les sots
Sur les mauvais médecins
Sur le reproche qu 'on lui a fait de copier l'antiquité
Les derivations
Set to the poems of Jacques de Cailly, these atonal songs feature vocal lines that are often quite disjunct and dissonant to the guitar. There are two instances where a sustained, forte C6 is required; one occurs at the beginning of the first song. The moods and settings within the cycle vary considerably. The third piece—with its *lento* tempo—is the longest, while the final song is rather lively and brief, lasting about fifteen seconds. The guitar part is rather demanding and contributes greatly to the work's abstract atmosphere.

Bredemeyer, Reiner
Drei Chamisso-Lieder (Neue—NM 2047)
German
Medium or low voice (G3–B4/B♭3–B4)
Medium difficult
Cycle of three songs (5')
Tragische Geschichte
Kanon
Nachtwächterlied
The early nineteeth-century poet Adalbert von Chamisso wrote the texts. Yet the composer wishes to relate the words to social topics relevant at the time of the cycle's composition (1987), as judged by the brief performance descriptions prefacing each song (i.e., "gorbatchovinistisch," "tschernobylytisch grün," and "ab - DDRitistisch"). This cycle is atonal, with angular, chromatic vocal lines set to accessible rhythms. The first and last songs are strophic, containing six and seven verses respectively. "Kanon" is quite short (30") and musically repetitive. The guitar part is dissonant and fragmented and lends greatly to the music's expression. The cycle is printed in the same edition as the composer's *. . . wie immer* (see below).

Bredemeyer, Reiner
. . . wie immer (Neue—NM 2047)
German
Tenor or Baritone (B♭2–F♯4/G3–G4)
Medium difficult
Cycle of three songs (5')
7.Juni 1931
Mai 1935
16. März 1937
Based on poems of Osip Mandelstam, each song is titled by dates of Russian significance. The cycle contains varied yet accessible chromatic melodies in an atonal setting. "7.Juni 1931" uses repeated voice and guitar motives. The last two songs are very short; the former is strophic, with four verses. The cycle is printed in the same edition as the composer's *Drei Chamisso-Lieder* (see above).

Bresgen, Cesar
Von Wäldern und Zigeunern (Tonos—7260)
German
All voices (B3–C♯5/E4–B4)
Medium difficult
Cycle of four songs (15')
Sich in waldern treffen
Im keller desgroßvaters des mörders
Losgelöstes inneres eines regens
Das leben der zigeuner
Hans Carl Artmann supplied the poetry for this cycle. The singer mostly speaks, with the words merely printed over the guitar music. The few sections specifying vocal pitches or rhythms are very brief and simple. The guitar part, being in the musical forefront, is often quite challenging.

Bresgen, Cesar
Zwei Lieder (Doblinger—GKM 169)
German
High voice (A3–G♯5/E4–E5)
Medium difficult
Group of two songs (5')
Meine Stadt
Am Hügel
Although tonal, the chromaticism within these songs yields frequent dissonance, especially in the guitar. The vocal lines are somewhat disjunct, but the intervals within are rarely larger than a perfect fourth. While meter changes occur regularly, the rhythms are not complicated. The guitar is often prominent yet technically accessible.

Britten, Benjamin
Folksong Arrangements, Volume 6 (Boosey—Boosey 18814)
English
High voice (C4–G5/G4–E5)
Medium difficult
Group of six songs (18')
I will give my love an apple

Sailor-boy
Master Kilby
The Soldier and the Sailor
Bonny at Morn
The Shooting of his Dear
The first five volumes of these well-known settings feature piano accompaniment; Britten arranged the final volume for voice and guitar at the request of Peter Pears and Julian Bream. The group contains folk songs of British and American origin, ranging from the ebullient "Sailor-boy" to the jovial "The Soldier and the Sailor" and the dramatic "The Shooting of his Dear." As in Britten's other volumes, the new and innovative accompaniments add fresh perspective to the original melodies without overshadowing them. The guitar part is quite varied and expressive and is not too demanding except for the virtuosic solo that concludes "Sailor-boy" (a simplified *ossia* is also provided).

Britten, Benjamin
Songs from the Chinese (Boosey—Boosey 18505)
English
High voice (E♭4–A5/E4–F♯5)
Difficult
Cycle of six songs (15')
The Big Chariot
The Old Lute
The Autumn Wind
The Herd Boy
Depression
Dance Song
These settings of ancient Chinese poetry (translated by Arthur Waley) were first performed by Peter Pears and Julian Bream at the 1958 Aldeburgh Festival. This cycle represents one of the finest contemporary works for voice and classical guitar. The songs expertly evoke a wide array of emotions and ideas, aided greatly by the varied and colorful writing for the guitar. The cycle is very chromatic yet tonal, with rhythms that are not too difficult despite many meter changes. "The Old Lute" maintains a parlando, quasi-ametrical feeling. "Depression" is extremely slow and emotionally quite moving, with the guitar playing glissando

throughout. The cycle concludes with the exuberant “Dance Song” in 7/8, which prominently features vocal portamenti.

Britten, Benjamin—see **Various Composers**

Brouwer, Leo
Dos Canciones (Doberman—DO 141)
Spanish
Medium voice (A♭3–F5/A4–C5)
Medium difficult
Group of two songs (5')
Poema
Madrigalillo
These tonal songs feature long vocal lines with disjunct melodic motion. Wide intervals, such as sixths, sevenths, and ninths, are common. The rhythms are not complicated, even in “Poema,” with its many meter changes. The texts, by the composer, have a folk-like simplicity. The two songs contrast greatly in tempo: the first is *tranquillo*; the second is *vivace*. Performance recommendations for both singer and guitarist are provided for “Poema.” English and French poetic translations are included. The varied guitar part is active yet technically accessible.

Campolieti, Cecilia Seghizzi
Gabbiani (Pizzicato—P. 131 E.)
Italian
Medium voice (D4–E5/E4–C♯5)
Medium difficult
The text was taken from the poetry collection *La specchio*, written by Vincenzo Cardarelli. The vocal melodies are chromatic, with contrasting sections of disjunct, speech-like rhythms and long, lyrical phrases. The song often uses melodic and rhythmic motives that shift back and forth between the voice and guitar. It concludes with a very long, sustained vocal C♯5 over a repeated sixteenth-note guitar pattern. The instrumental part is varied yet not complicated.

Carfagna, Carlos
Aipnos (Bèrben—E. 3828 B.)
Italian

Soprano (C4–A5/A♭4–F♯5)
Difficult
Inspired by an ancient Oriental poem, the text, subtitled "insonnia" (insomnia), was written by the composer. The song is atonal, with contrasting sections distinguished by changing tempi, ametricality, and speaking, all of which provide an ethereal ambience. The vocal lines are chromatic yet not too disjunct, and pitches are often doubled by the guitar. Rhythms for both performers are uncomplicated. The guitar part contains several technically challenging phrases but otherwise is quite accessible.

Castelnuovo-Tedesco, Mario
Ballata Dall'Esilio (Bèrben—E. 2252 B.)
Italian
Medium voice (A3–F5/D4–D5)
Medium difficult
The late thirteenth-century Italian poet Guido Cavalcanti wrote the text. This virtually diatonic song features many long, lyric vocal phrases. The slow tempo and minor key help to lend the work a brooding, plaintive quality. Notable contrasts in dynamics are required, especially for the singer. The mostly chordal guitar part is accompanimental in design.

Castelnuovo-Tedesco, Mario
The Divan of Moses-Ibn-Ezra (Bèrben—E. 1713 B.)
English (German—see below)
High voice (B3–A3/E4–F5)
Difficult
Cycle of nineteen songs
Part I—Songs of Wandering
When the morning of life had passed . . .
The dove that nests in the tree-top . . .
Wrung with anguish . . .
Part II—Songs of Friendship
Sorrow shatters my heart . . .
Fate has blocked the way . . .
O brook . . .

Part III—Of Wine, and of the Delights of the Sons of Men
Drink deep, my friend . . .
Dull and sad is the sky . . .
The garden dons a coat of many hues . . .
Part IV—The World and Its Vicissitudes
Men and children of this world . . .
The world is like a woman of folly . . .
Only in God I trust . . .
Part V—The Transience of This World
Where are the graves . . .
Let man remember all his days . . .
I have seen upon the earth . . .
Come now, to the Court of Death . . .
Peace upon them . . .
I behold ancient graves . . .
Epilogue
Wouldst thou look upon me in my grave? . . .
Moses-Ibn-Ezra (1055–1135), whose texts are featured exclusively in this major work, was a prominent Sephardic poet/philosopher. While widely varied in musical styles and expression, the songs are mostly diatonic with conventional rhythms. The guitar part is largely accompanimental yet quite rich and often challenging. A German version of this cycle is also available from the publisher as *Der Diwan des Moses-Ibn-Ezra* (E. 3276 B.).

Castelnuovo-Tedesco, Mario
Vogelweide (Bèrben—E. 2639 B.)
German
Baritone (A2–G4/G3–F4)
Difficult
Cycle of ten songs (30')
Schlimme Zeiten
Magdeburger Weihnacht
Die römische Opfersteuer
Gott unergründlich
Unnatur
Reimar, der Mensch und der Künstler

Presislied
Wahre Liebe
Der Traum
Unter der Linde
This cycle was written for Dietrich Fischer-Dieskau and Siegfried Behrend. The texts are taken from the poetry of German minnesinger Walther von der Vogelweide (c. 1170–c. 1230), one of the most famous poet-musicians of his time. The original Old German words are printed in each song along with the modern equivalent. The work features uncomplicated, often repetitive melodies that, like the guitar part, are mostly diatonic. A baritone voice with a secure G4 and the ability to easily sing lyric phrases that consistently lie within the range of C4–F4 is required. However, the importance of many of the lower-pitched phrases would make a tenor voice inappropriate. The guitar part is often chordal yet features several contrasting, difficult sections. An alternative piano accompaniment is also provided; it is essentially a note-for-note transcription of the guitar music. Given the notable differences required in writing well for both instruments, the piano version is not recommended.

Copland, Aaron—see **Various Composers**

Cordero, Ernesto
4 Works for Voice & Guitar (Chanterelle—ECH 708)
Spanish
High voice (D4–G5/E4–E5)
Medium difficult
Collection of four songs
Zenobia
La hija del viejo Pancho
Cadencia
El viaje definitivo
These diverse songs possess a distinct Spanish folk flavor. The fragmentation and tempo fluctuations in "Zenobia" lend the song an improvisatory air. "La hija del viejo Pancho" and "El viaje definitivo" are quite rhythmic and contain repeated vocal syncopations; those in the latter are more challenging. In addition, "El viaje definitivo" begins with an

ametrical solo voice passage and concludes with rapid melismas. "Cadencia" is slow and gentle, with lyrical vocal lines. The guitar part can be demanding at times and has many notable solos.

Davies, Peter Maxwell
Dark Angels (Boosey—B.&H.20296)
English
Mezzo-soprano (E♭3-B♭5/B♭3-F5)
Very difficult
Cycle of three songs (12')
The Drowning Brothers
Dark Angels (guitar solo)
Dead Fires
The piece features somber, morbid texts from George Mackay Brown's poem-cycle *Fishermen with Ploughs*. The work is atonal with much dissonance. The melodies are chromatic and highly disjunct, with many very wide intervals. The vocal rhythms are not difficult, despite the work's quasi-metricality. The guitar part is quite challenging and features some nontraditional performance techniques.

Donatoni, Franco
Ase (Zerboni—S. 10025 Z.)
Language—see description
Soprano (C4–C6/F4–A5)
Very difficult
This ten-minute piece is atonal and ametrical, with chromatic and highly disjunct guitar phrases that are fragmented and rhythmically intricate. The voice is featured quite sparingly, first consisting of isolated glissandi on phonetic sounds and later sustained tones on parts of the word "magnus."

Duarte, John W.
Five Quiet Songs (Bèrben—E. 1520 B.)
English (German—see below)
High voice (C4–G5/E4–F5)
Difficult
Group of five songs (12')

Dirge in Woods
Silence
An Epitaph
Omar's Lament
The Birds
This work, with texts by different authors, was written for Peter Pears and Julian Bream. The songs are tonal with many disjunct melodies. They vary in terms of chromaticism; the first two songs are most so. "Silence," written in a quasi-speech style, is often ametrical. The moods and themes vary within an overall air of introspection. The final song, "The Birds," deals with Christianity. The guitar parts are largely accompanimental. A German version of this work is also available from the publisher as *Fünf stille Lieder* (E. 3326 B.).

Duarte, John W.
Friends and Lovers (Columbia—CO 319)
English
High voice (A♯3–G5/E4–E5)
Difficult
Cycle of five songs (12')
When First We Met
Just Friends
A Complaint
Sing Agreeably of Love
Driver, Drive Faster
The texts, by various authors, deal with friendship and love. The cycle is tonal with moderate chromaticism and features much disjunct melodic motion. The rhythms within each song tend to be repetitive and simple. There is ample variety in terms of moods and musical settings. The lighthearted "Driver, Drive Faster" is best performed by a woman. The guitar part is not difficult.

Duarte, John W.
Hark, Hark, the Ark! (Columbia—CO 320)
English
High or medium voice (B♭3–F♯5/E4–E5)
Medium difficult

Cycle of six songs (10')
Tiger, Tiger Burning Etc.
The Lion
The Swans
Ant and Eleph-ant
The Flea
Silly Old Baboon
The texts for these short, lighthearted songs were taken from Spike Milligan's *Milliganimals* and *Silly Verse for Kids*. They are mostly diatonic with uncomplicated rhythms, and there is much contrast in tempi and musical settings. In addition to the amusing words, there are musical references to famous melodies, some quite obvious. In "The Flea," the singer surprises the audience at the song's end by yelling "OW!" and then scratching, with the guitarist doing likewise on the strings. In the concluding song, "Silly Old Baboon," there is a key reference at the end to a town in England—this could easily be changed to any other town name for some topical humor. The brevity and simple wit of the cycle (as well as its unstrenuous vocal demands) make it an ideal closing set for a concert. It also would be a superb choice in a performance for children.

Dvorák, Charles
The Bones of the Greeks (Orphée—DTMO-3)
English
Soprano (A♯3–A5/B3–G5)
Difficult
Cycle of three songs (15')
I Longed for Winds
Interlude (solo guitar)
The Passionate Bones
The texts are taken from an anthology of postwar Greek poetry, *Resistance, Exile, and Love*. Based on Greek modes, the cycle features chromatic, often disjunct melodies, with many lengthy phrases requiring good breath control. There are frequent dissonances between the voice and the challenging guitar part, which has substantial solo passages and an optional improvised modal cadenza.

Einem, Gottfried von
Liderliche Lieder (Universal—UE 17840)
German
Medium voice (C♯4–E5/E4–C5)
Difficult
Cycle of three songs (12')
Der Fetischist
Der Transvestit
Der Sodomit
The composer has set texts not normally associated with art song; Lotte Ingrisch's poetry centers on deviant sexual behavior. The music is frequently diatonic, but with some difficult chromatic sections. The melodic phrases contain many repeated pitch sequences. The rhythms are generally not complex despite changing meters, save for brief sections in "Der Transvestit" where the parts alternate in overlapping duple and triple meter. Although thinly textured, the guitar part is demanding due to many rapid passages.

Falla, Manuel de
Siete Canciones populares Españolas (Eschig—Nos. 1501–1507)
Spanish (French)
High or medium voice (D4–F5/F♯4–D5)
Medium difficult
Group of seven songs (12')
El Paño Moruno
Seguidilla Murciana
Asturiana
Jota
Nana
Canción
Polo
Best known in their original edition for voice and piano, these songs, as arranged by Miguel Llobet and Emilio Pujol, reveal how well suited the accompaniments are for classical guitar. The vocal melodies are not complicated, but they often feature ornamental patterns indigenous to the Spanish folk song style that may prove challenging to inexperienced singers. The final song, "Polo," demands a great deal of emotional

intensity from both performers. The richly varied guitar part is often demanding and very expressive. Each song must be purchased individually.

Farkas, Ferenc
Cinque Canzoni dei Trovatori (Bèrben—E. 1512 B.)
French
Medium voice (C♯4–E5/D4–E5)
Medium difficult
Cycle of five songs (7')
These short songs are not titled but numbered. The composer has set medieval *trouvère* melodies to original accompaniments that reinforce the simple directness of the vocal part. The second piece contains some demanding vocal ornaments and rapid melismas; the remaining songs are not difficult. Inexperienced singers may at first encounter some challenges with the songs' modality. The guitar part is varied and accessible to most players.

Frandsen, John
Seven Silly Songs (Reimers—ER 101145)
English
Mezzo-soprano (F♯3–F♭5/B3–E5)
Difficult
Group of seven songs (12')
Drinking Song
Gypsies in the Wood
The Turtle-Dove
Wishful Thinking
My Apple Tree
All the Pretty Little Horses
Promenade
The texts were taken from anonymous sources. The songs are tonal with much chromaticism; the vocal lines often are disjunct yet lyrical. Meter changes are common, especially in the fourth, sixth, and seventh songs; "All the Pretty Little Horses" changes virtually every measure, in diverse meters including 1/4, 2/4, 3/4, 3/8, 5/8, 3/16, 5/16, 6/16, and 7/16. "My Apple Tree" is extremely short (20"). The texts' humor is reinforced

through varied musical settings and effects such as glissandi, whispering, and *senza vibrato*. The guitar part is demanding and significant, often working independently of the voice.

Fricker, Peter Racine
O Mistress Mine (Schott—GA 210)
English
Tenor (C3–G4/G3–G4)
Medium difficult
Set to the famous text by William Shakespeare, this short song in *andante semplice* features diatonic yet markedly disjunct melodies, with many leaps of fourths and fifths. The rhythms are quite simple, consisting solely of eighth and quarter notes. The guitar part is lute-like, with many lightly textured chords.

Greeson, James
Three Poems by Stephen Crane (Willis—WMCo. 10824)
English
High voice (D4–A5/E4–E5)
Medium difficult
Group of three songs (7')
There Was Set Before Me a Mighty Hill
I Saw Man Pursuing
Ay, Workman
The first and last songs are diatonic and rhythmically uncomplicated, with simple, repetitive guitar accompaniments. The second song is the most demanding; it alternates between rapid sixteenth-note guitar phrases of varying length and short vocal passages that are disjunct and chromatic.

Guastavino, Carlos
Pueblito, Mi Pueblo . . . (Ricordi S.A.—BA 12443)
Spanish
Medium voice (D4–C♯5/D4–A4)
Easy

"Pueblito, Mi Pueblo . . ." is a short, Spanish folk-style song in an *andante nostálgico* setting. It consists of short rhythmic/melodic motives in both voice and guitar that are simple and repetitive.

Guastavino, Carlos
Severa Villifañe (Ricordi S.A.—BAl2444)
Spanish
High or medium voice (C4–E5/D4–D5)
Easy
With text by Leon Benaros, this is a strophic song in Spanish folk style. It features lively rhythms in an allegretto 6/8 with several syncopations in both parts that are not difficult. The long vocal phrases consist of varied yet accessible melodic motion. The guitar part features a prominent solo introduction; afterward it is mostly chordal and occasionally doubles the voice.

Hiller, Lejaren Arthur
Five Appalachian Ballads (Waterloo—WCG-310)
English
High or medium voice (B♭3–F5/D4–E5)
Difficult
Cycle of five songs (12')
Lord Randal
Barbara Allen
The Three Ravens
The Cruel Mother
The Two Sisters
This cycle was written for guitarist Thomas Binkley, who gave its premiere with singer Jantina Noorman at the Festival of Contemporary Arts at the University of Illinois in 1959. The composer has coupled the original Appalachian folk melodies with new accompaniments that are atonal and quite prominent. However, the guitar music does not pose any significant technical challenges.

Kutzer, Ernst
Drei Lieder (Preissler—JP 70210)
German

Medium voice (B3–E5/E4–D5)
Medium difficult
Group of three songs (7')
Anruf aus Neandertal
Schneckenparabel
Guter Rat
The satirical texts are by Otto Molz. The songs are diatonic with simple melodic motion and uncomplicated, repetitive rhythms in varied tempi. The largely accessible guitar part is mostly chordal and accompanimental in design.

Kutzer, Ernst
Fünf Lieder, Op. 93 (Preissler—JP 70211)
German
Medium voice (G3–E5/C4–E5)
Medium difficult
Group of five songs (10')
Meine Haut atmet Herbst
Vision
Mauern hat man um mich gestellt
Und schön dieses Mädchen
Herr, die Henker
This set is not to be confused with the composer's *Fünf Lieder, Op. 73*. Peter Coryllis is the author of the texts. These short songs are tonal with some degree of chromaticism and feature often disjunct yet accessible melodic phrases with simple rhythms. As a group, the pieces are varied in mood and tempo. The active and substantial guitar part is prominent and of moderate difficulty.

Kutzer, Ernst
Six Songs (Preissler—JP 70212)
German
Medium voice (A3–E5/C4–D5)
Medium difficult
Group of six songs (12')
Der ans Denken denkt
Verliebtes Regenlied

Ein fremdes Kind am Meer
Ich bin leicht
In mir bist Du
Leber schwänzen
Featuring texts by six different authors, these mostly diatonic songs consist of varied but uncomplicated melodies and repetitive rhythm patterns. They are somewhat varied in mood and style; perhaps most different is "Verliebtes Regenlied," with its simple folk-like melodic/harmonic design and strophic form. The accessible guitar part is essentially accompanimental due to its mostly chordal makeup.

Leisner, David
Outdoor Shadows (Merion—141 40018)
English
High voice (D4–B5/E4–F5)
Difficult
Cycle of five songs (12')
Slow
Homeward
Yes, What?
Seagulls
Sing a Song of Juniper
The texts are by Robert Francis. The cycle is primarily diatonic, with much stepwise motion in the vocal melodies. Most of the songs require strong, sustained high notes (G5–B5). "Slow" and "Homeward" feature long vocal lines, while the later songs are more fragmented and rhythmically challenging. Meter changes are virtually constant in "Seagulls," lending a feeling of ametricality, and "Sing a Song of Juniper" is in 7/4, with some unusual rhythmic subdivisions. The guitar settings are quite diverse and demanding.

Leisner, David
Simple Songs (AMP—79003)
English
High or medium voice (B3–G♭5/E4–E5)
Difficult
Cycle of six songs (10')

Exultation
Beauty
Madness
Letter
Humility
Simplicity
The texts of these short songs were taken from the poetry of Emily Dickinson. The musical and technical demands vary widely for both performers. "Exultation" and "Beauty" would be accessible to most singers, while "Madness" is more difficult, with its many leaps of sevenths and ninths. The lighthearted "Letter" features intricate speech-like rhythms over a percussive guitar, and "Simplicity" is virtually a cappella.

Lendle, Wolfgang
Cinco Canciones Populares Ecuatorianas (Margaux—em 5102)
Spanish
Mezzo-soprano (A3–G♯5/D4–F5)
Medium difficult
Group of five songs (12')
Duerme mi hijita
Niño lindo
Pajarito que cantas
Duermase mi Niño
Dicen que son flores
The words and vocal melodies are from traditional songs of Ecuador. As such, they are diatonic with varied yet simple melodic design. There are some distinctive features, however, as in the mostly 5/8 meter mixed with 3⁄4 and 6/8 in "Pajarito que cantas" and a quasi-recitative section in "Duermase mi Niño." The last song, "Dicen que son flores," concludes with a very long forte G5. The accompanimental guitar part is repetitive and uncomplicated.

Liani, Davide
Cjantis (Zanibon—G. 6043 Z.)
Friulian (Italian)
High or medium voice (D4–F♯4/F♯4–D5)
Medium difficult

Group of three songs (6')
Cjantute de Mari
Tal Clara di Luna
Cûr di Avrîl
Friulian is a dialect mixture of Northern Italian and Yugoslavian. These songs, with texts by various authors, have been transcribed for voice and guitar by Gianni Tombolato. They are diatonic with folk-like repetitive vocal phrases. The first two songs feature changing meters; "Cjantute de Mari" has sections of 7/8. The guitar part is quite accessible, consisting largely of chords.

Lilburn, Douglas
Sings Harry (Waiteata—1991 #44)
English
Tenor (D3–A4/E3–E4)
Medium difficult
Cycle of six songs (11')
Each song is untitled. Dennis Glover wrote the poems for this cycle, which originally was composed in 1954 for baritone and piano. Shortly after, the composer arranged it for tenor and guitar. The music is primarily diatonic with varied yet accessible melodies. Rhythm patterns change frequently but are not difficult. The text is introspective and often nostalgic, and every song ends with a phrase that includes the words "Sings Harry." The guitar part is simplistic, serving almost exclusively as background to the voice.

Maw, Nicholas
Six Interiors (Boosey—B.&H.20354)
English
High voice (G3–A♭5/E♭4–F♯5)
Very difficult
Group of six songs (18')
To Life
Neutral Tones
At Tea
In Tenebnis
I Look into My Glass

Inscriptions for a Peal of Eight Bells
The songs' texts are from poems of Thomas Hardy. The music is highly chromatic and often tonally elusive, featuring melodic motion ranging from stepwise chromaticism to leaps exceeding an octave. There are numerous meter changes and rhythmic challenges. Due to the scope of the texts, the songs' moods vary widely, aided by the expressive and complex guitar part. The lighthearted final song, "Inscriptions for a Peal of Eight Bells," features distinct musical settings for each bell portrayed. In this song, it is most effective if the singer can utilize different vocal timbres appropriate for each setting.

Mittergradnegger, Günther
Ich hab dir ein Lied gesponnen (Doblinger—GKM 173)
German
High voice (B3-A5/A4-F♯5)
Difficult
Cycle of six songs (8')
Glaube ist ein Baum
Unser Land
Die Nacht
Wenn der Mond kommt
Weit in der Ferne
Ich hab dir ein Lied gesponnen
Written for Peter Schreier and Konrad Ragossnig, these short songs are set to texts of African origin. The work is mostly diatonic, yet dissonance between the voice and guitar is not uncommon. Despite changing meters in all songs except "Glaube ist ein Baum," the rhythms are usually uncomplicated, save for "Die Nacht," which centers around 5/8 but makes frequent excursions to other eighth-note meters. Subtle changes in vocal timbre as well as spoken and declamatory styles are called for. The guitar part is quite varied and active.

Moreno, Ismael
Nunca Como Mi Querer (Ricordi S.A.—BA 12630)
Spanish
Medium or low voice (A3–C4/A3–C4)
Easy

This diatonic song is strophic with simple, somewhat disjunct melodies that are repetitive. The guitar part has an animated solo introduction, which then becomes a simple accompaniment of broken chords as soon as the singer begins.

Müller, Siegfried
Fünf Chansons (Neue—NM 354)
German
Medium voice (A3–E♭5/E4–D5)
Medium difficult
Group of five songs (10')
Russische Birk
Meine kleine Liebe
Ferien
Da steht ein Apfelbaum
Reglindis
The texts are by different authors. The vocal lines are often diatonic, with varied yet accessible melodic motion. "Meine kleine Liebe" and "Ferien" (which is quite fast) possess notable rhythmic drive; the same is true for the last half of "Reglindis," which is in 5/8. The first part of "Reglindis" is essentially an unmetered recitative. The songs are varied in both mood and tempo. The largely accompanimental guitar part has several somewhat challenging sections.

Müller-Hornbach, Gerhard
5 Gesänge der Schirin (Breitkopf—EB 9004)
Language—see description
Soprano (C♯4–B♭5/F4–G5)
Very difficult
Cycle of five songs (10')
Prefaced by a brief solo guitar *prolog*, the cycle is serialistic, featuring repetitive pitch/interval sequences. The untitled songs are ametrical, with rhythms notated mostly in approximate durations. The vocal line consists largely of repeated phonetic fragments except in the second song, which calls for humming throughout. Many detailed and unusual guitar sounds are specified.

Musgrave, Thea
Five Love Songs (Chester—JWC 454)
English
Soprano (C4–A5/E4–F♯5)
Difficult
Group of five songs (12')
These untitled songs feature texts by various sixteenth- and seventeenth-century authors. The work is tonally elusive with extensive chromaticism. Each song differs greatly in terms of technical difficulty and musical affection. The opening two songs are rhythmically intricate; the first features fragmented vocal lines, while the second contains demanding rapid melismas. Long yet disjunct vocal phrases are common in most of the pieces. The prominent guitar part is varied and quite active.

Musgrave, Thea
Sir Patrick Spens (Chester—JWC 55066)
Old English
Tenor (B♭2–A4/D3–G♯4)
Very difficult
This seven-minute song was written for Peter Pears and Julian Bream and premiered by them at the 1961 Aldeburgh Festival. Described in the score as "a ballad," it tells of a sailor who dies at sea. Set in Old English, the accurate pronunciation of many words requires research by the singer, since no information is provided in the score. The song is atonal with much disjunct melodic motion and features some intricate rhythms. The music is quite dramatic at times—a wide range of dynamics is required. The guitar part is complex and largely independent of the voice.

Nørgrd, Per
Libra (Hansen—4284 A)
Language—see description
Tenor (C♯3–D5/E3–B5)
Very difficult
This thirteen-minute *piece* consists of three movements: "Preludio," "Aria con Interludio," and "Postludio"; the outer two are for solo guitar. In the middle movement, the composer combines German text by Ru-

dolf Steiner and phonetic sounds in a setting featuring highly chromatic, disjunct melodic motives and complex rhythms. However, the slow tempo and sustained vocal phrases lend lyricism to the work. The tessitura is quite challenging; there are several long phrases that lie solely between E4 to B4 at dynamic levels of forte and louder. The singer is required to ascend to a sustained D5, which then must be sung subito piano in falsetto (an *ossia* passage a minor third lower is provided). The guitar part is quite virtuosic in its technical demands.

Nørholm, Ib
Blomster fra den Danske Posis Flora (Engstrøm—E&S 562)
Danish
High voice (B3–G5/E4–E5)
Easy to difficult
Group of eight songs (15')
Ud of en vinter
Åen
Salme
Genesis
Opvågnen
Juniakvarel
Løvsanger
Pusterum
All of the songs are strophic; many of them are rather brief. Due to varying degrees of tonality, dissonance, melodic motion, and meter changes, the songs have a wide range of difficulty levels for the singer, from the straightforward "Opvågnen" to the very chromatic and disjunct "Pusterum." Slow tempi and terse vocal rhythms predominate throughout the entire group. Like the voice part, the often harmonically interesting guitar varies in technical demands: "Opvågnen" is rather simple, while "Løvsanger" contains intricate, unusual rhythms.

Nørholm, Ib
Tavole per Orfeo (Hansen—WH 29139)
Danish (English)
Mezzo-soprano (A3–G♯5/B3–E♭5)
Very difficult

Cycle of six pieces (22')
I—Eurydike kalder
II—For Guitar
III—Eurydike spotter klippernes dans til Orfeus'sang
IV—For Guitar
V—Eutrydikes blod
VI—For Guitar
As indicated by the titles, this cycle consists of three songs alternated with three guitar solos. Paul Borum supplied the Danish text as well as its English singing translation. The work is atonal; the two outer vocal pieces feature chromatic, disjunct lyricism. The first song also utilizes frequent changes of unusual meters. The middle song, "Eurydike spotter klippernes dans til Orfeus'sang," is markedly different from the other movements in its virtually exclusive use of nontraditional performance techniques, especially for the singer. Also notable is the song's use of unconventional instruments (glass chimes and thundersheet, to be played by the singer as she sings), as well as a cigarette and balloon. The guitarist is expected to light and puff on the cigarette in mid-song (between playing notes), then suddenly burst a balloon with it at the song's conclusion (the balloon is to be attached to the guitar at the beginning of the song). The guitar music in the other five movements is substantive and demanding.

Orrego-Salas, Juan
Canciones en el Estilo Popular (MMB—X815001)
Spanish
High voice (C4–A5/A4–A5)
Difficult
Group of three songs (9')
Al Aire
A la Cebolla
Al Pan
The texts were taken from Pablo Neruda's *Odes Elementales*. These strophic songs of Spanish character feature much stepwise melodic motion and simple rhythms. The challenges lie in the voice's very high tessitura and its many dissonances with the accompaniment. The guitar part is active yet accessible, featuring chromatic, colorful harmonies.

Pinkham, Daniel
Antiphons (Ione Press—ECS 4169)
Latin
Medium voice (B3–F♯5/E4–E5)
Difficult
Cycle of seven songs (7'30")
These short, untitled songs are contemporary settings of medieval chant texts from *Liber Responsalis,* attributed to St. Gregory the Great (c. 540–604). The music is atonal, with much dissonance between the voice and guitar. However, the vocal lines contain only a few challenging passages despite extensive chromaticism. There are frequent meter changes and constantly varied, often asymmetrical rhythms. The guitar part is texturally quite sparse—it is primarily melodic, with few chords. A separate part for harp, in lieu of the guitar, is available from the publisher.

Pinkham, Daniel
Charm Me Asleep (Ione Press—ECS 169)
English
Medium voice (A3–F♯5/C4–E5)
Difficult
Cycle of ten songs (19')
Prelude (guitar solo)
To Music, to becalm his Fever
In Commendation of Music
Say that I should say
Absence
Chloris in the Snow
Upon a rare voice
A Report Song in a Dream, between a Shepherd and his Nymph
Man, dream no more
The Conclusion
This work features texts by nine Old English authors. The cycle is tonal yet frequently chromatic, with vocal lines of accessible and varied melodic motion. Four of the songs are somewhat strophic; the guitar accompaniment is repeated over slightly varied vocal melodies. The rhythms are uncomplicated, except in "Upon a rare voice" and "A

Report Song in a Dream," which contain some moderate challenges. The moods and musical settings are rather diverse, aided greatly by a stimulating guitar part that is not too difficult.

Pinkham, Daniel
Man, that is born of a woman (ECS—ECS 143)
English
Mezzo-soprano (F♯3–F5/A♭3–D5)
Very difficult
Cycle of three songs (8')
The texts to these untitled songs come from the Book of Common Prayer. The work is distinctive in that the guitar may be classical or electric. The music is atonal with much disjunct melodic motion (especially in the first song); many intervals exceed an octave. The tempo is generally slow with uncomplicated rhythms amid numerous meter changes. The guitar part is quite sparse, consisting mostly of single pitches, many of which are sustained. Nevertheless, the relationship between the voice and the guitar is primarily dissonant.

Rasmussen, Karl Aage
When I Was Happy I Wrote No Songs (Hansen—WH 29388)
Swedish (English)
Baritone (F2–F♯4/B♭2–D4)
Very difficult
The colorful, descriptive text was derived from anonymous gypsy songs and translated into Swedish by Katarina Taikon (the quite apt English version was written by John Bergsagel). Although described as "seven lyrical improvisations," this fourteen-minute piece has no cadences or pauses. Any sense of sectionalism is determined by changes in tempo and mood corresponding to new poetry. The work is unusual in that, in the composer's words, it "is best realized when the singer and instrumentalist are one and the same person," yet "the work is also suitable for performance by two persons." The music is atonal and ametrical, utilizing many unconventional performance techniques such as speaking, glissando, whispering, and relative pitch levels. The difficult guitar part often is fragmented.

Robinovitch, Sid
Canciones Sefardies (CMC—MV 1102 R656ca)
Sephardic
Medium voice (B♭3–G5/D4–E5)
Very difficult
Cycle of five songs (15')
Ir me quero la mi madre
Una muchacha en Selanica
El rey que muncho madruga
Rucu quere cama a la franca
Tres hermanicas eran
The songs are based on folk texts of the Sephardic Jews of Turkey, featuring a distinctive Judeo-Spanish dialect. Modern Spanish serves as a basis for the language, and a concise pronunciation guide is included. The music has a strong Spanish flavor, with colorful, often dissonant harmonies, and is quite varied in mood and musical setting. The first song contains rapid, highly demanding vocal phrases. There are frequent meter changes in most of the songs, especially in "Rucu quere cama a la franca," where alternations between 2/4, 3/8, 3/4, 4/4, 5/8, 7/8, and 9/8 take place virtually every measure. The third song, "El rey que muncho madruga," and the beginning of the fifth, "Tres hermanicas eran," are unmetered.

Rodrigo, Joaquín
Aranjuez, ma Pensée (Rodrigo—EJR 1784)
French
High or medium voice (B3–G5/B3–D5)
Difficult
With text by Victoria Kahmi, this song was adapted by Rodrigo from the popular "Adagio" of his *Concierto de Aranjuez* for guitar and orchestra. The vocal part consists of very long phrases of intricate rhythms that imitate the guitar melodies of the original piece. Thus, breath control and phrasing are key challenges in performance, as well as the accurate and legato rendering of the words. The guitar part is primarily chordal until its extended solo near the end of the piece.

Rodrigo, Joaquín
Coplas del Pastor enamorado (Schott— ED 7603)
Spanish
Soprano (B3–F♯5/E4–E5)
Medium difficult
This tranquil song, with text by Lope de Vega, incorporates many elements of Spanish folk style. It begins with a sparse, repetitive guitar solo, followed by several simple yet expressive unaccompanied vocal phrases. The voice and guitar then merge; long vocal melodies over active accompaniment alternate with quick speech-like phrases sung over sustained chords. Rapid vocal ornamentations are featured, and the guitar has a prominent accompanimental section of repeated thirty-second high notes over a low, ostinato-like eighth-note pattern. A German poetic translation is provided.

Rodrigo, Joaquín
Folias Canarias (Song from the Canary Islands) (Schott—ED 10600)
Spanish (English)
High or medium voice (A4–E5/A4–D5)
Easy
The song features brief, repetitive legato vocal phrases in an *andante* setting. Quick melodic turns in both parts as well as several short flamenco-like sections for the guitar help to lend a Spanish flavor. The guitar accompaniment, after a notable solo introduction, consists primarily of several motives that are repeated throughout the remainder of the work.

Rodrigo, Joaquín
Romance de Durandarte (Rodrigo—EJR 190174)
Spanish
High or medium voice (E4–F5/E4–E5)
Medium difficult
The song is diatonic with mostly stepwise melodic motion and simple, repeated rhythms. Set to a graceful *andante moderato* tempo, the very lyric vocal line incorporates elements of Spanish style such as numerous rapid melodic turns. The guitar part consists of a simple melodic motive that is periodically played over an E3 rhythm pattern.

Rodrigo, Joaquin
Three Spanish Songs (Schott—ED 10601)
Spanish (English)
High or medium voice (C♯4–E5/F♯4–D♯5)
Medium difficult
Group of three songs (6')
En Jerez de la Frontera
Adela
De ronda
This set would provide inexperienced singers with an excellent introduction to Spanish folk song. They are simple and strophic—the only challenge to the singer might be the brief yet rapid ornamental figures in the first and last songs. The guitar part is repetitive and technically quite accessible.

Ruiz-Pipó, Antonio
Cantos a la Noche (Bèrben—E. 1519 B.)
Spanish
High voice (B♭3–G♯5/F♯4–E5)
Very difficult
The text was written by the composer. The song is approximately eight minutes long and is atonal and mostly ametrical. The vocal part consists largely of short, detached phrases that are not difficult by themselves but are independent of and dissonant to the guitar. A wide dynamic range is required, and the music is quite dramatic at times. The guitar part is very expressive and demanding.

Rutter, John
Shadows (Oxford—ISBN 0-19-345756-3)
English
Baritone (A2–E4/D3–D4)
Difficult
Cycle of eight songs (23')
Shadows
Gather ye rosebuds
Sonnet
The epicure

Sic vita
O Death, rock me asleep
In a goodly night
Close thine eyes
The texts are by various sixteenth- and seventeenth-century authors, and the music displays many rhythmic and melodic qualities of the secular music of that period. The most challenging aspect is the frequent meter changes in songs such as "Gather ye rosebuds" and "In a goodly night." Several of the songs—"The epicure" and "Sic vita"—are almost strophic and rather straightforward in design. The cycle is quite varied in terms of tempi and musical settings. The guitar is generally not difficult and tends to be texturally lean, serving largely as an accompaniment to the voice.

Sanchez, Bias
Al Pie de la Cruz del Roque (Eschig—ME 7559)
Spanish (French)
High voice (G♯4–F5/A4–E5)
Easy
This short strophic song of four verses is diatonic with stepwise melodies and very basic rhythms. It is folk-like in its construct and textual content. The guitar accompaniment is active yet accessible, consisting mostly of eighth-note patterns at a lively tempo. A suitable accompaniment for piano is also included.

Sanchez, Bias
Arroro (Eschig—ME 7558)
Spanish
High voice (A3–G5/E4–D5)
Medium difficult
The song is mostly diatonic with uncomplicated melodic motion and rhythms. The song is very tranquil, yet the work is sectionalized by slight changes of tempo in which variations of the melody and accompaniment are featured. There is a brief section of humming in the middle. The active and varied guitar part is largely accompanimental in design. A French poetic translation is included.

Sanchez, Bias
Atardecer en Canarias (Choudens—A.C. 20.627)
Spanish
High voice (D4–G5/F♯4–E5)
Medium difficult
This brief *andantino* song begins softly and then gradually builds in intensity. After reaching its climax, the music quickly subsides, concluding as softly as it began. The accessible melodies feature repetitive rhythms that nevertheless contain subtle yet significant variations. Several rapid vocal turns befit the work's distinctive Spanish flavor. The guitar part is strictly accompanimental yet features some challenging rapid passages.

Sanchez, Bias
Ag, Barquita (Choudens—A.C. 20.268)
Spanish
High voice (D4–A5/D4–F5)
Difficult
This very fast and lively Spanish song contains lengthy vocal phrases with many wide melodic leaps. The piece concludes with a long, forte "Ay!" on A5. The largely accompanimental guitar part has an attractive yet brief solo in the middle of the song.

Sanchez, Bias
Ingenio (Eschig—ME 7556)
Spanish
High voice (D4–G♯5/F♯4–E5)
Medium difficult
The song is diatonic, with uncomplicated melodies and rhythms. It is divided into numerous short sections—most of which are repeated—distinguished by differing key, meter, tempo, melody, and guitar accompaniment. In the repeat of one section, the singer is required to hum for the entire phrase. Another section features many grace note ornamentations. The active and varied guitar part is primarily accompanimental.

Sanchez, Bias
Nananita Nana (Choudens—A.C. 20.266)
Spanish

Medium voice (B3–F♯5/A4–E5)
Medium difficult
This song is a lullaby, with long, legato melodic phrases. The vocal pitches, while largely consonant to the guitar's distinctive chordal outlines, are often not doubled in its part. The accompaniment consists solely of repeated thirty-second-note broken chord patterns in an *andantino* tempo.

Sanchez, Bias
Paisaje (Choudens—A.C. 20.265)
Spanish
Medium voice (D4–F♯5/D4–D5)
Medium difficult
This simply constructed song features diatonic melodies with straightforward rhythms in an *andante con moto* setting. The last fourteen measures are quasi-recitative, with tremolo guitar chords. Prior to that, the accompaniment consists mostly of Alberti bass-like patterns.

Santórsola, Guido
Cinco Canciones (Bèrben—E. 2406 B.)
Spanish
High voice (B3–B5/C♯4–G5)
Difficult
Group of five songs (12')
Mañana
¡Tú, Señor!
A Una Niña
Luna Triste
Tormenta de Nieve
With texts by Jesús Silva, these tonal yet extensively chromatic songs feature many detached vocal phrases consisting of repeated pitches with detailed rhythms, yielding a speech-like effect often requiring great dramatic intensity. The third song, "A Una Niña," is the most vocally "melodic." The very demanding guitar is usually much more prominent than the voice and often gives little accompanimental support.

Schmidt, Eberhard

Die Blätter an meinem Kalender (Neue—NM 415)
German
Medium voice (C4–E5/E4–E5)
Medium difficult
Cycle of nine songs (15')
Die Blätter an meinem Kalender
Die Wildgänse
Kalenderblätter
Der Sommer
Wiese, grüne Wiese
Kalenderblätter
Trip, trip, trop
Der Winter
Kalenderblätter

These nine short songs (texts from Peter Hacks's *Der Flohmarkt*) are interspersed with seven solo guitar interludes, entitled respectively "Zwischenspiel A," "Zwischenspiel B," and so forth. The third, sixth, and ninth songs are elaborations of the first. Often lighthearted, they feature varied melodies with uncomplicated rhythms. The guitar part plays a substantial role and is challenging at times.

Sealey, Ray

A Circle of Tears (Waterloo—WCG-31 3)
Latin
High voice (C♯4–A5/F♯4–G5)
Medium difficult
Cycle of seven songs (9')

Betsey Barker Price wrote the text for these short untitled songs. This cycle would be an accessible choice for those interested but inexperienced in contemporary nontraditional performance techniques. The work is mostly diatonic with accessible rhythms and stepwise melodies. Varied in tempo and mood, many of the songs utilize brief instances of humming, *parlando*, glissando, and optional wind chimes, none of which pose technical hardships. The guitar part requires some improvisation and unusual sounds such as string squeaks and tapping. Poetic translations in English and French are given.

Seiber, Mátyás
Four French Folk Soros (Schott—ED 10637)
French
High or medium voice (E4–E5/E4–E5)
Medium difficult
Group of four songs (10')
Réveillez-vous
J'ai descendu
Le Rossignol
Marguerite, elle est malade
At the behest of Peter Pears and Julian Bream, the composer took French folk melodies and provided new accompaniments that nonetheless preserve each song's traditional flavor. They are varied in mood and tempo, concluding with a fast and humorous song ("Marguerite, elle est malade"). The group's attractive melodies and overall "lightness" would make it an effective closing set in a concert. The active and expressive guitar accompaniment is somewhat challenging in several brief passages. Although edited by Bream himself, he later modified the guitar part for his own performances, as is evident in his recording with Peter Pears[14]; guitarists may wish to refer to it for suggestions.

Seiber, Mátyás—see **Various Composers**

Smith, Larry Alan
An Infant Crying . . . (Merion—141-40017)
English
High voice (D4–E5/E4–F♯5)
Difficult
Cycle of three songs (22')
Dover Beach
Come Up from the Fields Father
Oh Yet We Trust
The texts were written by three well-known nineteenth-century poets: Matthew Arnold, Walt Whitman, and Alfred Tennyson. The generally accessible vocal phrases are sung over often dissonant guitar lines that are nevertheless tonal. The musical settings are diverse and expressive, befitting the somber and contemplative poetry. "Come Up from the

Fields Father" contains a brief narrative passage. The guitar music is substantial and rather varied.

Strindberg, Henrik
Det första kvädet om Gudrun (Reimers—ER 101144)
Swedish
Mezzo-soprano (A3–A5/A3–C5)
Difficult
Roughly nineteen minutes long, this work features a twenty-five-stanza poem by Björn Collinder. It is mostly diatonic, yet its key signature contains only F♯ and G♯. The song opens with an optional four-minute recitation of the poem's first ten stanzas, many of which are separated by a fermata or single guitar chord. The music that ensues consists of long, generally accessible lyric phrases for the voice. The diverse guitar part, which calls for unusual tunings, is rather active and much more technically demanding than the voice.

Stucky, Rodney
Five Spirituals (Southern—V-98)
English
High or medium voice (A3–G♯5/E4–E5)
Medium difficult
Group of five songs (11')
Little David, Play on Your Harp
Give Me Jesus
Couldn't Hear Nobody Pray
Deep River
Hard Trials
These well-known spiritual melodies have been arranged with new accompaniments utilizing some colorful harmonies in a firmly tonal setting. Although the score states the voice type should be mezzo-soprano, the songs are appropriate for any voice comfortable with the tessitura. "Give Me Jesus" and "Couldn't Hear Nobody Pray" are a bit lower than the others and would be less suitable for high voices. The guitar part is technically accessible, with varied settings that help set the appropriate mood for each song.

Thomson, Virgil
What Is It? (Presser—111-40091)
English
High voice (E4–E5/G4–E5)
Medium difficult
Noted late Renaissance composer Thomas Campion wrote the text. The song is mostly diatonic with accessible yet varied vocal melodies in an andante 6/8 setting. The guitar part, based on conventional harmonies, is equally prominent due to its active, virtually nonstop accompaniment and can be challenging at times.

Tippett, Michael
Songs for Achilles (Schott—ED 10874)
English (German)
Tenor (C♯3–B♭4/G3–G4)
Difficult
Cycle of three songs (12')
In the Tent
Across the Plain
By the Sea
This atonal cycle requires great musical assertiveness from both performers. "In the Tent" is an *adagio* (quarter note = 48), with frequently changing simple meters. In this setting, the vocal part features very long, often sustained lines that must be dramatically rendered, while the guitar part consists largely of thirty-second notes. "Across the Plain" is more varied for both performers yet remains intense throughout due to its *allegro vivace* tempo and many brief, separated musical phrases. "By the Sea" has substantial guitar solos at the beginning and end and a recitative-like vocal section in the middle.

Various Composers (Benjamin Britten, Aaron Copland, Mátyás Seiber)
Twelve Folk Song Arrangements (Boosey—Boosey 6553)
English
High, medium, or low voice (A3–F♯5/D4–E5)
Medium difficult
Collection of twelve songs

The Foggy, Foggy Dew (arr. Benjamin Britten)
The Sally Gardens (Britten)
O Waly, Waly (Britten)
The Lincolnshire Poacher (Britten)
Four Greek Folk Songs (arr. Mátyás Seiber)
O my love, how long
Have pity on me
Each time, my love, you say farewell
O your eyes are dark and beautiful
I Bought Me a Cat (arr. Aaron Copland)
At the River (Copland)
Simple Gifts (Copland)
Ching-A-Ring Chaw (Copland)
Gregg Nestor has taken these well-known songs and transcribed their original piano accompaniments for guitar, occasionally transposing them for the sake of the instrument's capabilities. While the tessitura of the four Britten songs is best suited to a medium-range voice, most higher singers can perform them well. The *Four Greek Folk Songs* lie much higher and are best for tenor or soprano, although baritones and mezzo-sopranos comfortable with sustained and repeated E5 can consider them. These songs are more challenging than the rest of the collection. "O my love, how long" and "Have pity on me" contain many meter changes; the former centers around 7/8. "Each time, my love, you say farewell" features powerful phrases where the singer "wails" on rapidly repeated E♭5 and E5 with upper grace notes. "I Bought Me a Cat" and "Simple Gifts" are the lowest songs in the collection and very appropriate for low and medium voices. The other two Copland songs can be sung by medium or high voices. In attempting to remain as faithful as possible to the original piano music, the guitar parts pose some substantial challenges, especially in legato passages.

Walker, Gwyneth
As a Branch in May (ECS—ECS 4309)
English
Medium voice (D4–G5/D4–B4)
Easy

The text, by the composer, makes this song most suitable for a wedding ceremony, aided by the contemporary folk-like melody and accompaniment. Near the song's conclusion is a brief, unmetered a cappella section. It is only here that the highest pitches (E5–G5) occur; a lower *ossia* is provided. The guitar part features varied configurations yet is not difficult.

Walton, William
Anon. in Love (Oxford—OUP 157)
English
Tenor (C3–B♭4/E3–F♯4)
Difficult
Cycle of six songs (9'30")
Fain would I change that note
O stay, sweet love
Lady, when I behold the roses
My Love in her attire
I gave her Cakes and I gave her Ale
To couple is a custom
Written for Peter Pears and Julian Bream, this often sprightly and lighthearted cycle is set to anonymous sixteenth- and seventeenth-century love poems, several of which are somewhat risqué. Although generally tonal, the vocal lines vary in terms of chromaticism and melodic motion. "Fain would I change that note" is perhaps the most technically challenging; it is notably chromatic and disjunct, with numerous leaps of sevenths and ninths, yet must be rendered very legato. "I gave her Cakes and I gave her Ale" demands an exuberant and carefree delivery, while "To couple is a custom" ends the cycle with tongue-twisting lyrics, concluding with a rapid portamento from A3 to A4. The stimulating and varied guitar part is often challenging, especially in the rapid "My Love in her attire"—the easy and fun vocal lines will tempt the singer to "push" the music faster, but the guitarist must choose the tempo, lest it be unplayable for him or her.

Williamson, Malcolm
Three Shakespeare Songs (Weinberger)
English

High voice (C4–A♭5/E4–F5)
Difficult
Group of three songs (10')
Come away, death
Full fathom five
Fear no more the heat of the sun
The first song is set to an *allegretto* tempo, with accessible, lyric vocal melodies and repeated guitar arpeggios firmly rooted in traditional harmonies. "Full fathom five" is a cappella and tonally elusive, with chromatic, disjunct phrases. The final song, set to *largo*, shifts from major to minor in both parts but often at opposing times, with long, sustained vocal melodies. Piano can be substituted for the guitar, yet the accompaniment clearly sounds best on the latter instrument, despite the uncharacteristic two-stave notation.

APPENDIX—PUBLISHERS AND DISTRIBUTORS

AMP
Associated Music Publishers (U.S.—Leonard)
257 Park Ave. South, 20th floor
New York, NY 10010
www.schirmer.com

Bèrben
Edizioni Musicali Bèrben (U.S.—Presser)
via Redipuglia 65
1-60122 Ancona
Italy
www.berben.it

Boosey
Boosey & Hawkes, Inc.
35 East 21st St.
New York, NY 10010-6212
www.boosey.com

Breitkopf
Breitkopf & Härtel (U.S.—Presser)
Walkmühlstrasse 52
D-65195 Wiesbaden
Germany
www.breitkopf.com

Chanterelle
Chanterelle Verlag (U.S.—Mel Bay & GSP)
Postfach 103909
D-69029 Heidelberg
Germany
www.chanterelle.com

Chester
Chester Music (U.S.—Shawnee)
Music Sales Distribution
Newmarket Road
Bury St. Edmunds
Suffolk IP33 3YB
England
www.maxopus.com/publish/chester.htm

Choudens
Editions Choudens (U.S.—Peters & Presser)
38, rue Jean Mermoz
F-75008 Paris
France

CMC
Canadian Music Centre
Chalmers House
Ettore Mazzoleni Library
20 St. Joseph St.
Toronto, Ontario M4Y 1J9
Canada
www.musiccentre.ca

Columbia
Columbia Music (see Presser)

Doberman
Les Èditions Doberman-Yppan
(U.S.—GSP)
c.p. 2021
St. Nicholas, Quebec G7A 4X5
Canada
pages.infinit.net/doyp

Doblinger
Musikhaus Doblinger (U.S.—FMD)
Postfach 882
Dorotheergasse 10
A-1011 Wien
Austria
www.doblinger.at

EAM
European American Music Distributors LLC
15800 NW 48th Ave.
Miami, FL 33014
www.eamdc.com

ECS
E.C. Schirmer Music Co.
138 Ipswich St.
Boston, MA 02215-3534
www.ecspublishing.com

Engstrøm
Engstrøm & Sødring Musikforlag
Borgergade 17
DK-1300 København K
Denmark
www.steeplechase.dk/esmusic

Eschig
Editions Max Eschig (U.S.—Leonard)
215 rue de Faubourg Saint-Honore
F-75008 Paris
France

FMD
Foreign Music Distributors
9 Elkay Dr.
Chester, NY 10918

GSP
Guitar Solo Publications
230 Townsend St.
San Francisco, CA 94107
www.gspguitar.com

Hansen
Edition Wilhelm Hansen AS (U.S.—Shawnee)
Bornholmsgade 1
DK-1266 København K
Denmark
www.wilhelm-hansen.dk

Ione
Ione Press (see ECS)

Leonard
Hal Leonard Publishing Corp.
PO Box 13819
Milwaukee, WI 53213
www.halleonard.com

Margaux
Edition Margaux (see Neue)

Mel Bay
Mel Bay Publications, Inc.
4 Industrial Dr.
PO Box 66
Pacific, MO 63069-0066
www.melbay.com

Merion
Merion Music (see Presser)

MMB
MMB Music, Inc.
Contemporary Arts Building
3526 Washington Ave.
St. Louis, MO 63103-1019
www.mmbmusic.com

Modern
Edition Modern (U.S.— GSP)
Amalienstrasse 40
D-76133 Karlsruhe
Germany

Neue
Verlag Neue Musik (U.S.—GSP)
Köpenicker Strasse 175
D-10997 Berlin
Germany
www.verlag-neue-musik.de

Orphée
Editions Orphée, Inc. (dist.—Presser)
1240 Clubview Blvd.
N. Columbus, OH 43235-1226
www.orphee.com

Oxford
Oxford University Press, Inc.
200 Madison Ave.
New York, NY 10016
www.oup-usa.org

Peters
C.F. Peters Corp.
373 Park Ave. South
New York, NY 10016
www.edition-peters.com

Pizzicato
Pizzicato Edizioni Musicali
Via Monte Ortigara 10
I-33100 Udine
Italy
www.pizzicato.ch

Preissler
Musikverlag Josef Preissler (U.S.—GSP)
PO Box 101058
D-80084 München
Germany
www.accordions.com/preissler

Presser
Theodore Presser Co.
588 North Gulph Road
King of Prussia, PA 19406
www.presser.com

Reimers
Edition Reimers (U.S.—Presser)
Mårdvägen 44
Box 17051
S – 161 17 Bromma

Sweden
www.editionreimers.se

Ricordi S.A.
Ricordi Americana S.A.E.C. (U.S.—GSP)
Tte. Gral Juan D. Perón 1558
1037 Buenos Aires
Argentina

Rodrigo
Ediciones Joaquin Rodrigo, S.A. (U.S.—GSP)
General Yagüe, 11.4oJ
28020 Madrid
Spain
www.joaquinrodrigo.com

Schott
Schott Music (U.S.—EAM)
Weihergarten 5
D-55116 Mainz
Germany
www.schott-music.com

Seesaw
Seesaw Music Corp.
2067 Broadway
New York, NY 10023

Shawnee
Shawnee Press
49 Waring Drive
PO Box 690
Delaware Water Gap, PA 18327-0690
www.shawneepress.com

Sikorski
Hans Sikorski (U.S.—Leonard)
Johnsallee 23
D-20148 Hamburg
Germany
www.sikorski.de

Sonzogno
Casa Musicale Sonzogno (U.S.—Presser)
Via Bigli 11
1-20121 Milano
Italy
www.sonzogno.it

Southern
Southern Music Co.
PO Box 329
San Antonio, TX 78292
www.southernmusic.com

Tonos
Tonos Musikverlags GmbH (U.S.—Seesaw & GSP)
Holzhofallee 15
D-64295 Darmstadt
Germany
www.tonos-online.de

UME
Unión Musical Ediciones, S.L. (U.S.—Shawnee)
Marqués de la Ensenada, 4, 3o
28004 Madrid
Spain

Universal
Universal Edition Musikverlag (U.S.—EAM)
Bösendorferstrasse 12
A-1010 Wien

Austria
www.universaledition.com

Waiteata
Waiteata Music Press
School of Music
Victoria University of Wellington
PO Box 600
Wellington
New Zealand
www.vuw.ac.nz/music/waiteata

Waterloo
Waterloo Music Co., Ltd. (U.S.—GSP)
3 Regina St. North
Waterloo, Ontario N2J 4A5
Canada

Weinberger
Josef Weinberger Ltd.
12-14 Mortimer St.
London WIT 3JJ
England
www.josef-weinberger.co.uk

Willis
Willis Music Co.
PO Box 548
Florence, KY 41022-0548
www.willismusic.com

Zanibon
G. Zanibon Edition (U.S.—Boosey & GSP)
Piazza dei Signori, 44
1-35100 Padova
Italy

Zerboni
Edizioni Suvini Zerboni (U.S.—GSP)
via M.F. Quintiliano 40
1-20138 Milano
Italy
www.esz.it

BIBLIOGRAPHY

Maroney, James F. *Music for Voice and Classical Guitar, 1945–1996*. Jefferson, NC: McFarland & Company, 1997.

NOTES

This chapter comes from the original article published as James Maroney, "Contemporary Art Song for Voice and Classical Guitar—A Select Annotated List," *Journal of Singing 60*, no. 1 (September/October 2003): 9–26.

1. Marcia Drennen, liner notes for LP *Music for Voice and Guitar,* RCA AGL1—1281.
2. In string playing, the term "harmonic" refers to a high, flute-like tone produced by lightly touching a vibrating string at a nodal point. *Tamburo* is a percussive sound resulting from the side of the thumb striking the guitar's soundboard.
3. A capo is a movable bar that can be attached to a guitar's fingerboard to uniformly raise the pitch of all the strings.
4. Course refers to a set of strings tuned in unison or in octaves and plucked together to obtain greater loudness and richness. To simplify terminology, a single string is also referred to as a course. For example, the sixteenth-century lute generally had eleven strings in six courses: G2–G3, C3–C4, F3–F4, A3–A3, D4–D4, and G4.
5. Willi Apel, *Harvard Dictionary of* Music, 2nd ed., s.v. "Guitar" (Cambridge, MA: Belknap Press of Harvard University Press, 1969), 362.
6. Alexander Bellow, *The Illustrated History of the Guitar* (New York: Franco Colombo, 1970), 158–59.
7. Paul Hurley, "The Guitar in Song: An Introduction," *Soundboard* 16, no. 2 (1989): 33.

8. Bellow, *Illustrated History*, 160–61.

9. Paul Hurley, "The Guitar in Song: An Introduction. Part IV—The 19th Century," *Soundboard* 17, no. 1 (1990): 47.

10. Ibid.

11. Bellow, *Illustrated History*, 172.

12. Hurley, "The Guitar in Song: An Introduction. Part IV," 45.

13. Ibid.

14. *Music for Voice and Guitar*. RCA compact disk 09026-61601-2.

APPENDIX C

Why Neglect the Sacred Solo Duet?

Joan Frey Boytim

As a private voice teacher in a small community, I feel that my responsibilities are to prepare young students for college music departments and choral groups; to develop appreciation and performance skills for all styles of vocal music; to provide musical challenges, a musical education, and performance outlets for those many adults who are busy in their individual careers but who have an intense interest and latent talent in singing; and, most important, to develop among my young students and adults the type of church soloist dedication that will ensure a solid foundation of our church choirs for years to come. This latter responsibility leads us to my major interest at the present time: the "sacred solo duet."

Three years ago, the seeds of this interest were sown when I formed my first studio duet combination—two sisters (a college junior in this community and a high school sophomore) having light soprano voices with like flexibility, ability, and interest. After looking through the standard sacred duet collection, I was very disturbed and decided that there must be good material somewhere that is available in readily accessible form. After reviewing my SA octavo reference file, publishers' catalogs I had available, and the few song listings that included sacred duets, I decided to turn to the two-part octavo for my first material. The girls began with the very easy but effective duet "Saviour Like a Shepherd Lead Us" by Gluck-Holler (Gray) and "Come Ever-Gracious Son of God" by Handel-Hines (Elkan-Vogel). As we experimented with voicing (eventually deciding on the younger sister on the top part) and began developing the refined sensitivity and give and take that are essential for fine duet singing, we added "O Hold Thou Me Up" by Marcello-Weinhorst (Concordia), which is extracted from Marcello's *Fifty Psalms of David*. This requires two medium or high voices since the compass of both parts is basically the same. Now the girls were ready to tackle some more challenging material, and they added one of the recently published Moravian duets, "Like as a Father Doth Pity His Children" by Geisler-Nolte (Boosey and Hawkes), which is a late-Baroque-style composition in two sections, the latter cut time part moving a good bit faster than the longer first section in triple meter. We included also "I Waited for the Lord" by Mendelssohn (G. Schirmer) and "Laudamus Te" from the *Gloria* by Vivaldi-Martens (Walton Music). This last duet the girls performed in English, and it is certainly beautiful with clear, young, flexible voices.

You may have wondered why I have termed this the "sacred solo duet." The type of duet that I have mentioned holds true musical value for the performers and provides spiritual effectiveness for the congregation but requires two solo singers of similar abilities. Most of the duets I will list are written in a contrapuntal manner and require complete solo independence in addition to ensemble sensitivity and balance. At present, there are eight sacred solo duet combinations working in my studio. A duet blend is readily achieved when both persons involved are singing with the same basic vocal technique. This is a very important factor that should encourage teachers to form duet combinations within the studio.

Exactly how does one go about finding combinations? I can only relate what has worked for me. One of the first items I record on my permanent card for each new student is his or her church affiliation. I keep a yearly up-to-date list of all churches represented by my students for the primary purposes of choosing sacred solos and keeping the respective churches informed of newly developing talent. From this list I have carefully considered abilities, drive, personalities, and same church or closely related church affiliations and have thus formed my duet combinations. I have found that the most successful combinations come from closely interacting personalities and those with equal interest. A duet pair of matching voices that I formed earlier never became very successful simply because the drive and personality factors were too different. The voices should be of somewhat similar strengths, however, to achieve a proper balance, but even this can be adjusted when working with flexible persons. Of course, in a college setting, church affiliation would have little bearing on the picking of combinations.

You will notice that I have not mentioned voice types. After reviewing much of the literature, I have discovered that there is some available material for any type of combination. Even though most octavo duet compositions are listed SA, this to me means it is merely in two parts. An adult tenor student and I (a mezzo) have been doing mostly pieces listed SS or SA with the tenor singing the top part. My studio combinations presently consist of three soprano-soprano pairs, two soprano-alto pairs, one soprano-mezzo pair, one tenor-mezzo pair, and one tenor-alto pair. In the early stages, one must experiment to find out which voice on the upper and lower part provides the best balance, particularly in like voice types, and then pick music to suit these individual voices.

Needless to say, the response from my students and from the churches has been most gratifying. I am tremendously excited about the possibilities of exploring the field more thoroughly. In the remaining part of this article, several examples of suitable octavo repertoire presently available will be discussed. Most of the compositions listed will be of a general sacred nature. If there is further interest expressed among the membership, I would be willing to compile a more complete listing of available duet literature for general as well as the traditional church seasons and also possibly including duets available only in oratorio and cantata scores.

Some additional very easy beginning duets I would suggest include: "Thou, O God Art Praised in Sion" by Corfe-Harker (Oxford); "Thou, O Lord, Art My Shepherd" by Marcello-Martens (Concordia); and "Bless Thou the Lord" by Handel-Whitford (J. Fischer), which are all written for high and medium voices. The Handel has a short middle section solo that could be divided effectively. For medium and low voice, I add: "Lo, My Shepherd's Hand Divine" by Haydn-Barthelson (Walton Music); and for two medium high voices: "A Prayer of St. Richard of Chichester" by White (Oxford).

Particularly appealing to higher voices are these four interestingly and rather modernly composed canons by Lang (Oxford): "Let All the World in Every Corner Sing," "The King of Love," "O Let My Wish Be

Crowned," and "Jesu, the Very Thought of Thee." All four of these have beautiful flowing melodic lines that demand excellent legato singing and wide ranges. Teenagers especially enjoy the first one listed because it is a jubilant song of praise. Also for teenage appeal, I will list "Make a Joyful Noise" by Vance (Belwin) for high and low voices.

Earlier I mentioned one of the Moravian duets as excellent material. Several other Moravian compositions I definitely recommend are: "Bless the Lord, O My Soul" by Geisler-Nolte; "O Jesus, Show Thy Great Compassion" by Grimm-Nolte; "Lord in Thy Presence" by Gregor-Nolte; "O Thou Our Joy" by Geisler-Nolte; and "I Will Mention Thy Loving Kindness" by Antes-McCorkle. These are all published by Boosey and Hawkes. They are written in late-Baroque style and are of medium difficulty. The last one listed is written for a very high and a medium voice, and the others are written for high and medium low voices.

Maurice Greene (1695–1755) has written very effective works like the easy sustained "Show Me Thy Ways, O Lord" (G. Schirmer) for medium and low voices; "The Lord God Is a Light" (G. Schirmer) for high and medium voices; "My Lips Shall Speak of Thy Praise" (Oxford) for two medium flexible voices to handle the moving lines; and the almost cantata-length works each in three sections, "Like as the Hart" (Oxford) and "Blessed Those That Are Undefiled" (C. F. Peters), both for medium voices.

Some Couperin duets I would include are: "Be Joyful in the Lord" (Concordia), which is a fast song of praise for high and medium voices, and "O Clap Your Hands" (Concordia) for high and medium voices. Marcello has given us several possibilities from the *Fifty Psalms of David*, including the sustained "Give Ear Unto Me" (Concordia; Gray); the joyous "And With Songs I Will Celebrate" (Concordia); and the rather florid "As the Hart Panteth" (Gray) for two high voices.

Schein is well represented with the recent duet volume edited by Ludwig Lenel titled *Eight Chorale Settings for Two Voices from Opella Nova* (Concordia). This publication for the college student or musically mature adult is set for high and medium voices. Mercury Music (Presser) has published several of the Schütz duets from *Kleine Geistliche Konzerte* with English translations and edited by Boepple, which are set for medium voices. Three I would note are "Give Ear Oh

Lord," "Great Is Our Lord," and "O Mighty God Our Lord." Concordia and Augsburg have also published a number of fine Schütz duets. For the really advanced duet combination, many of the florid Bach cantata duets published in octavo form by E. C. Schirmer, Presser, Oxford, and Concordia may prove to be an interesting challenge.

There are a number of settings of the old standards that have a definite place in the repertoire, such as: "The Lord Is My Shepherd" by Smart (Gray); "Peace I Leave with You" by Roberts-Deis (G. Schirmer); "O Lord Most Holy" by Franck-Ehret (Boosey and Hawkes); "O Magnify the Lord with Me" by Mueller (Carl Fischer); and "Ave Verum" by Mozart, of which there are at least six different two-part arrangements. I prefer the Gray edition with the title "Jesus Calls Us" (the other words can be substituted) mainly because it is the only one that brings the contrapuntal effect into the lower voice part in the second section.

Space does not permit including the fine sacred duets of Saint-Saëns, Mendelssohn, Schubert, Fauré, Gretchaninoff, and the moderns such as Peelers, Pinkham, Larkin, Thiman, Willan, and Clokey. I would call your attention, however, to a new, worthwhile, singable contemporary sacred duet collection by Cassler called *Sacred Duets for Equal Voices* (Augsburg). This includes five duets, all for high voices, and the duets are medium in difficulty.

I hope after reading through this sampling of sacred duet literature possibilities that you will give some serious thought to forming duet combinations in your studios and your church choirs. The possibilities of providing service through song with the sacred solo duet are endless. Will you give it a try?

NOTE

This chapter comes from the original article published as Joan Boytim, "Why Neglect the Sacred Solo Duet," *Journal of Singing 28*, no. 3 (February 1972): 13–14, 37.

GLOSSARY

A415: Approximate baroque tuning system in which A4 (above C4 or "middle C") resonates at a frequency of 415 Hz, approximately a semitone below modern tuning.

A440: Standardized modern tuning system in which A4 (above C4 or "middle C") resonates at a frequency of 440 Hz.

Ballade: One of the three fixed forms of secular musical and poetic repetition in fourteenth- and fifteenth-century France in AAB form.

Basse musique: Soft music or instruments of the Middle Ages and Renaissance such as stringed instruments.

Bell: The open end of a wind instrument.

Cantata: Sacred or secular baroque vocal genre with varying sections of solo or multivoice recitatives, arias, and choruses.

Cantus Firmus: Preexisting melody on which a polyphonic composition is based.

Continuo: Thoroughbass over which numbers indicate intervals and chord quality.

Contratenor: Third vocal line between the discant (highest voice) and tenor voice in fourteenth- and fifteenth-century music.

Downbow: Drawing the bow away from the stringed instrument.

Embouchure: Placement of mouth (including lips, tongue, teeth, facial muscles, and jaw) on mouthpiece of wind instruments.

Fioritura: Vocal embellishment or "flowering."

Formes Fixes: Fixed forms of secular musical and poetic repetition in fourteenth- and fifteenth-century France that included the *rondeau*, *virelai*, and *ballade*.

Frottola: Secular Italian form of medieval music.

Galant: Light, homophonic style of the early classical period (*rococo*).

Haute musique: Loud music or instruments of the Middle Ages and Renaissance such as trumpet.

Homophonic: Music in which one line has melodic emphasis and supporting accompaniment is often chordal. All parts move together rhythmically.

Homorhythmic: All parts sharing the same rhythm.

Lied: German art song.

Madrigal: Italian song form of the fourteenth century with stanzas of verse and ritornello. Traditionally polyphonic and unaccompanied, madrigals in the 1600s were performed with basso continuo and other instruments.

Melisma: Multiple notes, often sung on a single syllable.

Mélodie: French art song.

Minnesinger: Medieval German musician poets who composed monophonic songs focused on courtly love.

Monophonic: Denoting a single melodic line.

Motet: Influential sacred vocal genre that evolved from the polyphonic setting of sacred Latin texts in the medieval period.

Multiphonics: Sounding two or more simultaneous pitches.

Musica Ficta: The addition of symbols written over pitches with implied chromatic adjustments in repertoire prior to 1600.

Obbligato: An accompanying instrumental part.

Polyphonic: Consisting of two or more melodic lines.

Portamento: The continuous connection of all notes between two pitches.

Rococo: A term borrowed from French visual arts to describe graceful and lightly ornamented music of the early eighteenth century.

Rondeau: One of the three fixed forms of secular musical and poetic repetition in fourteenth- and fifteenth-century France in ABaAabAB form.

Rubato: Expressive slowing or acceleration of the given tempo.

Scordatura: The practice of tuning stringed instruments in an unconventional manner.

Seconda Prattica: Championed by Claudio Monteverdi (1567–1643) in the early seventeenth century, a revolutionary and unconventional dissonance treatment that prioritized text declamation.

Sprechstimme: Speech-song, or approximate intoning of pitches.

Timbre: Distinctive quality of sound or tone color.

Tessitura: A part's average or most commonly occurring pitch range.

Troubadour: Medieval southern French musician poets who established a genre focused on courtly love in regional vernacular.

Trouvère: Medieval northern French musician poets who composed monophonic songs focused on courtly love in regional vernacular.

Upbow: Drawing the bow toward the stringed instrument.

Urtext: An original manuscript without additional editorial markings.

Vibrato: Pitch fluctuation used as an aesthetic tool based on variations in air flow regulation, embouchure, or manual manipulation on an instrument.

Viol: A term that denotes early string instruments from the sixteenth through the eighteenth centuries, including the *viola da gamba*, *viola d'amore*, and *bartyon*.

Virelai: One of the three fixed forms of secular musical and poetic repetition in fourteenth- and fifteenth-century France in AbbaA form.

INDEX

ABOUT THE AUTHOR AND CONTRIBUTORS

Susan Hochmiller is assistant professor of voice at the Sunderman Conservatory of Music at Gettysburg College and director of Orvieto Musica's Art of Song summer vocal chamber music festival in Orvieto, Italy. She is an avid recitalist and has performed chamber music in Italy and across the United States. She holds a BM in vocal performance from Susquehanna University and an MM and DMA in voice performance and literature from the Eastman School of Music. Hochmiller has presented at national and regional conferences, including College Music Society (CMS) and National Association of Teachers of Singing (NATS). An active member of NATS since 2007, Hochmiller was one of twelve voice teachers from the United States and Canada selected to participate in the prestigious 2012 NATS Intern Program, and she has served as president of the Allegheny Mountain Chapter since 2016. Her students have received numerous awards in both classical and music theater divisions at district and regional NATS student auditions in Pennsylvania and Colorado, have been accepted into competitive graduate and summer programs, and have sung with professional opera companies.

* * *

Wendy LeBorgne is a voice pathologist, speaker, author, and master class clinician. She actively presents nationally and internationally on the professional voice and is the clinical director of two successful private practice voice centers: the ProVoice Center in Cincinnati and BBIVAR in Dayton. LeBorgne holds an adjunct professorship at University of Cincinnati College-Conservatory of Music as a voice consultant, where she also teaches voice pedagogy and wellness courses. She completed a BFA in musical theater from Shenandoah Conservatory and her graduate and doctoral degrees from the University of Cincinnati. Original peer-reviewed research has been published in multiple journals, and she is a contributing author to several voice textbooks. Most recently, she coauthored *The Vocal Athlete* textbook and workbook with Marci Rosenberg. Her patients and private students currently can be found on radio, television, film, cruise ships, Broadway, off-Broadway, national tours, commercial music tours, and opera stages around the world.

Scott McCoy is a noted author, singer, conductor, and pianist with extensive performance experience in concert and opera. He is professor of voice and pedagogy, director of the Swank Voice Laboratory, and director of the interdisciplinary program in singing health at Ohio State University. His voice science and pedagogy textbook, *Your Voice: An Inside View*, is used extensively by colleges and universities throughout the United States and abroad. McCoy is the associate editor of the *Journal of Singing* for voice pedagogy and is a past president of the National Association of Teachers of Singing (NATS). He also served NATS as vice president for workshops, as program chair for the 2006 and 2008 national conferences, as chair of the voice science advisory committee, and as a master teacher for the intern program. Deeply committed to teacher education, McCoy is a founding faculty member in the NYSTA Professional Development Program (PDP), teaching classes in voice anatomy, physiology, acoustics, and voice analysis. He is a member of the distinguished American Academy of Teachers of Singing (AATS).

James Maroney is associate professor of music at East Stroudsburg University (Pennsylvania), serving as director of choral and vocal activities, and is a member of the voice faculty at Muhlenberg College. He is one of the foremost authorities on music for voice and classical guitar, having authored a book on the subject, *Music for Voice and Classical Guitar*, as well as an article in *Journal of Singing*. As a tenor, he has performed the repertoire extensively over several decades with a number of guitarists and was awarded a grant through the Pennsylvania Faculty Professional Development Council to perform concerts of that genre throughout Pennsylvania and neighboring states.

Maroney has concertized extensively in recital, oratorio, and opera over three decades, including many solo programs and more than thirty operatic roles. He has served as president of the Lehigh Valley Chapter of the National Association of Teachers of Singing as well as the Pennsylvania Collegiate Choral Association.

Maroney received grants to give lecture-recital performances of Schumann's *Dichterliebe*, Copland's *Twelve Poems of Emily Dickinson*, and Schubert's *Die schöne Müllerin*. He has researched the opera arias of George Frideric Handel written specifically for the tenor John Beard during the composer's years at Covent Garden.

Maroney received degrees from Columbia University, University of Hartford, Ithaca College, and Western Connecticut State College.

Joan Frey Boytim is nationally known in the field of voice instruction. In her workshops and presentations at many events over the years, especially at the conventions of the National Association of Teachers of Singing, she has shared her expertise with thousands of other voice teachers. Through her ability to articulate to other teachers the special issues in guiding young singers, Boytim has become the most recognized American expert in training the young voice.

For more than sixty years, Boytim has taught voice in her private studio in Carlisle, Pennsylvania. It is unusual that a teacher of Boytim's caliber has devoted herself almost exclusively to teaching teenagers and community adults to sing, which has been her passion.

Boytim is the compiler of sixty vocal anthologies including *The First Book of Solos Parts I*, *II*, and *III* and the *Second Book of Solos Parts I* and *II* for soprano, alto, tenor, and baritone. Other volumes are devoted to Broadway, sacred, Christmas, sacred and secular duets, and a variety of very easy teaching literature and other specialty categories. As of 2015, sales have surpassed one million copies.

Her revised book *The Private Voice Studio Handbook (A Practical Guide to All Aspects of Teaching)* is a favorite book for new teachers developing private voice studios and is often used as a supplemental book in college vocal pedagogy classes.

Boytim was educated at Indiana University of Pennsylvania, where she received a bachelor's of science degree in music education and a master's of education in music education. Her continuing education included thirty graduate credits in voice and vocal pedagogy at Indiana University in Bloomington and a year's study at the Staatliche Hochschule für Musik in Munich, Germany.

In 2007, she was awarded a Distinguished Alumni Honor from Indiana University of Pennsylvania. In 2016, she was awarded the Lifetime Achievement Award from the National Association of Teachers of Singing at the Chicago conference.

Lightning Source UK Ltd.
Milton Keynes UK
UKHW042104170119
335659UK00001B/36/P